THE TURNSTONE

A Doctor's Story

GEOFFREY DEAN

LIVERPOOL UNIVERSITY PRESS

First published 2002 by
LIVERPOOL UNIVERSITY PRESS
4 Cambridge Street
Liverpool, L69 7ZU

British Library Cataloguing-in-Publication Data
A British Library CIP record is available

ISBN 0-85323-757-3 *cased*
ISBN 0-85323-767-0 *paper*

Typeset in Monotype Bembo
by XL Publishing Services, Tiverton, Devon
Printed and bound in the European Union
by Bell and Bain Ltd, Glasgow

This book is dedicated to my family, colleagues and friends,
who have turned over many stones with me.

They are not long, the weeping and the laughter,
Love and desire and hate:
I think they have no portion in us after
We pass the gate.

They are not long, the days of wine and roses:
Out of a misty dream
Our path emerges for a while, then closes
Within a dream.

Ernest Dowson, *Vitae summa brevis*

Contents

Foreword

by Sir Richard Doll

This book is not for the squeamish, the religiose or the prudish. Surprising perhaps, seeing that it is the autobiography of a physician; but then Geoffrey Dean is no ordinary physician. Brought up in Liverpool in a family with Irish ancestry, he seemed set on a standard medical career, but not liking the scramble for places on the professional ladder in Britain after the war, he went to seek his fortune in South Africa, leaving a newly wed wife with her parents. The gods, it is said, help those who help themselves and this has seldom been illustrated more clearly than by the incidents that set Geoffrey on his feet as a consultant physician in Port Elizabeth with his membership of the Royal College of Physicians but no previous consultant appointment.

But if he was fortunate in the way he got established locally, it was Geoffrey's own perspicacity that led him to follow through the strange attacks of paralysis that had baffled colleagues and to discover a new strain of porphyria that affected thousands of the descendants of one of the early Dutch settlers, just as it had earlier led him and a colleague to the discovery of cylinders of oil contaminated with orthotricresyl phosphate that were causing Liverpool dock workers to develop peripheral paralysis.

No one who reads this book can fail to be enriched by it, by the insight gained into the pressures on the crews of RAF bombers, the procedures by which medical discoveries are made, the extent of the cover-up of police atrocities during the apartheid era in

South Africa, and the effects of personal tragedy on religious belief. Geoffrey Dean's historical hero is Thomas More and I leave it to the reader to decide whether Geoffrey has succeeded in his aim of also being a 'man for all seasons'.

Oxford, December 2001

Acknowledgements

This book has been more than seventeen years in preparation, and there have been many additions and improvements as the years have gone by. I would like to thank the many friends who have helped me to prepare this book, not least my personal assistant Hilda McLoughlin and my secretaries Maureen Moloney and Susan Murray. I thank them for their patience. It was Dr David Nowlan of the *Irish Times* who recommended Jonathan Williams to me as a literary adviser, and he has helped me to avoid many solecisms. At Liverpool University Press, Robin Bloxsidge, my publisher, Andrew Kirk and Simon Bell have been fine advisers and friends. I would also like to thank all those who have worked with me who are not mentioned in this book.

CHAPTER 1

The Seed and the Soil

If you can look into the seeds of time,
And say which grain will grow and which will not.
William Shakespeare, *Macbeth*

My father, Richard Dean, known as Dick, was born in 1887 at the Manor House near the village of Upholland in Lancashire, where his father, John, lived the life of a prosperous squire. The Dean family had lived in the area for many generations and the name comes from the nearby village of Dean; it means a valley or dell. John Dean's eldest child, Ellen, aged sixteen, was accidentally shot by a gamekeeper in 1894 and died a few days later. The gamekeeper did not recover from the accident and died shortly afterwards. At the end of the Boer War, in 1901, there was a major slump in the value of farm produce and John Dean found himself in serious debt. In June 1902 he shot himself, accidentally or on purpose no one is quite sure. He left four sons and two daughters.

In 1902, following his father's death, Dick, now aged fifteen, had to leave Upholland Grammar School. He went to work for Parr's Bank, which later amalgamated with the Westminster Bank, in the nearby town of Wigan, at a salary of £20 a year, out of which he had to pay his train fare from Upholland. Dick's mother, Ann, and later his youngest brother, Joe, continued to farm Prescott Farm, which alone remained from the Manor House estate.

In August 1914, the first week of the Great War, Dick joined the cavalry, thinking, as many did, that the war would be over in a few months. He was extremely short-sighted, having inherited myopia from his mother, Ann Kerfoot. To pass the eyesight test for the army, Dick learned by heart the 'Snellen Type', the letters used in a standard eye test. Unfortunately – or I should say fortunately – during his basic training on horseback at Aldershot he rode straight at the colonel whom he could not see. His severe myopia was discovered and he was discharged from the army and returned to work at the bank. This near accident undoubtedly saved his life since there was little chance of survival for those cavalry charging German machine-guns.

My mother, Agnes Irene, was the daughter of Henry Fleetwood Lloyd and Josephine Murphy. Josephine Murphy was one of the four daughters of John Murphy, whose father, Daniel, had emigrated to Liverpool from Wexford in Ireland during the potato famine of the 1840s. Daniel started work in Liverpool at Muspratts Chemical Works which made acid and alkali from Cheshire salt. His eldest son, John, my mother's grandfather, also began work at Muspratts and then started to manufacture acid and alkali on his own account in a shed in a yard. He prospered and in 1870, having married Ann Briscoe, the daughter of a successful cooper, he bought a large chemical works which had the tallest chimney in Liverpool. Ships sailing up the Mersey used 'Murphy's chimney' as a landmark. It no doubt poured forth highly poisonous fumes, destroying much of the vegetation in the vicinity.

My grandmother, Josephine Murphy, married Henry Fleetwood Lloyd against the wishes of her father, John, and her sisters because Henry was not a Catholic but a Methodist. Josephine died within a year of my mother's birth, according to her three sisters from 'a broken heart', although her death certificate states that she died from pulmonary tuberculosis. Perhaps her sense of guilt lowered her resistance. Tuberculosis was very common among the Irish settlers in Liverpool and the husband of Josephine's sister, Anne, and two of Anne's children also developed tuberculosis.

Following the death of Josephine Lloyd, my mother, Agnes Irene Lloyd, was raised by her three aunts in upper middle-class Victorian style in John Murphy's large mansion, 'Kingston', in the suburb of Aigburth in Liverpool. My mother recalled the green baize door, beyond which she was not allowed to go, which separated the main part of the house from the servants' quarters.

She was never permitted to meet her father, although he called to the house hoping to see her on a number of occasions. The aunts told her that he was an alcoholic, but undoubtedly the main problem was his religion. Some years ago I decided to find out what had happened to my grandfather and discovered that he had lived to the age of seventy-four and had died in 1930. He never saw his grandchildren.

During the Great War, middle-class women, who in normal times would not engage in paid work, replaced many of the men who had been conscripted into the armed services or who made munitions. My mother first worked as a censor because of her good knowledge of languages and then, in 1917, joined the Widnes branch of the Westminster Bank, where she met my father. They fell in love and wanted to marry.

Marriage, however, presented a major problem because my father and all his family were staunch members of the Church of England. The three aunts who had brought up my mother refused to countenance marriage to my father unless he converted to the Roman Catholic faith. Even if he agreed to do this, they were very unhappy about the marriage because he was a poor bank clerk, while their niece was 'a lady of means'. If she did marry a non-Catholic, she would, according to her grandfather's will, lose her considerable yearly income – over £500 a year in 1901 – from the Trust he had founded for his three daughters and his grand-daughter, Irene.

My father was in a quandary. He had grown up in rural Lancashire where there was a strong Church of England tradition and where Roman Catholics were regarded as very strange folk indeed. The little he knew about Catholics was from John Foxe's *The Book of Martyrs*, which relates the martyrdom of such Protestants as Cranmer and Ridley, burnt at the stake at Smithfield in the reign of 'Bloody Queen Mary', as the Protestants called her. The only Catholics he had met were the 'Paddies' who came from Ireland every autumn to work in the potato harvest. They lived in a separate building, the Paddy House, and my father would often escape to join them in a supper of potatoes and bacon and to listen to stories about life in Ireland.

One day in 1917, Dick, travelling on the train to London, found himself in the same railway carriage as Bishop Chavasse, the

Anglican Bishop of Liverpool. They started talking and Dick told the Bishop his problem: how could he join a religion that believed that Jesus was born of a virgin? Bishop Chavasse replied: 'This is a cardinal belief of the Church of England.' My father, who knew little theology, was very surprised. He must have recited the Nicene Creed without thinking about it! He decided that if the Anglicans also believed in such improbabilities, he might as well become a Catholic.

Dick married Agnes Irene Lloyd in the Catholic Church on 16 February 1918, a few days after a gruelling interview with the three aunts' legal advisers. I was born on 5 December 1918, less than a month after the end of the First World War, in Wrexham, Wales, where my father was at the time the manager of the local branch of the Westminster Bank. He had become a manager at a very young age, probably because most of the older men were in the armed services.

At that time a bank official was not permitted to marry until he was thirty-three and was earning £150 a year. My father had not quite reached this age and earned only £140 a year but, because his fiancée had a good income, he received permission from head office to marry. After my birth, my parents had two more children at three-yearly intervals: Pauline and Helen, the latter named after my father's sister Ellen, who had been killed in the shooting accident.

My earliest memories are of living over the bank in Cressington, a suburb of Liverpool, near Aigburth. The bank house had stables where my father kept his car, a Standard with a folding roof and detachable windows, and a loft where I had many pigeons. I had started with 'Reddie', a male, and 'Bluey', a female. I can still remember the first two eggs 'Bluey' laid.

In Cressington the bank was situated opposite the Catholic church, St Austin's, which was serviced by priests from Ampleforth, a Benedictine school and monastery on the North Yorkshire moors. Two of my mother's three aunts lived in Cressington Park, an estate of large, late Victorian houses just around the corner from the bank. Later, my father bought a large house in the Park. We would visit Aunt Etta, who was unmarried, and Aunt Annie, whose husband, Dr David Donnelly, had died from tuberculosis many years before. Aunt Etta was a very frail lady lying in bed and apparently 'dying from asthma'. She looked as if a puff of wind would blow her away and received every attention, including daily calves' foot jelly, from Annie. She outlived her two sisters and died at the age of eighty-four. My mother's third aunt, Liz, who had looked after the Vauxhall Road Chemical Works for some years after John Murphy's death in 1901, lived in Aigburth.

Cressington was like Mrs Gaskell's village, 'Cranford'. Although a suburb of Liverpool, it was largely self-contained. In a row of shops there was Dennerly the chemist, Stevenson's the cake shop, Irwin's the grocer, Dugdale's dairy – with cows in the cowshed – the sweet shop and, on the corner, the Westminster Bank.

My father was a successful bank manager. He took risks in lending money, usually to house-builders, but nearly always made a good profit for the bank. He was a popular, outgoing man and I was proud of him and also of my mother, who, besides speaking Italian, German and French, was also an accomplished pianist. She had been to school in Germany and had lived for some time in Naples, where she played the piano in the orchestra at the opera house. She was well-read, witty, amusing, and excellent company.

My father had a great fondness for the novels of Sir Walter Scott, for poetry and for riddles. As small children we would be brought down to the sitting room at half past five, after tea, by our 'nurse' (there was always a nurse, a cook and a maid) and would spend half an hour or so with our parents. I would sit on my father's knee while he recited, in a fine deep voice, poems and prose from an old nineteenth-century book, *Studies on Elocution* by Alfred Lowry. I still have, ringing in my memory:

And then they knew the perilous rock,
And blest the Abbot of Aberbrothok.

He would also ask us 'teasers' that he had, in turn, heard from his father, such as:

A man without eyes saw plums on a tree,
He neither took plums,
Nor left plums,
Pray, how can that be?

CHAPTER 2

School

It is customary, but I think it is a mistake,
to speak of happy childhood;
Children are at the mercy of those around them.
John Lubbock, *The Pleasures of Life*

When I was five I attended La Sagesse, a convent school run by French Sisters, a few hundred yards from the bank. We would start each day with the greeting, 'Bonjour, Bonne Mère'. This was a happy time of my life, although on one occasion my friend Kenneth Smith and I decided to run away and live, like the Red Indians, in a nearby wood. We stole tins of food and matches, settled under a tree and lit a fire. It started to pour with rain and we decided to give our parents one more chance. The next day we had to go and see Bonne Mère. She gave us each an apple and suggested that we wait until we were older before starting to live like Red Indians.

Our big adventures usually took place in the farm at Dugdale's dairy. There were high beams in the barn and Kenneth and I would dare each other to walk along the beam the length of the barn. It was very foolish, but fortunately neither of us fell and our parents never knew. On Saturday we would often go to one of the two local cinemas, the Lyceum and the Empire. Those were the days of silent films, although the piano played and the music suited the events on the screen. The hero was cheered and the villains booed. Two films in my memory of this time were *Chang*, about Indian elephants, and *Svengali*, a frightening film about hypnotism.

While at La Sagesse, I developed a rash and was diagnosed as

7

having scarlet fever. I was immediately taken by ambulance to Fazakerly Fever Hospital and was not allowed home for twelve weeks. The three fever hospitals in Liverpool were kept full with scarlet fever and diphtheria patients. Scarlet fever, now uncommon, is caused by a streptococcal sore throat. My sister Pauline also developed rheumatic fever, now seldom seen in the developed world, which is also a reaction to the streptococcus. Rheumatic fever often caused damage to the heart muscle and scarring of the mitral valve. Fortunately, it did little damage to Pauline's heart.

In 1926, when I was seven, my parents sent me to a preparatory boarding school, Bishop's Court, at Freshfield, between Liverpool and Southport, and I was at this school for five years. It was the custom, if parents could afford it, to send their children to boarding school, and my mother, no doubt because of her upbringing, was very class-conscious. Bishop's Court was owned by Miss Trevor and Miss Robins and they employed three or four other teachers. It was a dreadful school and I was desperately unhappy there. The food was abominable and we used to keep envelopes or small tins in our pockets so that we could hide some of the food and later put it down the toilet. We did this because our plates had to be left absolutely clean. We never received an egg unless a boy had a birthday and the parents paid extra fees so that each boy could have one boiled egg. We would have to stand up and Miss Trevor, the headmistress, would say: 'Three cheers for Robinson' or whatever the boy's name was. 'Hip, hip, hoorah. Hip, hip, hoorah. Hip, hip, hoorah.' Of course those were harsh times in many boys' schools.

The mistresses would bang the children's heads against the wall for minor mistakes in their class work and there was a dreadful system known as conduct marks. A child could be given a conduct mark for either a bad exercise in class or for some misdemeanour, such as talking in the corridor or in the dormitory. Every Friday, at three o'clock, the conduct marks were read out by the headmistress, and those who had five or more, which I nearly always had, were placed on what was known as the 'black list' for the following week. Being on the black list meant that you were deprived of the one teaspoonful of brown sugar on your plate of porridge for breakfast. You also lined up in your pyjamas outside the headmistress's room that evening, so that she could beat each child on his bare bottom with a three-tongued strap, giving as many strokes as there were conduct marks.

I was utterly miserable at this school. Unfortunately, they instilled into us the idea of loyalty to school and I did not tell my parents much about what went on there. Our letters home, which we had to write every Friday after hearing the conduct marks, were read by the headmistress before being posted and we could make no criticism of the school in them. There was a beautifully furnished hall where visiting parents were entertained for tea. At the Prize Day, the Catholic Archbishop of Liverpool, Dr Dick Downey, would attend and praise the school after we had all sung 'Ecce sacerdos Dei'. The boys always knew their catechism well, but it was a hateful place. It was drilled into me that I would never make anything of my life or do any good in the world.

I remember waking up one morning in the dormitory at Bishop's Court with the Matron standing over my bed and saying: 'Dean, we know you did it.' For once I did not know what it was that I had done. When we went downstairs, we saw that much of the main study, directly under the headmistress's flat, had been on fire. Miss Trevor and Miss Robbins had narrowly escaped with their lives. They had no idea who had started the fire, although they pretended to know, and for three days there was an inquisition of boys individually and in groups.

The priest came to hear confession and Miss Trevor said: 'Will any boy in mortal sin go to confession?' Nobody moved for a minute and then she took the first boy to hand by the scruff of the neck and bundled him into the confessional box. Eventually, on the evening of the third day, Miss Trevor announced to the assembled boys: 'We know who did it, but we want to give him a last opportunity to confess and so save his eternal soul. He will not be expelled. He will not be punished.'

The next morning a boy, surnamed George, had disappeared. The headmistress announced that George had set the study on fire. Later I believe George went to Stonyhurst, a famous Jesuit school. The Jesuits must have known what life was like at Bishop's Court. George did very well in life and became an officer in the regular army.

I shall never forget the school song, taught to us by Mr Borristan the music master, which we sang every Friday.

Where the butterfly and the bumble bee and the birds and the wild flowers are, is our Alma Mater, Bishops Court, let's sing with joyful chorus.

> Long live Bishops Court
> Loud let our voices ring
> God keep us true
> To our Faith
> To our School
> To our Country
> To our King.

At that time the Catholic teaching about sex was extremely Jansenistic. We were taught that to harbour a sexual thought was in itself a mortal sin. Masturbation was always a mortal sin and, unless we went to confession and the mortal sin was forgiven, we were condemned to hellfire forever. From the age of about twelve I was tormented with guilt about this and was condemned to hell quite regularly by my thoughts and deeds. I could find no peace until I had confessed my sins. I remember that other boys were in the same situation. This was an atrocious way to torment young boys. Fortunately, more common sense prevails in the Church today. Many of the priests in Liverpool were Irish and had come straight from Maynooth Training College, near Dublin, which at that time held extreme views about 'sins of the flesh'.

On Sundays during the holidays we would often spend the day at Uncle Joe's Prescott farm at Upholland and always finished with a sing-song around the piano, played by Joe's wife, Mary. Uncle Joe sang 'Sailors Beware of the Terrors of the Deep' in a deep bass. Pauline and I would spend two or three weeks each summer with Uncle Jack and 'Aunt Edythe' at Tower Hill farm, near Prescott farm. We would go to the market in Wigan with panniers containing a hundredweight of potatoes. There were twenty panniers in a cartload, and they were sold for four-and-sixpence each. We had a great time riding on the horses, Tommy and

Queenie, and feeding the ducks and hens. Uncle Joe was enterprising. He found coal about twelve feet below ground on his farm to supply his own grate and, later, a small but profitable coalmine was developed on the farm.

During the holidays I became interested in the wireless and in photography. The first wireless my father gave me was a crystal set, with a 'cat's whisker', a fine wire in contact with a crystal of lead sulphide to detect radio signals. My father then gave me a 1921 wireless built on a large 30-inch by 20-inch bakelite panel. There were four valves and coils of wire, all of which required adjustment, during which there would be blood-curdling squeaks from the loudspeaker. The set had three batteries: high-tension, low-tension, and 'grid'. By the age of twelve, I had learned enough about the wireless to make sets for my father's friends. My father also taught me how to take good films and develop them with metol hydroquinone in the darkened pantry lit by a red light. I made brown-coloured prints from the negatives, using a special frame and exposing the print to sunlight. My father had also inherited a Kodak camera that used a glass plate negative. It produced an excellent film.

When I was due to leave Bishop's Court, my mother said to me, 'Geoffrey, we would now like to send you either to Stonyhurst or Ampleforth. Stonyhurst is an excellent Jesuit school, very strictly run. Ampleforth is a Benedictine school and is much more relaxed.' Naturally I chose Ampleforth, and was admitted to the junior house.

Ampleforth is on the edge of the North Yorkshire moors, about twenty miles from York. The monks trace their origin back to the Abbey of Westminster and there is still an Abbot of Westminster besides the monastic abbot at Ampleforth. During the Reformation, the Westminster monks fled to Dieulouard in Lorraine and then returned to England, arriving in Ampleforth in 1802. The monks were, and are, highly educated and cultured men.

When I arrived in the junior house, the housemaster was Father Illtyd, known to the boys as Bacchus because he liked wine. He was a kind and good man. I was well behind the other boys in classwork, but within a term I had caught up. From being at the bottom of the class in Bishop's Court, I suddenly found myself at the top. Ampleforth was and is a great school; the atmosphere was relaxed, discipline was reasonable (there was hardly any corporal punishment, and then only by ferula, a short piece of hardened leather, on the hand). We were free every afternoon, from lunchtime until a quarter past four, to play rugger or cricket. On Wednesday afternoon we went beagling with the school's pack of beagles, across the moors. We generally ended up at a nearby village, Helmsley, and had a ham and egg tea. On our return we would have a cinema show, sometimes a Réné Clair film. I can remember seeing *The Ghost Goes West* and *Le Dernier Milliardaire*.

After a year in the junior house, I jumped a class and joined the upper school in a newly formed house, St Edward's, with Father Raphael Williams, Bacchus's brother, as housemaster. He was known as Flaps because of his big ears. Flaps was a good house-master and a talented painter; many of his paintings are still in St Edward's House. To begin with, there were only twelve boys, but the number increased in a couple of years to thirty or forty. I had good friends, in particular David Gillott, with whom I spent delightful weeks during the summer holidays at his parents' beau-tiful home on Lake Windermere.

I had difficulty translating English into French or Latin until Flaps made me commit to memory a passage of French and a page of Latin from Caesar's *Gallic Wars*. I can still clearly recall what I learned, beginning: '*La femme du Colonel mourante exprima le désir d'être enterrée au milieu d'un petit bois où elle aimait à se promener*' and '*Prima luce cum summus mons a Labieno teneretur ipse ad castrium hostis non longius quam mille et quingentis passis.*' I soon had a better under-standing of Latin and French idiom.

At the age of sixteen I was not sure whether I wanted to become a Benedictine priest or a doctor. We had a Retreat at Ampleforth given by Father Ronald Knox, chaplain of Trinity College, Oxford, who had made a fine translation of the Bible into modern English. He was also well known for limericks. In answer to W.N. Ewer, who had written: 'How odd, of God, to choose the Jews', Knox had replied: 'But not so odd, as those who choose, a Jewish God, and hate the Jews.' I talked to him and told him about my quandary: should I become a priest or a doctor? He said to me: 'Geoffrey, become a doctor.' It was the right advice.

After two years in the upper house, I passed the necessary six subjects with credits in the school leaving certificate which would give me entry to the Medical School at Liverpool University. I had to return to school for two more terms and the headmaster, Paul Neville, six foot six with a commanding personality, called me to his office and said, 'Dean, you have been studying maths, science, and biology to get into Medical School. Take my advice for the remainder of this year: forget these subjects. Study only English, history and economics, and read. You can read any of the books in our main library and any of the books in my private library. Keep a list of what you read and I'll tell you what books I enjoyed myself.' I followed this advice and often read a book a day. Not only would I read during the daytime; after lights out at nine o'clock I would leave my room and sit on the stairs, where there was a good light, to read. It was not a good idea to read in my room because the light could be seen from outside. Among the books I particularly remember from this time are T.E. Lawrence's *The Seven Pillars of Wisdom*, which was in Father Paul's private library, and *Wuthering Heights*. One night I was reading on the stairs when suddenly there was a hand on my shoulder. It was Flaps. 'Dean', he said, 'what are you reading?' 'Lawrence', I said. 'D.H.?' asked Flaps, 'No, T.E.' 'That's all right, go to bed.'

It was during that year that I developed a great admiration for Thomas More, whom I still regard as my patron saint. I always admired him because he was such a practical man of affairs and, unlike some of the earlier Christian saints, did everything he reasonably could to avoid the wrath of Henry VIII; but when it came finally to the heart of the matter – who was head of the Church, the Pope or the King? – he kept to the Catholic tradition, although it cost him his head. He was so different from the early Christian saints, who more or less asked to be thrown to the lions.

During the summer holidays at Ampleforth, we had to attend Officer Training Corps camps, usually on Salisbury Plain. One year I volunteered to be a 'runner' for the General who was in charge of manoeuvres. Runners were provided with a horse and had a much more pleasant time than the cadets, who were moving on foot or very often on their bellies. I had learned to ride on holidays in North Wales. When I was interviewed by the General, he asked, 'One of the Gloucester Deans?' 'No sir, Lancashire.' 'Must be related, must be related. You'll do fine.' One day he said to me, 'Dean, go and tell Captain Fox he's a bloody fool. What the devil does he mean having those men on the skyline?' I galloped away and translated to Captain Fox, 'Captain, the General suggests that it might be a good idea to take your men to lower ground where they are not so easily observed.'

For two years I shared a room at St Edward's House at Ampleforth with an Irish boy, Jerningham Corballis. During the summer he invited me to stay with him at his home, Rosanagh, in Ashford, County Wicklow. This family lived in great style. There were horses and paddocks, a beautiful haunted chapel and a resident chaplain, and plenty of servants to look after the large country house and gardens. Jerningham had a five-year-old sister, Jennifer. During Mass one morning she sang a song she had composed about her horse, 'My Beautiful'. I was about fourteen at the time and I looked at her and thought, 'This is the most beautiful girl I have ever seen!' Later I called one of my daughters Jennifer because of this memory.

The sudden change in my life, and in my self-image – from failure to success – which followed the move from Bishop's Court to Ampleforth, made me realise for the first time the immense importance of environment. Genetically, I had not changed, but in a good environment I had become a different person. The interaction of inheritance and environment, the seed and the soil, has remained my greatest interest ever since and has been the main inspiration for much of the medical research I later undertook.

CHAPTER 3

Medical School

The human soul shares a universal mind.
Aberoes or Ibn Rashid

In 1936, at the age of seventeen, I started my life as a medical student at Liverpool University. In the first year we took four subjects: chemistry, physics, botany and zoology. In physics we had to work in pairs and I found myself with Sam (John) Bradshaw, an ex-Saint Francis Xavier school Liverpool boy who had won a rarely given state scholarship to university.

One of my memories of my first year as a medical student was the difficulty we had in getting our electrical experiments to work. At the time we did not know the reason for the problems we had with our galvanometers, but I know now that Professor James Chadwick, the professor of physics, who had worked with Ernest Rutherford and who had discovered the neutron in 1932, had a cyclotron in the basement of the Physics Department and his experiments with it made our galvanometers act independently of our experiments. I particularly enjoyed zoology, studying the anatomy of the frog, the dogfish, the rabbit, the earthworm and the cockroach.

The first operation I saw was with Sam. It was a gastrectomy, the removal of a stomach, at Garston Hospital near Cressington. We had asked the surgeon, Philip Hawe, a friend of my father, if we might attend one of his operations. Hawe made the first large incision in the abdomen and then, without looking up, said, 'Catch him' as Sam fainted.

In the second year we studied anatomy and physiology.

Professor Wood, the professor of anatomy, told us that we must remember two things. One, that in the tram going home we must not talk about our 'parts', being the parts of the body that we were dissecting – an arm, a leg or a thorax. Secondly, we must not take our 'parts' home with us. Once a fellow student did take an arm home wrapped in brown paper. As she was jogging along in the tram, she was surprised when the lady opposite to her stood up and then fainted. Looking down, the student saw that the corpse's hand on her lap had come out of the brown paper!

In 1937 it was becoming more and more clear that there had been a great military build up in Germany associated with strong anti-Jewish propaganda. This had also happened to a lesser extent in England, particularly with Oswald Mosley's Black Shirts. I wanted to go to Germany to see for myself what was happening there. My parents could not give me the money to go because they not only supported me at university but also paid fees for my two sisters at expensive private boarding schools. I had the idea of writing to Nelson Rockefeller in New York, whom I had heard was the richest man in the world. I asked him to provide me with enough money to spend some months in Germany. To my surprise, I had a letter back in just over two weeks. Enclosed was a cheque for $500, so that I could go to Germany; $500 was equal at that time to £100. To make a comparison of money value, my father's salary in 1937 as a bank manager was about £800 a year. Rockefeller made one condition: I must send him a report on my return.

The summer holidays were almost over, so I travelled by train to Frankfurt and then went canoeing with other students on the river Main. I returned to Frankfurt in the summer holidays of 1938 and attended the university to learn German, staying with a German family. Every day I would bicycle to the university to attend my German classes and I generally lived the life of a German student.

The young men were in the Hitler Jugend and the girls in the Bunde Deutsche Madchen (BDM). Inge, the daughter in the house where I was staying, was a BDM. She was a statuesque girl and very athletic; she used to swim several miles up the Main and back every Sunday. Being rather lazy, I would bicycle part of the way and then swim the rest with her.

I remember going to the Opel Works in Mannheim and was surprised to see that this large American-owned General Motors factory was manufacturing tanks, although it looked as if a war, in which the United States would probably oppose Germany, was imminent. I also went youth-hostelling with the Hitler Jugend, but I refused to sing the 'Horst Wessel' song, an aggressive anti-English marching song.

I had some English friends in Germany, in particular a young man of my own age, Forbes A'Brassard. One day Forbes and I were swimming naked in a quiet rural branch of the Main when a canoe approached paddled by two young women. We climbed a leafy tree, hoping to hide ourselves until they had passed. When the canoe was immediately beneath the tree, they stopped, waved up to us and said 'Wie gehts'. My friend flew through the air like a monkey into the water, while I stayed bashfully in the tree!

Some in England at that time had admiration for what appeared to be the anti-decadent Nazis, who, according to the propaganda in certain newspapers, would be a bulwark against communist and atheist Russia. In Frankfurt great anti-Jewish feeling was being stirred up by Julius Streicher, the *gauleiter* of Bavaria. He published a most scurrilous newspaper, *Die Sturmer*, including caricature pictures of hideous Jewish men raping blonde Aryan girls. Every day copies of this paper were placed behind glass at the street corners. I remember reading the slanderous story of how the 'Elders of Zion' were not only plotting a communist dictatorship, but had a ritual in which they ate Christian babies. The Jewish shops, the few that remained, had 'Jude' written on them. I used to buy my cigarettes at a shop owned by an old Jewish lady. There would be a stormtrooper in a brown uniform at the door with a camera, photographing everybody who went in, but I was bloody-minded and bought cigarettes more frequently than I really needed.

One day a crowd had gathered to watch a group of stormtroopers force two old Jewish men to wash the street with a scrubbing brush, kicking them and laughing at them while they laboured. The German onlookers jeered at the two Jews. I protested to the crowd but I was ignored. Even today, more than sixty years later, I cannot emotionally like the Germans.

Back in England, I wrote Nelson Rockefeller an account of what I had seen in Germany, saying that I thought that the Germans were preparing for a war in which they hoped to conquer Europe, if not the world. I also said that what I had seen happening to the Jews looked to me as if it was a prelude to a massacre. Of course I never thought the Germans would methodically gas six million Jews, a crime that will not be forgotten in a thousand years. I did meet a number of older lecturers and professors at Frankfurt University who were aware of the way things were going. They were frightened to say very much, but they told me enough to make me realise that they, at least, were horrified by it.

On 1 September 1939, Germany invaded Poland and at eleven in the morning of 3 September, Neville Chamberlain announced over the radio that Britain was at war with Germany. Heavy bombardments of British cities were expected and my father decided that we should stay with his eldest brother, Josiah, at Ormskirk, outside Liverpool.

Uncle Jos had been an artillery officer in the First World War. He had been very badly injured, with shrapnel through his face, in the third battle of Ypres in 1917 and was awarded the Military Cross. He was in hospital until 1921. He and his wife, Dorothy, had one child, Gordon, aged sixteen in 1939. I remember him as a quiet sensitive young man with whom I played table tennis.

I spent my time with Dr Haslam Fox, a general practitioner who ran the Ormskirk Hospital. It was he who first showed me the importance of asking patients for a good history of their complaints. I remember the first woman with puerperal fever, due to streptococcal septicaemia, in Ormskirk, whom Dr Fox gave the new sulphonamide wonder drug, M and B 693. She recovered. I would give injections of another wonder drug, Neosalvarsan, or 914. This was the successor of the drug Salvarsan or 606, the first effective treatment for syphilis – discovered by the great German chemist, Paul Ehrlich. '606' stood for the 606th arsenical chemical, which Ehrlich had studied to kill the spirochaete of syphilis. This drug was injected intravenously to as many as thirty patients in the afternoon and I became quite expert at finding a vein.

Dr Fox also had the good sense to ask me to do a post-mortem examination on patients who had died in the hospital, with the permission of the relatives, and to show him what I had found. Up until then I had dissected only in the university's anatomy department. These examinations made me realise how wrong doctors could sometimes be in the diagnoses they made. After a few weeks living in Ormskirk, we returned to Cressington and when term began I continued lectures and started clinical ward rounds at the hospitals.

During the Christmas holidays of 1939, I worked in the shirt department at Lewis's large store in Liverpool. My salary was 21 shillings a week, plus a penny commission on each pound of goods sold, that is one-240th of a pound. Lord Woolton, the managing director, would walk around the store and if he saw shop assistants chatting, he would give them a chit to take to the cashier for their wages; they were fired. On Christmas Eve, there was a party with wine and snacks for the staff after the shop closed. My take-home pay with commission was about 28 shillings a week, not very much for a single person, and poverty for a man with a family. Later I made some money by buying, with a borrowed £20, two microscopes from a pawn shop and selling them at a profit to the parents of the first-year students and then doing the same again in the following years. Although my pocket money was only four pounds a month, out of which I had to pay my bus fare to town, I found I had enough money. In the autumn I also sold the apples from our very fruitful apple tree.

In 1941 I fell in love with Cicely Lyons, a first-year medical student and a sister of Morris, a student in my year. She had taken a degree in English from Oxford before studying medicine in Liverpool and she introduced me to the world of poetry. I read with her Baudelaire's Les fleurs du mal and still have and read The Oxford Book of English Verse, which she gave me for my twenty-first birthday. Her father had a restaurant in the centre of Liverpool. Meals, even in the best restaurants, were restricted to a maximum cost of five shillings and were of poor quality. At Cicely's house, however, there was always a plentiful supply of chicken and steak. Once I was invited to spend an evening with her, when her parents were away. I found soft lights in the sitting room, Mozart on the gramophone and cushions arranged on the floor. Thinking about it now, it was the perfect seduction scene, but in fact neither of us was seduced. I was either very slow or very innocent. Perhaps both. She married Captain Roosevelt Weil, a captain in the American army, and qualified as a doctor at Tulane University, New Orleans, in 1947.

In May 1940 France fell and there was the retreat from Dunkirk. This was followed in July by the Battle of Britain and in September by the bombing of London. So many doctors had been conscripted that medical students were instructed to act as 'house men' or 'doctors' in the hospitals. In Liverpool the posting of medical students to the hospitals was organised by a surgeon, Keith Waldergrave Monsarrat, the father of Nicholas Monsarrat, author of *The Cruel Sea*. In April 1941 I was called to see Mr Monsarrat (surgeons are always called 'Mr' because in the old days surgery was performed by barbers). He told me that I was to be the casualty officer at the Stanley Hospital, a small hospital in Bootle, near Liverpool docks. I was in my fifth year as a medical student and was to continue attending lectures and ward rounds whenever possible. I had only been casualty officer a few days when, on 1 May, there was a bombing raid on Liverpool. There was a further raid the next night and many fires were started. On 3 May there was a devastating raid by 500 bombers and much of the city was destroyed. An ammunition ship in the docks near the hospital had a direct hit and exploded, with great loss of life.

On the third night the Stanley Hospital was hit by a number of fire-bombs; the roof in one area collapsed and there were small phosphorous fires in the hospital. Hundreds of wounded were lying on the floor of the casualty department. The dead were piled on top of each other in a room off the large main casualty room. The windows had been smashed; there was no light and no running water. All my colleagues and I could do was to fill a syringe with morphine and inject a quarter of a grain of morphine into those who were in pain. We stopped haemorrhages and applied first-aid dressings. One woman was trapped in a part of the building that had collapsed; only her face was exposed and a fire was burning in the rubble beneath her, reaching up to her legs. I gave her half a grain of morphine into her cheek, the only part of her I could reach. She died a few hours later.

That same night, to my great sadness, I unfortunately killed a patient. He was badly burned and I wanted to remove some of his clothing to apply dressings. He was in such pain that I gave an injection of pentothal anaesthetic into a vein in his arm in order to induce a light sleep. His breathing and his heart stopped. I know now that it was wrong to give a shocked man pentothal and if I had not done so he would probably have stayed alive. There must be few doctors who do not have at least one death on their conscience.

The situation in Bootle was chaotic: roads were blocked with fallen buildings and hundreds of people were trapped in the debris. During the night a lorry arrived with casualties. I went out, climbed onto the back of the lorry and gave morphine to about ten men who were in great pain. One man's legs had been blown off, but he was still just alive. I explained to the lorry driver that it was impossible to take the injured into the hospital because there was no room on the floor of the casualty department, no light and no water, and suggested he should go to another hospital where they could be treated. I then closed the double doors. He crashed through the doors with his lorry but, seeing the chaos, he then reversed and left.

When it was light and we were working among the injured, I was surprised to see my old friend from Ampleforth, David Gillott, arrive in the uniform of an army lieutenant. He had come to see if any of his men were casualties because a number of them were missing. David said that his platoon had been guarding one of the ammunition ships and they had spent the night getting casualties out of the ship and the bombed warehouses. His sergeant described to me how during the night, when David did not have enough men, he went down an air raid shelter and asked a group of dock-workers if they would come and help, which they refused to do. He went up to the spokesman and knocked him out with a blow to the chin. Then he asked again if the men would come and help. They decided that they would. Gillott and his men, and the dock-workers who helped, saved many casualties that night and he was rightly awarded the George Medal. David Gillott was killed during the allied invasion of Sicily in August 1943 at Zefferana.

The May 1941 bombing of Liverpool caused great distress because many were killed or injured. Roads were blocked with rubble. Soldiers were drafted to the city and there was a free distribution of eggs and bacon, which were in very short supply. Our main problem was to get the casualties from the Stanley Hospital to other hospitals outside Bootle. The hospital was so damaged it was no longer able to function. Soldiers helped to move the casualties.

On the night the Stanley Hospital was fire-bombed, Morris Lyons, the brother of my girlfriend Cicely, and another student were killed while working at Mill Road Hospital, and a third student lost his eye after being buried in rubble for several days. He was in an operating theatre and everyone else there except him and the patient, who was unconscious on the operating table, was killed.

There were some things that we could have done better. We were right to give morphine, to stop bleeding and to apply first-aid dressings. If it happened again, I would try to organise tea. It would have been possible, I think, to have found some way of heating water, although there was no electricity or gas. We would have had to use a fire. The distribution of hot tea would have helped prevent shock and certainly would have raised morale. During the night a priest arrived and started to give the last rites to the dying. I said, 'Father, you were very brave to come out tonight.' He replied, 'Doctor, I would have been much more brave to have stayed at home.'

When the casualties had been evacuated, the hospital was closed. I had worked there for only a week and was paid eight shillings, in cash, for my efforts. The hospital larder was emptied and I collected a dozen eggs and a seven-pound jar of jam before walking the nine miles home to Cressington, through the heavily bombed streets, in my filthy 'white' doctor's coat.

A few days later when Morris Lyons's body had been recovered from the debris, I went with my friend Stephen O'Reagan to the funeral. Only the men attended the synagogue and neither Stephen nor I knew that we had to cover our heads. I did not have a hat, so I placed a handkerchief on my head. The rabbi said to Stephen, 'Put on your hat.' This he didn't want to do because it was a green 'pork-pie' with a large feather in it, yet he did put it on.

During the rest of our clinical training we continued to work in the hospitals. Perhaps we did some good; at least we kept up morale. It was strange to be called 'doctor' when we were only medical students. We had great practical experience.

It was while I was a student at the Royal Infirmary that Hubert Wolfenden, a senior surgeon, one day took a barium meal X-ray of his stomach. We went with him to see his X-ray films. An indentation in the stomach, which looked like a cancer, could be seen. Wolfenden said to me, 'Dean, what do you think?' 'It could be an ulcer', I replied. Wolfenden said, 'Don't be silly. It's cancer! Now who else must we see this morning?' He carried on working until a few days before he died in 1940.

As part of our training as medical students, in our fifth or sixth final year, we lived for two months in a hostel opposite the Liverpool maternity hospital. We had to go out 'on the district' and deliver twenty mothers at their homes, usually normal deliveries. There was great poverty in Liverpool and often we had to use a drawer as a cot for the baby, lining it with newspaper.

The warden of the hostel where we lived was an alcoholic and he became most unpleasant when he was drunk. He also liked the ladies. One of my fellow students warned him that an important part of his anatomy would become gangrenous if he continued to get drunk. He was very drunk two days later and when he awoke in the morning he found, to his horror, that what had been foretold had occurred. Part of his anatomy had been painted black with Indian ink. He ran across the main street in his pyjamas to find a doctor in the maternity hospital. He did not become drunk again while we were in his hostel!

Another girl I greatly admired was Sheila Straw, who was also admired by my best friend Sam Bradshaw. She was a medical student and she later became a well-known paediatrician, Sheila Tyrrell. Sheila was the daughter of a former consul to the Argentine. She introduced me to the works of the novelist Charles Morgan. I read his book *Sparkenbroke* (1936), which gives a clear picture of disseminated sclerosis, as multiple sclerosis was called at that time. It was a much better description than could be found in a medical textbook.

In 1942 I met Nonie Devlin, who had been a medical student for a year. Nonie left medical school so that she could chauffeur her father, Dr Frank Devlin, who did not drive. He ran a practice in a poor part of Liverpool near the university and they lived in the suburb of Childwall. Nonie was a gentle and beautiful girl and we fell more and more in love. There were a number of doctors in her family, including her brother Brian and, later, her younger sister Rosaleen. Brian had qualified a year ahead of me. He was a man of exceptional courage and, on qualifying, he went as a ship's doctor on a convoy to the Far East. He saw many of the ships in the convoy being sunk. Later he had a distinguished career in the army and took part in the airborne attack on Arnhem. He was captured, but with the help of the Dutch Resistance he later escaped.

Life for a doctor in general practice in Liverpool was hard. Dr Devlin would see perhaps thirty to forty patients in his surgery in the morning, some only for repeats of their medicine, and then make up to twenty home visits and see another large surgery of patients in the evening. He was a kind and good man, a Catholic from County Down. He was distressed by the poverty he saw around him.

After passing the Bachelor of Medicine examinations in anatomy and physiology, at the end of our third year we started ward rounds and we were attached for about three months to a physician or surgeon. For a term I was 'on the firm' of Dr Robert Coope, an excellent teacher, who had made clear the difficult subject of diseases of the chest in a very readable textbook. This was unusual; most medical textbooks were heavy-going. Another very well-written textbook on diseases of the eye was by Dr Bernard Chavasse, the son of Bishop Chavasse, the Anglican Bishop of Liverpool. He described how the word pupil came from *pupilla*, the Latin for 'girl', who saw her reflection in her lover's eye.

Perhaps our best teacher was the professor of medicine, Henry Cohen. He was a brilliant man who had been awarded the chair when he was only thirty-two. He later became Lord Cohen of

Birkenhead. He would arrive at the Royal Infirmary to find his registrar, housemen and students waiting for him at the front entrance. His registrar would take his cloak and then Professor Cohen would often play the piano in the doctors' quarters, before starting his ward rounds with the doctors, sisters and medical students in attendance. He was a showman, a bachelor, and a great supporter of the Liverpool Repertory Company. The star of the company, Ruth Lodge, would sometimes accompany him to medical dinners.

Henry Cohen was a good teacher and a wit, although I am not sure if he was the originator of all his witticisms. He once said, 'One of the characteristics of a man with pseudo angina is a tendency to drop dead.' When a particularly stupid answer was given to one of his questions, he replied: 'O'er the gate of Salamanca University is writ: "What nature denies, Salamanca cannot provide".'

In our fourth year we studied pathology. The professor of pathology, Tom Davie, was a great teacher; he later became the Vice-Chancellor of Cape Town University. He would hold what the students called irreverently a 'meat class' every Saturday morning, at which specimens were produced from patients who had died at Liverpool hospitals during the week. The specimen on a dish would be passed to a student and he or she would be asked what pathology was present. Attending Davie's classes was very dramatic, like attending the theatre. We were encouraged to have enquiring minds.

In July 1942, while still a student, I was appointed house physician at Broadgreen Hospital. Broadgreen had been built at Childwall, on the outskirts of Liverpool, as a First World War hospital on an open plan, a lane of wards with paths from one to the next. One ward was reserved for tuberculosis patients. I, and another young doctor named Scott, looked after these patients as part of our duties. One of the patients with open tuberculosis took pleasure in spitting his tubercular purulent sputum into goblets around his bed. Scott started to get headaches and then a fever. He had an X-ray taken of his chest and was found to have miliary tuberculosis or 'galloping consumption'. He also developed tubercular meningitis. It was terrible to watch him suffering dreadful headaches. Over three or four weeks he became more and more demented and used the most blasphemous language as he slowly died. At that time tubercular meningitis was a death sentence. Two other students out of our year of sixty also developed tuberculosis and one of them died.

We were fortunate as medical students in the first three years of the war that, of necessity, we had to take much more responsibility as 'house men' than we would have done in normal times. There was a great sense of purpose, exhilaration and enthusiasm among the consultant staff, who made it their business to convey to us knowledge and also some wisdom. They did their best to prepare us to become good doctors. I passed my final exams in medicine and in obstetrics and gynaecology in June 1942, and in surgery that December. I had to continue as a house physician at Broadgreen Hospital until the end of June 1943.

While waiting for my call-up papers, I decided to do one or two locums. The first one was for a fortnight in Cheshire in a well-to-do practice, at a salary of £16 a week. My chief memory of this was attending a nurse who was having her first delivery at home and who was three weeks overdue. She had refused to go into hospital and it proved to be a very difficult delivery because it was a large baby. After the head was born, the baby would come no farther, because its arm and shoulder were stuck. I could see the baby's head becoming more and more blue from asphyxiation. I tried to bring the arm down but could not move it. Suddenly I heard a 'click' as the humerus broke and then, thank God, the baby came away with no difficulty. The infant was well, the humerus, I later heard, healed and the mother was delighted with her child.

After this, I did a two-week locum for a doctor in the North Riding of Yorkshire. He had a main surgery at his home and two subsidiary surgeries in neighbouring villages. It was not a busy practice. In his main surgery he had a number of medicines marked 'for cough', 'for constipation', 'for diarrhoea' and so on, but in the subsidiary surgeries he kept two large Winchester bottles, one containing a concentrated red liquid and the other a foul-tasting blue liquid. In the subsidiary surgeries, there were notes on the patients' cards such as '3-1', which meant a proportion of three red to one blue. For anyone who was seriously ill, a bottle of medicine was made up at the main surgery.

After I had been there for two or three days, a mother brought her three-month-old infant to see me because he was coughing at night. I worked out how much I must dilute the medicine 'for cough', calculating the dilution by the weight of the baby, and told the mother to give the baby a teaspoon of the medicine each evening. That night, at about twelve o'clock, there was a knock on the front door. I came down in my pyjamas to find the mother standing there. She said: 'Doctor, I'm worried about my baby because he is only breathing about once or twice every minute.' I realised at once that there must have been some opiate drug, such as codeine, in the cough medicine to which babies are particularly susceptible. We rushed to the house and I gave the baby an injection of a respiratory stimulant – coramine. Within half an hour he was breathing normally.

Naturally I was extremely relieved that the child had not died. What was my surprise to find that, during the remainder of my stay, every night mothers were bringing their infants to see me because I now had a reputation for being good at treating sick babies!

It was borne in on me at this time that one's reputation in practice does not depend on how good a doctor you are. This was confirmed by another event that happened in the same practice. I was called to see a wealthy farmer who had cut his throat. I found him lying on the floor of the kitchen. There was blood everywhere; he had cut his throat from ear to ear. Fortunately, he had thrown his head back, thus protecting his carotid arteries and had cut only through the veins. He was unconscious and pulseless. I put clamps on his veins, bled one of his neighbours for blood and crossmatched the blood with the farmer's blood on two slides, simply, and then poured blood into a large vein, using a funnel and rubber tubing. After about an hour and two pints of blood, the farmer regained consciousness. I called for an ambulance and when his condition had improved, he went off to hospital.

I was delighted with myself for the successful way in which I had treated the farmer and thought the family would be pleased with me, but this did not prove to be the case! Apparently he had been an extremely difficult and garrulous old man and his sons were waiting for his death in order to inherit his large farm!

CHAPTER 4

Bomber Command

They shall not grow old, as we that are left grow old;
Age shall not weary them, nor the years condemn.
R. Laurence Binyon, *Poems for the Fallen*

In August 1943 I received my call-up papers to join the Royal Air
Force as a medical officer with the rank of flying officer. This rank
was equivalent to that of a first lieutenant in the army. The newly
recruited doctors first reported to a training centre where there
were about ten other doctors who had been conscripted at the
same time. We were given a wcek's preliminary training: how to
salute, how to march reasonably in step and the structure of the
RAF. Since I had been in the Officer Training Corps at Ampleforth, this was straightforward.

After a few days of basic training, we were sent to a large air
force station at Halton, Buckinghamshire, to learn something about
aviation medicine and tropical medicine. In order to impress on
us how important it was to use oxygen, we were put into a decompression chamber. As the atmospheric pressure was lowered, we
were asked to do simple sums, such as 13 take away 6. I wrote
down the wrong answer. I remember little after this until I woke
up on the floor of the decompression chamber, the sergeant in
charge having plugged in my oxygen mask. We were not likely to
forget the importance of using our masks. On another occasion an
aeroplane flew overhead and dropped an irritant gas, such as is used
to disperse a crowd, so we quickly appreciated the importance of
always carrying our gas masks. Fortunately, poison gas was never

used in the Second World War.

The officers' mess at Halton had formerly been a palace belonging to the Rothschild family. There was a magnificent hall in which we normally took afternoon tea. After I had been at Halton about ten days, I was talking to my friends in the hall while having tea and was leaning negligently against one of the tables. A red-faced and portly officer, an air vice-marshal, approached me and, to use an air force slang expression, 'tore me off a strip' for slouching against the table. I was very surprised by this and apologised three or four times. Off he went. It suddenly occurred to me that he had no right to be reprimanding an officer in front of the mess servants. The senior officers of air rank had a private room where they had tea and their drinks in great comfort, sitting in large leather armchairs by a roaring log fire. I knocked on the door of this sanctum, and somebody shouted 'Come in'. I went up to the officer who had reprimanded me – I later learned he was the mess president and an unpopular man – and said to him, 'Sir, once again I apologise for leaning against the table, but I do take the strongest exception to being reprimanded in front of the mess servants.' He flushed crimson as if he was going to have a stroke, blew out his cheeks and said: 'If you have any complaints, put them in writing.' I noticed that the other air marshals and air vice-marshals were tittering behind their newspapers. Once again I said I was sorry and left the room.

I was told by my instructors, who I now think found it very amusing, that I would probably find myself posted to a malarial swamp in Central Africa, where it could be pretty well guaranteed that I would be dead within six months. Alternatively, they said, there was a base in the Arctic Circle where the medical officer had recently died from frostbite. So I was surprised when I was given what was considered to be a very good posting to a Wellington bomber station at Bitteswell, near Lutterworth in Leicestershire.

Bitteswell was both an operational and a training station. The planes were twin-engine Wellington bombers. The buildings were built of wood as a temporary wartime measure and were very cold. I flew on training flights two or three times a week. I had never flown before. The purpose of doing this was to make it clear that the medical officer was aware of the problems of flying and to study the aircrew's reactions in the air. I flew once, sitting behind the pilot, in a fighter plane which was practising attacks against bombers. I have never been so sick in my life. Each time the fighter plane zoomed up or down to attack the bomber, my one prayer was that the pilot would misjudge and crash. Air sickness is much worse than sea sickness!

A high proportion of the aircrew at Bitteswell were Poles who had escaped after Poland had fallen to Germany and Russia. They were extremely courageous men and were greatly admired by the young women in the Women's Auxiliary Air Force, the WAAF. Most of the Polish airmen had girlfriends in the WAAF or living in the vicinity. No one was allowed to leave a RAF station without a kit, which consisted of condoms and a bactericidal jelly. Only senior officers were permitted to catch the 'clap' from a lavatory seat; for anyone else, it was a punishable offence!

The courtyard outside the sick quarters at Bitteswell was inches deep in mud and this made it difficult to carry stretchers to the main entrance. Fortunately, some tarmacadam had been left at the end of a newly made runway and there was also an old steamroller. I piled the tarmacadam on to a truck, brought it to the courtyard outside the sick quarters, spread it on the ground with the help of my sergeant and then, with the steamroller, made a reasonable courtyard.

One morning several sackloads of cats were delivered to the sick quarters with instructions from the Commanding Officer that I was to dispose of them. I remembered that there was some morphine which was not 'indented', that is it was not officially on my list of drugs and for which I did not have to fill in any forms; I decided to give each cat two grains of morphine, enough to kill a man. After injecting the cats, they became active and amorous, purring, rubbing against my legs and showing an embarrassing amount of affection. I telephoned the local vet and he explained that morphine acts as a stimulant in cats. When the cats eventually quietened down, all I could do was put them in a truck, leave the engine running, and close the garage door. Before doing this, I picked out the most attractive kittens and 'accidentally' let them free. I found it very hard to kill them.

After three months I was posted to Waterbeach, in Cambridgeshire, which, unlike Bitteswell, had been a peacetime RAF station and had well-built red-brick buildings, including a small hospital. Waterbeach was a Lancaster bomber operational base commanded by a group captain. An air commodore was in overall command of Waterbeach and two other stations nearby. The Waterbeach station commander was Group Captain C.M. Heard. The purpose of the station was to make it possible to send out up to twenty four-engined Lancaster bombers in raids over Europe two to three times a week and sometimes more often, unless flying was impossible because of fog.

On a Lancaster there was a crew of seven: the pilot, observer/navigator, flight engineer, wireless operator, bomb aimer and the middle and rear gunners. The loss per raid varied but averaged in 1944 about five per cent. On a bad raid, twenty planes would go out and perhaps twelve or fourteen would return. With an easy raid and good luck, perhaps all twenty would come home. There were often a number of injured in the returning planes, particularly rear gunners.

Before each raid there would be a briefing of the aircrew, which I and David Stafford-Clark, the senior station medical officer, would attend. Before starting on a long operation, many of the crew would take amphetamine tablets, known as 'Wakey, Wakey' pills. These acted as a stimulant and would keep the men alert for eight hours or longer.

We would wait for the planes to return in the early morning. German fighter planes would sometimes return with the bomber stream, when they could not be picked out, and shoot planes down when they were coming in to land. We would go in the ambulances and collect the injured aircrew and the remains of the dead. When a plane crashed, which sometimes happened close to the airfield, there was a splash of flame into the sky over a hundred yards high. It was impossible to get near to the wreckage because of the heat.

Before an operation over Europe, and on their return, aircrews were given a bacon-and-egg meal. Only aircrew on operations ever received this luxury. On their return from an operation, which might have lasted eight or nine hours, they were debriefed. The aircrew were often so excited that it was necessary to knock them out by giving them two or three capsules of a pentobarbitone sedative, Nembutal – yellow capsules which were known as 'Sleepy Sleepies'.

It was a murderous business. The aircrew, particularly the pilots, were the pick of Britain's and the Empire's young men, often university graduates. They needed high qualities to stand the strain of long flights over Germany and attacks by fighter planes and anti-aircraft fire. They knew, once they saw the loss rate, that their chance of completing a 'tour', which consisted of thirty operations, was small. The few who survived had to return six months later for a second tour of twenty 'ops'. Hardly anyone survived two tours.

David Stafford-Clark was an exceptionally gifted medical officer. He was also a courageous man and went as a passenger on a bombing raid once or twice, something that was strictly forbidden for medical officers. He had, incidentally, published a book of poetry, *Autumn Shadows*. After the war, he became a famous psychiatrist and director of the York Psychiatric Clinic in London; for some years he was also 'television psychiatrist' for the BBC. He was twice mentioned in despatches and should have had a military honour.

If a member of aircrew refused to fly on an operation, he was considered to be 'lacking in moral fibre' (Lmf). This was a dreadful disgrace and meant dismissal from the RAF and sometimes a posting to the pioneer corps of the army to work on the roads in India. To be discharged as Lmf was a difficult thing to explain to family and girlfriends and it did not occur often. Aircrew would come to us and say 'Doc, I refuse to fly'. We had to persuade them that they had to fly or they would be Lmf.

On the nights of 23, 24 and 25 November 1943 there were particularly dangerous raids on Berlin, with heavy losses. On the afternoon before the third raid, some aircrew came to the sick quarters and said, 'Our nerves are shot – we are not going to fly.' We talked to them, individually. They all flew that night. David and I felt depressed and drank a good amount of beer on the fourth night when there was a 'stand down' and no planes were flying. On occasion, illegally, we would mark a man as medically unfit for flying, making some medical excuse, because we knew that if he was given a rest for a few days he would then return to flying. We also succeeded in obtaining permission for a number of aircrew, who had perhaps survived twenty-five or twenty-six raids, to escape the last four or five raids on the grounds that they had become physically and mentally exhausted. During a three-month tour of operations, those who survived appeared to visibly age. It was not possible to avoid flying because of a state of anxiety with perhaps quite marked symptoms, such as tremor. This, after all, as was pointed out in Joseph Heller's *Catch 22*, was normal. The Commanding Officers and the medical back-up, including when necessary, psychiatrists, were tough. The medical officers were expected to fly and did with aircrew on training flights. Over London we were once attacked in error by our own anti-aircraft guns, which I found very scary.

There was a large field near the airfield where the cars of aircrew who had been lost were left – several hundred cars, some of which were in excellent condition. Petrol was strictly rationed, and while I couldn't obtain an extra six gallons of petrol for the car for a weekend's leave, I could get a friend to fly to the nearest airport in a Lancaster on a 'training flight', using perhaps a thousand gallons of fuel.

Once I was flown to Liverpool's Speke aerodrome so that I could visit Nonie. The ground was covered by thick smog and we could not see the airfield. During the war the factories were encouraged to produce smoke and much of England was usually covered in smog. I said to my pilot: 'This is hopeless. Let's go back.' He said, 'No, Doc. I promised I'd get you to Liverpool and I will.' I said, 'But you can't see where to land.' 'I think I can see the river and the runway leads to the river.'

He insisted on landing and we approached the runway at about 180 miles an hour. I was sitting beside the pilot and saw the Mersey about thirty yards in front of us. It looked as if we were going to go straight into it. The pilot revved up the four engines to full throttle and somehow managed to get airborne just before we reached the water. I could feel the perspiration running down my neck. I had forgotten about Nonie and had only one wish: to get back to Waterbeach. 'For God's sake', I said, 'don't try that again.'

'I've got the feel of it now, Doc. I'm coming in once more.' This he did successfully. I think this was my most frightening experience in the RAF.

I am quite sure that the aircrew who had volunteered to fly in Bomber Command had not realised before starting their training how heavily the odds were stacked against them. More than 60,000 aircrew were killed in Bomber Command during the Second World War. One strange phenomenon was the 'jinx girls'. An attractive WAAF would have a lover who would be killed when the plane was shot down. She would get another boyfriend and a few weeks later the same thing would happen. She might be able to find a third and a fourth. At this stage her friends would start to say 'You're a jinx.' If a girl had the reputation of being a jinx, it meant that if you 'slept' with her, you would die. The aircrew became so frightened of 'jinx' girls that often they would not accept a cup of cocoa from one. Several jinx girls had to be posted to other non-operational stations and one hanged herself with a lavatory chain.

Superstition among aircrew was rampant. Most had lucky charms; a monkey's paw was a favourite, and the religious-minded might have rosary beads or a special medal. Nothing helped.

David Stafford-Clark had trained at Guy's Hospital in London. The senior physician there was also the senior physician of the RAF, Air Vice-Marshall Sir John Conybeare. Conybeare had written the standard textbook on medicine for British medical students. He visited us at Waterbeach on a number of occasions and was always addressed, at his wish, as 'Cony'. We were extremely busy but, in spite of this, he would send David and myself notes from London such as: 'Dear David and Geoffrey, please each send me an essay on emphysema by the end of the month. Yours ever, Cony.' He chose difficult subjects, which required considerable thought.

Cony once visited us with a number of senior Russian officers and insisted on leaving his footprints on the ceiling of the officers' mess, along with the Russians and other officers. A group of perhaps twelve men on the ground supported six men on their shoulders, and then three men on their shoulders, and eventually a man on top, held upside-down with his feet on the ceiling. The whole line would move slowly forward while the man on the top left his foot-prints on the ceiling, his shoes having been blackened with soot. Very often the whole mass of men would collapse halfway, which of course it did when Cony was leaving his footprints. The next morning he called David to see him and said: 'I've one hell of a pain in the right side of my chest. Would you have a look at it for me?'

The right side of his chest was dull on percussion; there was no resonance and no sounds of breathing could be heard. Clearly the right side of his chest was full of fluid. David said, 'Cony, you have fluid on the right side of your chest. It's probably blood from the fall you had last night.' Cony replied: 'Shut up about it. Call my driver. I am going back to Guy's. I'll get it fixed up there. Don't say a word.'

In the later part of 1943 and in 1944, when bombing raids were at their height and losses were high and when Britain had not opened a second front in Europe, senior Russian generals would be brought to Waterbeach where they were shown that Britain was 'bombing the hell out of Germany'. They would always come with crates of vodka and political commissars who could speak English, all very tough men. On one occasion one of the Lancasters could not fly on an operation because an engine had been damaged in a raid the night before. A Russian general said, 'Why is that plane not flying?' Group Captain Heard replied, 'One of the engines is damaged and has to be replaced.' The Russian said, 'Are your men frightened of flying a plane over Germany on three engines? My men will fly it for you.' Heard answered: 'No you will not. This is not your plane.'

Before the Russians came, we were told that they were our great allies and that we would have been defeated without them holding the German line on a 2,000-mile front; that we must tell the Russians everything they wanted to know, but if anybody mentioned any of the details about how certain radar apparatus worked, they would be in great trouble!

Sometimes a bombing plane would return with a blockbuster bomb, weighing perhaps 10,000 pounds, partly in and partly out of the bomb bay because the release mechanism had been damaged.

When this happened to American planes, all the aircrew would parachute to earth after the plane had been set on automatic pilot to fly over the Atlantic. The RAF could not afford to lose bombers in this way and the rule in Bomber Command was that all the aircrew parachuted out except the pilot, who then brought the plane in to land, praying that the bomb would not explode. Quite often it did not since there was a propeller device at the end of the bomb which rotated as the bomb fell before it reached the ground and exploded. Nevertheless, the impact of the dislodged bomb when it hit the ground as the plane landed would be so great that it could easily detonate. On three occasions a plane returned to Waterbeach with a large bomb only partly released, but only once did the bomb explode on landing, on a seldom used runway, blowing out all the windows for miles around and leaving a large hole in the ground. The joke was going around that a plane had returned from Germany with a bomb half out and the group captain gave instructions on the radio that the pilot should fly over the North Sea and try and shake it off. He was unsuccessful, and had only half an hour's fuel left. The CO said: 'Everybody except the pilot bale out.' The pilot replied, 'All my crew are out, sir. I'm coming in to land. Are there any further instructions?' The Commanding Officer replied, 'Yes, say after me "Our Father which art in Heaven".'

After a bombing raid the medical officers would be waiting with the ambulances to go to the planes. All we could do immediately was to stop haemorrhaging, apply dressings and splints and treat cases of shock with intravenous fluid. Aircrew had morphine in small tubes, called tubunics, with a needle attached, sewn into their tunics, and they gave themselves or other members of the crew morphine by injection if they were injured and in pain. Once they had recovered sufficiently, we would send the injured aircrew by ambulance to the specialist RAF hospital in Ely, five miles away. Planes would sometimes return with the rear gunner half shot out of the cockpit, dead and frozen rigid. The temperature at 20,000 feet was perhaps minus thirty degrees. Getting these bodies out of the plane was part of our work.

There was nothing as unpleasant as dealing with the scraps that remained after a plane had hit the ground and caught fire. This happened on a number of occasions. All that could be found after the fire subsided would be pieces of rib cage or charred limbs. We would pick up these pieces of bodies and place them on the floor of the ambulance. Once this happened when a plane had crashed about three miles from Waterbeach. I went with my sergeant and collected what human remains we could find and brought them back to the station hospital where I obtained a list of the seven men who should have been in the crew. The remains were placed in seven coffins; a name was placed on each coffin so that they could be sent to the railway station to be returned to their relatives. A message then came that there had been only six men on board; the plane had been on a training flight and one of the gunners was unable to fly because he had caught flu. Fortunately his 'coffin' was recovered.

While at Waterbeach I had had hardly any leave because bombing raids two or three nights every week meant that both medical officers were needed on the station. On another occasion Nonie stayed a few days at a guest-house near Waterbeach. Nonie was, and is still in my mind, very beautiful. She had green eyes, dark hair, and an 'Irish complexion'. We were in love and we became engaged. In retrospect, I should have made sure that Nonie did not become pregnant. We also should have waited to get married until after the war was over. Nevertheless, on 7 June 1944, we married in the Catholic church in Cambridge. I drove myself to Cambridge in one of the two station ambulances with some of my friends piled into the back. After the ceremony we returned to Waterbeach and had a wedding party at a house in the village. We then returned to Cambridge and had a romantic weekend in an attractive hotel. We were probably in the bridal suite because two white doves spent the morning on our windowsill. Nonie then returned to Liverpool to continue as her father's chauffeur.

The Germans sometimes dropped what were called butterfly bombs over airfields. These were small anti-personnel bombs with metal flaps on their sides (hence their name) which would fall gently in the grass. If they were accidentally kicked or trodden on, they would explode, generally blowing off a man's feet. The planes were dispersed on the large airfield in case they were attacked from the air. The Germans did not bomb Waterbeach, although later in the war we would watch the unmanned 'doodlebugs' flying over, usually because they had overshot London. Sometimes our own bombs would explode, generally while a plane was being loaded. On one such occasion all that was left after a large 'blockbuster' had exploded was a colossal hole. What these bombs did to German cities could be seen on the aerial photographs that were taken of the bombing missions: whole cities devastated and every building without a roof. After one of the blockbusters exploded at Waterbeach there would be a roll call to see who was missing. One man, who was on the periphery of the bomb blast, had simply wandered away in a state of shock. He turned up a few days later.

A fighter plane crashed near the aerodrome and Sergeant Smith, the sick-quarters sergeant, and I rushed across fields in the ambulance to the crash. The plane was on fire and machine-gun bullets were exploding with the heat. We could see the pilot in the cockpit, apparently dead. As I ran around the plane to see if there was any way to get the pilot out, Smith said: 'Sir, this is bloody silly. Let's get to hell out of it.' Until the fire engine arrived, we could do nothing. He was quite right.

Gordon, the only child of my Uncle Jos, joined the RAF in 1941 and was trained as an aerial observer/navigator in the United States and Canada. He died on the night of 16–17 April 1943 when his Lancaster was flying on a mission to attack Plzen (Pilsen) in Bohemia (Czechoslovakia); the Skoda works were there. His plane crashed in France and Gordon's body was found by a lady in her garden at Conde-Sur-Marne, where he is now buried. The remaining six members of the crew were found sixteen kilometres away, so perhaps the plane exploded in the air. I named my youngest son Gordon, in his memory.

Not all the aircrew who were shot down over Europe died; some of them managed to get out through the escape hatch and parachute to safety. The escape hatches were small and difficult to get through, particularly in the dark in a burning plane. Aircrew had sewn into their tunics survival kits, containing compressed rations, amphetamine tablets to allay hunger and keep them awake, maps, a compass and so on. Some made their way, often with the help of the Resistance, from France to Spain and from there back to England.

I had a friend, David Rosenthal, an Oxford graduate, a tall handsome man and a courageous pilot. He was a Jew and when his plane was missing, we all hoped that he was not a prisoner of the Germans. About four months later he turned up to complete his tour of operations. He had escaped through occupied France, with the help of the Resistance, into Spain and so back to England. He survived another ten operations before his plane was shot down.

Because Waterbeach was a major Lancaster bomber station and not far from Bomber Command and London, we had visits not only from Russians and Americans but from 'Bomber Harris', the Air Marshall commanding Bomber Command. King George VI came to Waterbeach and visited the patients in the station hospital. David Stafford-Clark said to him: 'Sir, would you like to see the operating theatre?' He replied, 'Oh Doctor, don't you think we should go to the mess and have a drink?' He was a sensitive man who had never wanted to be king. On the abdication of his brother Edward VIII in 1936, he accepted the throne with, I suspect, great reluctance.

Quite by chance I discovered that there was a community of Carmelite nuns living near the base. With the war they had been forgotten about because they were an enclosed Order. I found that they were not getting the meagre civilian food rations. When I could, I would bring food that was left over from the sick bay in a bucket, and pass it through the grille to the Reverend Mother. The sisters did not speak except from dire necessity, and they slept on concave beds and left their day clothes outside their cells at night so that they would 'go to God' owning nothing. They made Nonie's trousseau for our wedding. One of the sisters was a good painter and when I left Waterbeach, the Reverend Mother gave me a painting by her of 'Christ in the Sepulchre', watched over by the Virgin Mary. On the back of the painting was inscribed: 'Lord, make Thou my life one dying, so that when Thou deemest best to call my soul, it comes replying, "consumatum est"' – too idealistic an approach to life, I fear, for me. Perhaps the prayers of the sisters helped us.

In November 1944 I developed a series of carbuncles and then a high fever and was diagnosed by Cony as having staphylococcal septicaemia. I was sent to Nuffield House, the private wing of

Guy's Hospital, and given, by injection, 16,000 units of the new wonder drug, penicillin, every four hours. Penicillin at that time was prepared in a black soup. It was in short supply and was used only for servicemen. I was lucky to get it and no doubt it saved my life, but the injections themselves were agonisingly painful. It was not the penicillin that caused the pain but the soup in which the fungus had been cultured. I asked to be given first an injection of novocaine, a local anaesthetic, and that the needle should be left in position and then the penicillin injected into the same area. This made the pain tolerable. As I recovered, I wrote a letter to *The Lancet*, my first communication to a medical journal, saying that doctors did not appreciate how painful these injections were, and novocaine should be injected first. It later became the custom to mix the novocaine with the penicillin, which made the injections much less painful. As penicillin was purified, the problem was overcome.

In February 1945 Nonie, now near full term, gave birth to a stillborn boy. She had had a very difficult time during her pregnancy because there was little food available and she had had to drive her father on his many house calls. I was able to get 48 hours to go to Liverpool and see her in a maternity hospital. She accepted the loss of our child with great fortitude.

With the virtual collapse of the German airforce in the spring of 1945, the Lancaster bomber losses were greatly reduced. Germany surrendered unconditionally on 7 May 1945, but the war with Japan continued and it appeared probable that much of the RAF would be transferred to the Pacific theatre of war. This all changed on 6 August when, without warning, the atomic bomb was dropped on Hiroshima, with enormous destruction. Three days later a second bomb was dropped on Nagasaki and the following day the Japanese sued for peace. The surrender was signed on 2 September 1945.

I remember walking up and down a country lane after the bombing of Nagasaki, thinking that the atomic bomb and the release of nuclear energy was the most important happening in man's history since he had learned how to use fire; for the first time

41

it was possible for the human race to destroy itself and perhaps make planet earth uninhabitable.

The morality of the RAF's area bombing of German cities (rather than strategic military objectives) can be questioned, although it was never allowed to be at the time and only the most courageous became conscientious objectors. In retrospect, I realise that Britain, with the help of the Commonwealth, the USSR and the USA, was fighting the greatest evil that the world has known. The Nazis – and at the time most Germans supported the Nazis, although many of them were to deny it later – looked upon themselves as the master race and were undoubtedly determined on world domination. If they had invaded Britain and not the USSR in 1941, they might have achieved it, although at a great human cost.

When the war was practically over, the saturation bombing of the beautiful city of Dresden by RAF Bomber Command and the US Strategic Air Force was inexcusable. Even Churchill, who had been in favour of bombing German cities, wrote to his chief military adviser, General Hastings Ismay, on 28 March 1945: 'The destruction of Dresden remains a serious query against the conduct of Allied bombing.' Harris, who commanded Bomber Command, was never made a Lord after the war.

At the end of the war, David Stafford-Clark was placed in charge of training post-war medical officers for the RAF. I believe he was offered a peacetime commission on the understanding that he would shortly become the RAF's senior medical officer – which would have meant a knighthood. However, he decided to train to be a psychiatrist and became a famous one.

At this time I had lost considerable weight and became very depressed. The reasons were probably multiple: the strain of the war years, the septicaemia which had left me with some kidney trouble, the loss of our child, and the uselessness of being in the RAF now the war against Germany and Japan was over. I was told to report for a medical board and was pleased to be demobilised, given my airforce gratuity, an army issue blue civilian suit – which quickly became threadbare on the seat of the trousers – and a rail pass to return to Liverpool.

CHAPTER 5

Peace

War lays a burden on the reeling state,
And peace does nothing to relieve the weight.
William Cowper, *Conversations*

On returning to Liverpool in September 1945 I found life very dreary; it was a great anti-climax after the excitement of Waterbeach and Bomber Command. Rationing had become worse; even bread was rationed. Nonie was pregnant again. We found a first-floor flat at 29 Ullet Road, near Sefton Park, and I bought a 1939 Morris 8 from Nonie's brother Brian for £120. There had been remarkably little inflation during the war because of the government's tight control of prices and wages. Nevertheless, great social changes had occurred. The poor people in Liverpool were better fed than they had been before the war because, as a result of food rationing, price control and work for all, everyone could afford the limited rations and, for children, there was a free issue of milk. We were able to afford a live-in maid at a salary of £1 per week and, since her father had retired from practice after the war, Nonie had a relatively easy life. Nevertheless, there was general gloom from the strict rationing of food and clothes.

I called to the medical school to see Professor Tom Davie, the professor of pathology, who had been appointed Director of Post-War Medical Establishments. Although it was not immediately apparent, Britain was moving rapidly towards a National Health Service and, in order to help re-establish discharged doctors from the services, additional registrar posts had been made available at the teaching hospitals at a salary of £600 a year, paid by the state.

I was fortunate to be appointed medical registrar to Robert Coope with whom I had worked in 1942 at Broadgreen Hospital. He was a consultant physician at the Liverpool Royal Infirmary.

As more and more doctors were demobilised and given registrar posts, the number of registrars at the Royal Infirmary was two or three times what it had been before the war, and so the amount of work for each doctor was not great. Once again I went back to the study of medicine; my enthusiasm had been increased by the encouragement I had received from Cony while I was in the RAF. I also attended the dramatic ward rounds of Henry Cohen.

As a medical registrar at the Royal Infirmary, I was responsible for teaching six to eight medical students and found that teaching helped me greatly to learn more about medicine; students quickly found any gaps in my knowledge! I also decided to take a correspondence course for the exam to become a Member of the Royal College of Physicians of London. This was, and is still, the examination all aspiring specialist physicians are expected to pass. The correspondence school, in Red Lion Square, London, employed senior medical registrars and consultants as coaches. Certain reading was recommended each week, followed by a three-hour examination paper which had to be answered without the aid of books. The essays were posted to the tutor in London, who returned them with his criticisms. This course had the double effect of encouraging study in a disciplined manner and of improving one's ability to express thoughts clearly.

On 25 January 1946, our first child, John, was born. He was a small baby and developed jaundice about a week after he and Nonie arrived home. It was at this time that our maid left and, in the middle of winter with no heating, it was difficult to dry nappies and clothes. Looking back, I could have made life easier for Nonie if I had given her more of my time and been prepared to spend more money from the small amount that I had saved. Life must have been dull for her because petrol was strictly rationed, and I was out all day. After our meagre supper of spam or dried egg, I would study for three hours. I found John's crying irritating when I wanted to work. Life for Nonie was hard and lonely.

My life, in contrast to Nonie's, was very interesting; I was getting a much better understanding of medicine and was attending ward rounds with some of the best teachers in Liverpool. I must have been very difficult to live with because my life revolved around study and, selfishly, I paid little attention to domestic difficulties. Since demobilisation, Nonie and I had had one weekend holiday in Wales. It was in the middle of the harsh winter of 1946/47. Nonie, John and I motored through North Wales in deep snow and stayed at a pleasant farm guest-house. For two or three days we had real food, such as bacon and fresh eggs.

One morning Robert Coope said to me: 'Geoffrey, as you know, I have been examining doctors in London who are aspiring to the higher degree of MD. One of the candidates has written an essay for the MD on "Propaganda in Medicine". Give me your opinion about it.' I immediately recognised David Stafford-Clark's writing. The next day I said to Coope: 'I must tell you I know who this is. I was on a bomber station with him. The essay is brilliant!' Coope replied: 'Yes, I thought so too.'

In the second half of 1946, when thousands of doctors had been demobilised, it was essential that I pass the London Membership Examination soon. The number of candidates for the examination was great – at this time it took place four times a year – and there was a very high failure rate. The examination consisted of three parts, two three-hour papers, a practical exam with patients and pathology specimens, and then if the first two parts were passed an interview with the President of the College and the censors. I would travel to London, by train, to take the two written examinations. In London I stayed at Cony's flat. I first took the written examinations, too soon, in June 1946 and failed, but the experience was useful. The letter I received from the examiners said: 'We do not consider that it would be worth your while to continue with the examination.' I tried again in September, passed the papers, and was called back for the clinical second part of the examination. When I did eventually pass, if I remember correctly, 43 candidates were successful out of 560 entrants. At this time few candidates passed, perhaps because many doctors were taking the exam and highly qualified doctors were being discharged from the services.

In March 1947 I was delighted to receive a letter telling me that the censors considered that I had passed the written part of the exam and that I should return to London for the clinical exam. At this time I developed parotitis, or mumps, and the left side of my face was swollen. Fortunately, the swelling had gone down by the time I had to attend at St George's Hospital for the clinical examination. Before going into the ward to examine a patient, we were shown a card which read something like this: 'Under no circumstances may a rectal examination be carried out on a patient. Such an examination will result in immediate and permanent disqualification from the membership.' The reason was that the same patient might be seen by more than one candidate.

My patient was a man of about sixty who was complaining of unsteadiness in walking, shooting pains in his legs, and a constant feeling that he needed to go to the toilet. On examination, I noted he had small pupils that did not react when a light was shone into them. The 'jerk reflexes' in his arms and legs were absent. I diagnosed that he had *tabes dorsalis*, as a result of syphilis. I asked him if he had had injections into his arm and he told me that he had been receiving intensive treatment during the previous four years at St Bartholomew's Hospital.

I found it hard to believe that a man who had had such intensive treatment would still have the symptoms of tenesmus – the constant desire to pass a bowel motion. I would have liked to have made a rectal examination with my finger, but knew that I could not ask for a screen to go around the patient's bed in order to do this, nor could I ask for a glove because we were strictly forbidden to make this examination. Nevertheless, I asked the patient if he would mind if I examined him under the bedclothes. This was without a screen and in an open ward, with the censors, who were responsible for the examination, walking up and down. He agreed and, with great trepidation, I made an examination with my finger which I had moistened with spittle. I found a marked obstruction in his rectum, which I thought was due to cancer. I had just completed this examination, and was of course unable to wash my hands, when the chief examiner, Sir Adolph Abrahams, arrived at the bedside to examine me.

Sir Adolph was elegantly dressed with a large diamond pin in his tie. He was well known to be a ferocious examiner and had examined and failed me on a previous occasion. His brother, Harold Abrahams, had been a famous sprinter who represented Britain in the 1924 Paris Olympics. Sir Adolph asked me to tell him the history of the patient and what I had found on examination. He then asked me for my diagnosis. I told him that the patient had *tabes dorsalis*. He asked me whether or not the irregular pupils, which did not respond to light, might not be due to some other disorder, perhaps an unusual abnormality called an Adie Holmes pupil, but I disagreed. He kept saying to me, 'What else could it be? Yes, and what else, and what else?' I then said, 'In addition, sir, he has a neoplasm of the rectum.' Neoplasm was a word for cancer which, at that time, was not generally understood by patients. Sir Adolph went red in the face. He said 'What?' and asked me how I knew. I admitted that I had made a rectal examination. There was a long silence; then he asked me if I had been shown the card saying that I would be disqualified if I did a rectal examination. 'Yes.' He turned around and walked away.

At this point I felt foolish and did not know whether to leave the ward or stay where I was. A few minutes later Sir Adolph returned with a sister pushing a trolley and two nurses with a screen. The screen was placed around the patient's bed. Sir Adolph put on a glove and some vaseline on his finger, told the patient to lie on his side and then examined him. He then turned to me and said, 'Dean, how do you know that is not a gumma?' A gumma is an inflammatory condition which can result from syphilis, which of course the man had had. I replied, 'Sir, he has been receiving treatment at Bart's for the last four years. It is impossible that he would have a gumma after such treatment.' Sir Adolph said, 'Go away.'

I returned to Cony's flat and told him my sad story. He laughed and laughed and said, 'Geoffrey, they must pass you now.' Apparently, within a couple of days the story had gone round the London hospitals about the candidate who had broken the cardinal rule at the membership examination. When I was examined by the other censors, they asked me one or two questions and dismissed me. They were obviously taking no real interest in how I did. The same happened in the pathology section of the examination.

I returned home to Liverpool and received, to my delight, a

letter saying that I had to return for the third and last part of the exam. This was held in the main boardroom of the Royal College of Physicians, at that time in Pall Mall. Lord Moran, the President of the Royal College of Physicians and also Winston Churchill's private physician, asked me to sit in the leather armchair by his side at the head of the table. Around the table the eight censors were sitting. Lord Moran said, 'Dean, are you the candidate who broke our most sacrosanct rule that under no circumstances will a candidate make a rectal examination of a patient?' 'Yes, sir.' 'We think you are a fit and proper person to be a member of the Royal College of Physicians. Congratulations!'

On this, my fourth trip to London, Nonie had come with me. We left John, who was now a fine one-year-old, with her parents. We celebrated by going to see Noel Coward's play *Brief Encounter*. During the eighteen months I had been studying for the membership, Nonie had been a great support and had never complained about the dreary life she was living. I loved John but it was Nonie who kept him happy and quiet while I studied.

Back in Liverpool, I went to see Tom Davie because my term as medical registrar to Robert Coope had ended. He offered me a job as registrar for the Liverpool School of Tropical Medicine. This famous school had a ward for patients with tropical diseases in the Liverpool Royal Infirmary. I would carry on working at the Royal Infirmary but would also attend lectures in tropical medicine and, in time, take the Tropical Medicine Diploma examination.

During 1945 and 1946 a number of patients were admitted to the Royal Infirmary in Liverpool suffering from paralysis; some had one limb paralysed, others had all four. Most of them were dock-workers. The paralysis came on insidiously over a few days; it was not associated with fever and it was not like poliomyelitis. A friend of mine from medical school, Dick Hotston, and I made a map of the area of residence of those who had developed paralysis. While some came from the dockland areas of Liverpool, a number came from Wrexham, my birthplace. We went there and stayed at a local pub. One of the men in the pub remarked that he had noticed that those who were affected by paralysis bought their fish and chips from, say, Taffy Jones. Those who went to Dai Williams's fish and chip shop were all right. This was such a marvellous clue that Hotston went to Taffy Jones's fish and chip shop, ordered six pennyworth of fish and chips, and brought them to Professor Roberts, a chemist and the Liverpool City Analyst. Roberts found that the oil in which the chips had been cooked contained a poison, Orthotricresyl Phosphate (OTCP). OTCP damages the nerves, causing paralysis in one or more limbs. The police were informed and raided the chip shop in Wrexham. They found two barrels of oil there stolen from a ship that had docked at Liverpool en route from the United States to Russia. On further enquiry it was found that other barrels had been stolen and the oil distributed among dock-workers. The poison was in the sealant for the barrels. I often wondered what happened to the Russians who ate the cooking oil after the cargo had been discharged. This was my first introduction to epidemiology.

My best friend from university, John Bradshaw, had been demobilised from the army in July 1946 after serving in Burma. He decided that he would try to make his living by writing a book. He and I, before the war, had made a pilgrimage to T.E. Lawrence's cottage in Dorset and John had made friends there with a Mrs Knowles, who had attended Lawrence until his death in a motorbike accident in 1935. Her sister, Mrs Forde, invited John to lodge with her while he wrote. This book was not published, but he subsequently published other books, including *Doctors on Trial* and *Drug Misuse and the Law*, both of which sold well.

While studying tropical medicine and attending lectures at the Liverpool School of Tropical Medicine, I became friendly with Dr Wilson, the senior company doctor for the Alfred Holt Shipping Line. At this time there were about 160 ships belonging to the Alfred Holt, or Blue Funnel Line, and we frequently examined seamen from these ships suffering from malaria or other tropical diseases. It would be many years before I would be senior enough to obtain a consultant post in England and I was considering emigrating because by 1947, the pre-war hospital registrars, some of them five to ten years older than me, had been demobilised and were first in line for consultant posts. Dr Wilson told me that there was a ship, the *Priam,* sailing for South Africa with sixty passengers and that, legally, a doctor should be on board. The ship's doctor had become ill and another doctor was only available to join the ship in South Africa to continue the journey to Australia. Wilson asked me if I would be interested in acting as ship's surgeon for the voyage to South Africa. After consulting with Nonie, and because prospects in England appeared to be bleak, I said 'Yes'.

While in the airforce I had bought, at a bargain price, a Queen Anne mahogany table and eight chairs. To acquire some funds before leaving England, I decided to sell them, and also a skeleton from my student days. My economical advert in the 'For Sale' column of the *Liverpool Echo* read: 'Queen Anne table and eight chairs. Also skeleton.' *Punch,* the satirical magazine, reprinted the advert, under the heading: 'Queen Anne's Dead', and sent me £5. I sold the furniture and the skeleton!

I could foresee big problems because I had only about £200. Nevertheless, I obtained letters of introduction to physicians in Cape Town from Cony, Robert Coope and Henry Cohen. My Uncle Jack gave me a gift of £50, but my parents and parents-in-law were very much against my leaving England and would give me no encouragement or financial help. It was highly impractical for Nonie to go with me, because we had a young son and no obvious means of support in South Africa and, in any case, I could not find them a passage. It was arranged that Nonie and John would live with her parents and join me later. I embarked at Liverpool docks on 6 June 1947.

It was a pleasant but uneventful trip and I had practically no work to do. I still have my discharge certificate stating: 'Conduct very good, ability very good, alcohol moderate.' I was paid a nominal one shilling for the trip!

CHAPTER 6

South Africa

The most stately thing, and the fairest
Cape we saw in the whole circumference of the earth.
Sir Francis Drake

The view of Cape Town nestling under Table Mountain when I arrived on the *Priam* on 24 June 1947 confirmed the words of Francis Drake. At that time, Cape Town was a relatively liberal city. Jan Smuts was the Prime Minister of South Africa and the leader of the United Party, which mainly represented the English-speaking white population, descendants of British settlers. The opposition Nationalist Party represented the Afrikaner white community, who predominated in the rural areas, but Afrikaners had also moved into the cities. Descendants of the Boers, they spoke Afrikaans, a dialect of Dutch. In 1947, the white population was 2.4 million. There were also people of mixed race in the Cape, known as the Coloureds, descendants of early white Dutch-speaking settlers and their Malay and Hottentot (Koi) slaves; they spoke Afrikaans. There were a million Coloured people in South Africa, a third of a million Asian, mostly of Hindu origin and living in Natal, and seven million black or, as they were known at the time, Bantu ('Bantu' meaning 'the people'). Democracy was restricted to the white population. When the early Dutch settlers first came to South Africa in 1652, the native people of the Cape were the Hottentots. The Bantu people, at that time invading from the north, had reached the border of the Cape Province at the Fish River but not the Western Cape.

On the day we docked, the ship's officers decided to take the unattached ladies from the ship to dinner. We wandered around the streets of Cape Town and found what appeared to be a pleasant place for supper. When we sat down, we were told that only drinks were served and so we decided to leave. The proprietor, a Portuguese, then told us that we could not leave without paying an entrance fee of £2 per head. There were fourteen of us. We continued to argue, but the manager would not let us to leave and locked the door! It looked to me as if we were going to have an unpleasant quarrel and perhaps a fight because some of the waiters had put on knuckle-dusters. It would have been an unfortunate way to arrive in Cape Town. Suddenly there was a shout from the other side of the door: 'Open the door or I shall shoot the bolt in!'

The owner of the club opened the door, and there stood a captain of police with two policemen. He told us to go quietly and keep to the main streets. While we were arguing with the owner, the ship's chief engineer had managed to find a telephone near the toilet and had telephoned the police. After this, the club was closed for three months.

Cape Town was fortunate in having two fine professors of medicine: Jack Brock and Frankie Forman. Brock was a handsome man with a moustache, in his mid-forties. He had been a Rhodes Scholar at Oxford, where he had become an enthusiastic supporter of the Oxford Group known as Moral Rearmament. This group had been founded by an American evangelist, Frank Buchman, and was broadly based on ecumenical Christianity. It emphasised the pursuit of four absolutes: purity, unselfishness, honesty and love. Although I admired Jack Brock greatly and was later invited to join the group, I declined, largely because I did not relish the idea of confessing my faults at their meetings. Frankie Forman was a gifted teacher. He retired early as professor in Cape Town so that he could continue hospital work and teaching in Israel. He did no private practice.

I decided I should learn some Afrikaans and placed an advertisement in the *Cape Times*: 'English Doctor, newly arrived in Cape Town, looking for accommodation with an Afrikaans-speaking family.' There were two replies: one from the Predikant, or Domine, of the Dutch Reformed Church at Rondebosch, the other from a Detective-Sergeant Ferreira, who lived at

Observatory, down the road from Groote Schuur Hospital, the main teaching hospital. I first went to see the Domine. He would not speak one word of English and I was unable to speak any Afrikaans. I then went to see the detective and decided it would be wiser to stay with him. We agreed that I should pay two pounds ten shillings a week for lodging and three meals a day.

During my first evening with the family, I asked Sergeant Ferreira's daughter, Margrieta, to teach me some Afrikaans. I asked her the Afrikaans for goodbye. She replied, 'Cheerio'. This was my first Afrikaans word! I then said, 'Tell me an Afrikaans saying', so this fourteen-year-old said playfully: 'Say after me "N'Lekker coppie coffee, en n'kuckie daarbye, Vra jy Ma om by my te vry".' I asked her what this meant and she replied, 'A nice cup of coffee and a cake with it. Let us ask your mother if we can make love.' Margrieta taught me some most useful basic Afrikaans.

A car was essential, although I had very little money. Even a poor white man in South Africa had a car. I went to a car mart and bought a Hudson for £80 at auction. Within two or three days I realised that it was not a question of what was wrong with the car, but was anything right with it. I took it back to the mart and it was sold again at the following auction. I lost £20 on the deal. Sergeant Ferreira then told me that he had a friend, an engine driver, who had a 1934 Chevrolet that had been looked after well; he was willing to sell the car for £160. I had a look at the car, which was in spotless condition. It had apparently clocked up only 40,000 miles, but the clock may have been going round a second time! The seats were covered in the best railway leather, and the engine, which had been looked after at the South African railway workshops, purred. I decided to buy the car and for the five years that I ran it, it gave me no trouble.

One of the great pleasures of Cape Town is climbing Table Mountain. From a distance the mountain looks like a table, often with a tablecloth of cloud on the top. It is beautiful. I had been in Cape Town only a week when I decided to walk up the mountain. On the way up, to my amazement, I met Jan Smuts coming down alone and said to him: 'Good morning, Prime Minister.' He asked me who I was and recognised my English accent. I told him I had just come to South Africa but hoped to settle there. He said: 'Walk down with me and I shall tell you about South Africa.' I walked down with 'Oom Janie' (Uncle Jan) until he reached his waiting car and he gave me a brief history of South Africa. In my opinion he was a great man and an outstanding statesman. If he and his party had won the 1949 general election, and not the Nationalist Party of Dr Malan, South Africa would have been spared the horror of apartheid.

After a month in Cape Town, and since my money was running low, I decided that I had better travel around the country and see if there were any good prospects of settling as a physician in another city. I drove along the garden route on the south coast to Port Elizabeth, 400 miles to the east of Cape Town. Much of the road, at this time, through the beautiful Knysna Forest where elephants roamed, was unmetalled with gates to be opened and closed along the way.

I arrived in Port Elizabeth late at night and, when I reached the town hall, asked a passerby to recommend a hotel. I was told to drive up a steep hill and at the top I would find two hotels, the Grand and the King Edward. I booked in at the Grand. The following morning, at breakfast, the head waiter, an Indian named Tony, asked if I would join two other doctors who were staying there: Professor Don Craib and a young doctor, John Russell. What luck meeting two doctors from Port Elizabeth on my first day!

Don Craib, of Scottish and Afrikaner ancestry, was a delightful, humorous man of about fifty, and we soon became very good friends. He had been professor of medicine at the Witwatersrand, Johannesburg, Medical School and had a great reputation as a teacher. As a young man he had worked with Sir Thomas Lewis, a famous cardiologist, at University College Hospital in London and was the first man, in the early 1920s, to expound the theory of bipolar electrocardiography. For many years his ideas were ridiculed, but it is now known that his concepts were correct. Craib had served as the senior physician in the South African Army and then, after the war, following some disagreement with the administrators at Witwatersrand University, he decided to practise as a consultant physician in Port Elizabeth and immediately built up a large and well-deserved consultant practice.

John Russell was at that time a young doctor who had just joined the practice of George Dunlop in Port Elizabeth. Dr Dunlop was a general practitioner with a well-to-do practice; he always dressed in a black, striped suit and was a dry, sardonic Scot. He was the senior honorary physician to the Provincial Hospital in Port Elizabeth. There was only one other consultant physician in Port Elizabeth besides Don Craib; he had a small practice and was on the point of retiring.

I spent a few days at the Grand Hotel, visited the hospital and met a number of the doctors. Don Craib told me that if I decided to settle in Port Elizabeth, I would be able to rent a consulting room at Elizabeth House, the offices where he practised in Park Drive. Elizabeth House, facing the city's central park, had previously been a nursing home and had been converted into rooms for consultants. There was already a radiologist, Duxie Osler, in practice there, an excellent surgeon, Sandy Stewart, and a gynae-cologist, Langley Gace.

After a few days in Port Elizabeth I continued by car to East London, 200 miles along the coast. This was a smaller city than Port Elizabeth with one consultant physician, George Nesbitt. Dr Nesbitt was an excellent physician who had been professor of medicine at the Royal College of Surgeons in Ireland. He had resigned as professor in 1930 and settled in East London. I then continued to Durban, a further 400 miles up the east coast. Durban is a predominantly English-speaking city. From Durban I motored inland to Johannesburg. I found it to be a brash modern city built on the wealth of the Witwatersrand gold mines. I then motored on to Pretoria, the former capital of the Boer Republic of Transvaal and with Cape Town, a twin capital of South Africa. In Pretoria all the physicians were Afrikaners and it seemed likely that I would never make a living there without a good knowledge of Afrikaans. Finally, I returned to Cape Town via the capital of the Orange Free State, Bloemfontein, where, again, Afrikaans was the main language

By now it was October 1947 and my funds were exhausted. I realised that I had to make up my mind quickly and decided that I would settle in Cape Town or Port Elizabeth. In Cape Town it would be difficult for me to earn a living in a reasonably short time. I became friendly with a young physician, Hennie Muller, and his wife Jean, who was also a doctor. His family was well known in Cape Town and he wanted to stay there. It did not appear to be a good idea for both of us to start practice in Cape Town, so I made up my mind to settle in Port Elizabeth. I returned there to stay at the Grand.

Don Craib advised me that I should learn something about the way the Afrikaners lived on their farms. The hinterland of Port Elizabeth, the Karroo, is dry and the farms are large sheep farms, often of 10,000 or more acres. Craib had grown up in a country town, Somerset East, 120 miles inland from Port Elizabeth. (His mother was a Hofmehr; his grandfather had been Domine Hofmehr of Somerset East.) Don arranged that I should spend two weeks on the farm, Kaalplaats (Dry Place) with Meneer and Mevrou Botha (Mr and Mrs Botha).

It was a great experience living with the Botha family. Meneer Botha had a white beard and was about seventy. He and his wife would lie in their big double bed drinking coffee in the morning as the farm servants came to the bedroom window for their instructions for the day. They would each say: 'More, Baas' ('Good morning, sir'). I went out shooting springbok with Meneer Botha, who spoke to me in English or simple Afrikaans. He would say: 'Look, Geoffrey, at that buck over there in the bushes.' I would see no sign of a buck. Meneer Botha would then place his rifle to his shoulder and shoot. After we had walked about half a mile I would see the dead buck.

In Somerset East I was surprised that the children in the village always called me 'Oom' or 'Uncle', until I realised that this was the customary address of young people to their elders. Older women were called 'Tante' or, in its familiar form, 'Tannie' or 'Aunt'. It is a good idea and a reminder that we all belong to an extended family.

I was interested to see that the white wool farmers took a paternal interest in their black servants; they were not well paid but they were well fed and each family received a sheep every month. On

the other hand, strict discipline was maintained; there was no tradition of equality between white and black.

I had applied – it was *chutzpah* – to be registered by the South
African Medical Council as a consultant physician. The Medical
Council, quite rightly, did not accede to this request, saying that,
although I had a higher degree in medicine, I had not had enough
years in specialist training. I decided to see members of the Medical
Council in Pretoria about my medical registration. John Russell
had a girlfriend, later his wife, Joan Bull, who lived with her parents
in Pretoria. He had a Piper Cub aeroplane and was flying to Pretoria
to see her. He offered me a lift to Pretoria and we flew from Port
Elizabeth, following the railway line and intending to stop at
Bloemfontein, about halfway, to refuel. As we followed the line,
we realised that we had exceeded the expected number of miles
and also that our fuel tank was empty. We became concerned
because there was no sign of Bloemfontein and we thought we
would have to land in the veld. The engine started to splutter. At
this point we saw a town with a large hole in the middle of it and,
both at the same moment, gasped 'Kimberley'. We both knew
about the enormous hole in the city from the digging for diamonds.
We had followed the wrong railway line! We managed to make a
safe landing at Kimberley airport and the rest of our journey was
uneventful.

In Pretoria, I went to see 'Ockie' Oosthuizen, the chairman of
the Medical Council, to discuss my application to be on the
specialist register. He told me that I could be registered as a doctor,
but that he would have to wait for the next meeting of his
committee to see about registration as a specialist physician. I registered as a doctor and returned to Port Elizabeth.

By then my funds were depleted and I decided that I had better
try to earn some money. I had already visited the Catholic Nursing
Home, St Joseph's, in Port Elizabeth, run by the 'Blue Sisters', and
they had introduced me to a number of the schools and to some
of the doctors in the town. I paid courtesy visits to the doctors. I
remember calling to see George Dunlop and being shown into the
sitting room by the maid. When George came in he said, 'Dean,
whoever said you could come into my house?' This shook me
rather badly. He then told me, plainly, that if I stayed in Port

Elizabeth, he would see to it that I would never be appointed as a physician at the hospital and that I would starve! Although George Dunlop was a general practitioner and not a consultant physician, he was the senior physician at the hospital and perhaps he did not relish the idea of a young physician in the city.

With the help of Don Craib, who asked me to see a few patients when he was too busy, and because I was called to attend to a few sick children from the boarding schools, I was just about able to pay my hotel bill. After dinner I would often be approached by guests who wanted free advice about their health. One evening I was surprised to see, at the window of the lounge, a ghostly face and a finger beckoning me to come out. I went outside and there, to my surprise, was George Dunlop, who said 'Dean, come and see a patient with me.' He was not as intimidating as he had appeared.

Over Christmas 1947, my old friend and mentor, Cony, came to South Africa with the senior surgeon from Guy's Hospital, George Doherty, to lecture and for a holiday. He visited Port Elizabeth for a couple of days. I was surprised early in January to receive a note from my bank, the Standard Bank, to say that my account had been credited with £70, and even more surprised the following day when a second letter arrived to say that it had been credited with an additional £400, which put my account in credit. I could not understand where this money had come from, so I phoned the bank manager and asked him. He told me that it had been paid into my account by Sir John Conybeare. The next day I received a letter from Cony which said, 'Dear Geoffrey, I have some money left over in South Africa and don't want to bring it back to England. You would be doing me a great favour if you would use it and pay it back to me at a later date.' It could not have come at a better time. I wrote a letter of thanks and about a year later was able to pay the loan back in full.

My first bank in South Africa was at the main office of Barclay's Bank in Cape Town. I went to see the chief accountant and asked him if I could have an overdraft of £200. He asked what security I could offer for the money. I told him none, but that I was a doctor and hoped to make a good living. He replied, 'What do you think we are? A charitable institution?' I decided to remove my £17 from Barclay's Bank and opened an account instead with the Standard Bank, who were much more understanding. It has been my bank ever since. It is strange how difficult it is to borrow money from a bank when one really needs it.

During the six months I had been in South Africa, Nonie had a difficult life in Liverpool. She and John were staying with her parents. Food and fuel were still very strictly rationed. In January 1948, she and John flew by Sabena from Brussels to Johannesburg, her father having paid the fare. John was not yet two. I drove to Johannesburg to bring them to Port Elizabeth. We travelled the 1,000 miles back to Port Elizabeth through the small dorps – or villages – of South Africa. Nonie was enthralled to find the country so beautiful and food plentiful; she had not eaten so well for years. Poor though we were, she found South Africa a paradise and John thrived. It was at this time that I really appreciated and loved her.

Nonie had spent only about two months with me in Port Elizabeth when I heard from the Medical Council that I could not be placed on the specialist register as a physician without a further period as a medical registrar at a teaching hospital. I was told I should apply again after three months. I would have to work at a hospital attached to a medical school and I had no money left. I decided that we had better go to Cape Town. Mother Frances, the prioress of the Priory Convent in Port Elizabeth, rang me up and said, without being asked, that Mother Thomas, an old nun who had been the previous Reverend Mother, would like to look after John until we were settled in Cape Town or returned to Port Elizabeth; she reasoned that it would be difficult and not fair on John if we did not find suitable accommodation in Cape Town. With great heartache we agreed to leave John with Mother Thomas, who became very fond of him. With hindsight, I realise that this was a mistake. It would have been better to bring John with us. He should not have been separated from both parents at such an early age.

Back in Cape Town, I went to see Jack Brock, and told him that I needed to be a medical registrar for some months. To my delight and surprise, he said that they had just lost the doctor who looked after the health of the nurses and that he would appoint me to this post, with the rank of medical registrar, at a salary of £50 a month. He said that the work of looking after the health of the nurses would not be great and I could spend the remainder of my time attending ward rounds and examining patients.

We looked for cheap accommodation in the town, but the cheap rooms we saw were incredibly dirty and probably verminous. Arthur Kipps, a surgeon attached to Groote Schuur Hospital, told me that on his brother's vineyard, at Constantia, a beautiful area outside of the city, there was a rondavel, a round thatched hut, which was empty and we could rent it. We went out to see the rondavel. Next to it was a second hut which could be used as a bedroom. We accepted the offer, bought a second-hand bed, used orange boxes as tables and chairs and bought an electric hot-plate which we placed on an orange box and attached to an electric light plug. Each day I went to the hospital by car and Nonie would help in the vineyard. Any food we required I would buy on the way home and we were able to live cheaply. We paid £10 per month rent for the rondavel and hut.

Once again I applied to be placed on the specialist register and in June 1948 my application was approved. We had been away from Port Elizabeth for just under three months and we had heard from the Priory Convent during this time that John had been happy. If I had not been accepted on the specialist register, we had intended travelling by car to Port Elizabeth and bringing him back with us. To have fetched him from Port Elizabeth would have meant a four-day round trip. Nevertheless, it was a mistake. We did not then appreciate the importance of young children staying with one or both parents. We should have gone back for John and, ever since, I have regretted not doing so.

CHAPTER 7

Practice and Lauries Bay

Is there no pity sitting in the clouds,
That sees into the bottom of my grief?
William Shakespeare, *Romeo and Juliet*

Nonie and I returned to Port Elizabeth and stayed at the Grand Hotel. I was now accredited by the South African Medical Council as a consultant physician, but still had no practice. I was able to rent a consulting room and shared a waiting room at Elizabeth House and a secretary with Dr Gace. In South Africa, every consultant physician had an electrocardiograph, and most patients, at least those over fifty, were expected to have an electrocardiogram (ECG) with their consultation. Heart attack rates among the white and Indian South Africans were the highest in the world, although the rates have fallen since the 1940s and 1950s because of changes in lifestyle.

I approached my friendly bank manager and, with a further loan of £200, bought a Sanborn electrocardiograph. At this time the electrocardiogram was recorded on photographic paper and I was able to arrange with the radiologist, Duxie Osler, that I could develop my cardiograph film in his darkroom. If I required an X-ray examination for any of my patients, I would take them downstairs to Duxie. The fee for the electrocardiogram was two guineas, which brought the consultation and ECG fee to five guineas.

One of the first doctors to ask me to see a patient was Robert Grieve, a good general practitioner with a big practice. He knew I was looking for somewhere to live and one day he phoned me to say that one of his patients, George Letherby, who lived in a house next door but one to my consulting rooms, had just lost the tenant in the semi-detached house next to his. Dr Grieve suggested that I should go and see Mr Letherby quickly and that he might let me rent the empty four-bedroomed house.

George Letherby was a remarkable eighty-five-year-old man when I first met him. He had come to Port Elizabeth from England at the age of nineteen and had started work in a men's outfitters shop. On hearing that gold had been discovered on the Witwatersrand, he borrowed money and bought jackets, trousers and boots to fill up a wagon and trekked to the Rand, where he sold the clothes at a very big profit to the miners. He returned to Port Elizabeth, bought more clothes, wagons and oxen and returned to the Rand. Within a short time he had made enough money to buy a large area of land in the centre of what is today Johannesburg. By the time he was thirty, with the rapid development of the new 'city of gold', he was a very rich man and he decided to retire and take up his hobby of microscopy. George Letherby became world famous for his articles in nature journals on the microscopy of various South African flora and fauna.

When I called on him, I found that he was stone deaf. I wrote to ask if he would rent me his house. He replied: 'Young man, your calligraphy is indecipherable!' I wrote my request again in capitals, telling him that I was a doctor who had just arrived in the city. He rented me the house. Letherby had a daughter, Enid, who was the only person at that time in Port Elizabeth with disseminated sclerosis. Enid had been born in South Africa but had spent many years in England as a child. She also had a brother living with her who had the disease in a much more acute form. Disseminated sclerosis occurs more frequently than would be expected in two members of the same family. Although Enid's first attack of the disease was at the age of nineteen, she was still, at sixty, able to walk with a stick. Nonie and I bought the minimum essential furniture and moved into 88 Park Drive.

Attending ward rounds at Groote Schuur Hospital, I had been surprised to find that disseminated sclerosis was very uncommon. Disseminated sclerosis, now known as multiple sclerosis or MS, is the second most common disease of the nervous system in Europe and North America. At Liverpool every medical student learnt neurology by examining patients with disseminated sclerosis, and there were one or two such patients in every medical ward. Yet in South Africa the doctors at all the hospitals I subsequently visited told me it was extremely uncommon and some of the physicians said that they had never seen a patient with the disease. While I was in Cape Town, I went through the records of the patients admitted to the hospital over the previous ten years. There was an excellent diagnostic register. Only three white people and no Coloured people had been found to have disseminated sclerosis, which was indeed strange because the physicians at Groote Schuur had trained in England and would not have missed the disease if they had seen it.

In my travels around South Africa I had collected copies of the records of all patients diagnosed as having disseminated sclerosis at the teaching hospitals, which kept a diagnostic index – in Cape Town, Pretoria and Johannesburg and also from the physicians in East London, Durban, Bloemfontein and Port Elizabeth. During the previous ten years I could find the records of only 29 white patients diagnosed as having disseminated sclerosis; fifteen of them were immigrants from Europe, although the European immigrants were less than 10 per cent of the white population. Ten of the remaining fourteen were white South Africans of British stock and only four were Afrikaans-speaking, although Afrikaners were 60 per cent of the white South African born population. For some reason, disseminated sclerosis was uncommon among those born in South African, especially among the Afrikaners.

In 1947 there had been an article in the medical journal *Brain*, describing how four out of seven veterinary workers carrying out research into a disease of sheep, swayback disease, on Bradwell Moor in Yorkshire, had developed disseminated sclerosis. Swayback disease affects the brain of lambs, causing them to sway as they walk. It is somewhat similar to disseminated sclerosis and can be prevented by feeding the ewes small amounts of copper. Except for one small area around Knysna, in the Southern Cape, swayback did not occur in South Africa, probably because of the high copper content of the country's soil. I wrote an account of the 29 patients in the main South African hospitals diagnosed as suffering from disseminated sclerosis, and pointed out that the disease was clearly uncommon in the country. Copper supplements we found did not prevent relapses in disseminated sclerosis.

In Port Elizabeth, as a newly arrived physician, I was asked by other doctors to see a number of patients who appeared to be close to death. 'Let us try the young doctor from England!' Within the first six months I was asked to see eight patients who had become paralysed. At first I thought I was seeing an epidemic of Guillain-Barré syndrome, a form of paralysis that sometimes occurs in epidemics, and I wrote a short report for the *South African Medical Journal* describing these patients. I was soon to realise that I was wrong and that some of these patients had a very different condition: acute porphyria. This was to prove the start of a twenty-year study.

I had been back in Port Elizabeth about a month when Dr Douglas Laurie consulted me. He had qualified in Edinburgh in 1908. He worked in a casualty clearing station in France during the First World War and was awarded the OBE. In 1922 he came to South Africa and started practice in Port Elizabeth. When I saw him in 1948 he was living in the house he had built on the coast about 15 miles from Port Elizabeth. The bay where the house was built was named after him and is known as Lauries Bay. The bay is part of a large farm owned by the Lovemore family, Bushy Park.

Harold Lovemore had come to South Africa, paying his own passage, with the settlers who arrived in 1820 and who founded the new city of Port Elizabeth. He bought a large tract of land to the west of the new town, known at the time as Claaskraal, extending for about ten miles along the coast. The name Lovemore was rumoured to be a fictitious one and it was said that he was an illegitimate son of King George III of England. He certainly named his farm after one of the royal parks, Bushy Park. I am not convinced of the story.

In 1925 Bushy Park was owned by his descendant, also named Harold Lovemore, known as Hal. Colin, his five-year-old son, developed a seriously infected knee joint. This was so life threatening that amputation of the leg was being considered. Colin's father asked Dr Douglas Laurie, who had a great reputation in Port Elizabeth, to tend to his son and after the removal of a large thorn from the knee joint the infection subsided and Colin kept his leg. Harold Lovemore was deeply grateful to Douglas Laurie and he gave him the right to select a site anywhere on Bushy Park farm for the purpose of constructing a home. Laurie chose a site on a small bay known as Whiteheads Bay which subsequently became known as Lauries Bay and it is so named on the ordnance map. The chosen site was fenced off and measured approximately five morgan (ten acres). Free right of access across Bushy Park farm to the property was granted. There was no written agreement but it was understood that the rights granted to Douglas Laurie were intended to be transferable at his option, as will appear from subsequent events.

Laurie had a most inventive mind. He had designed the standard operating table in the British Army in the First World War. He had invented the glass drip system known as the 'Laurie Regulator' which regulates the flow of fluid when a transfusion is given; it is still used. He had the idea of using an electromagnet to withdraw metal objects, such as nails, from a child's stomach. The small, greased magnet would be passed down the child's throat attached to wires covered by protective rubber tubing. Under an X-ray screen, the magnet would be brought into contact with the head of the nail, the current would be turned on, making the electromagnet active, and the nail would be withdrawn.

Laurie had invited me to visit him at Lauries Bay. His property there consisted of a splendid house with five bedrooms and three bathrooms and accompanying it were two cottages, a dairy, workshop and a swimming pool. Laurie had been using the house and cottages as a guest farm, thus making a living. I persuaded him that he should have a course of the new antibiotic, penicillin, and this greatly improved his health. He decided to accept an offer to teach the boys at a famous private school, Michaelhouse in Durban, some of the skills at which he was expert, for example, how to build a house, organise a drainage system, provide electric light and so on. He was intrigued by this idea and wanted to sell Lauries Bay to me. However, I had no money, though Laurie was asking only

£1,000. So he sold the house in 1948 to Mr and Mrs R.G. Gibbings, who ran it as a guest farm.

The house that Laurie had built expressed the originality of his mind. It was built on concrete stilts so that, if there was a high tide, the sea would flow under the house and not into it. He had first built one room, now the central dining room, and then added to it room by room until it appeared like a small castle. The doors closed with wooden catches, so they never shook if there was a strong wind. Originally the water to the house had been pumped by a windmill from a spring to a large tank on top of the hill above the house. Water pressure came from the height of the tank. The water was heated by an old-fashioned stove in the kitchen. Laurie had built a well-equipped workshop next to the dairy and a cowshed for six cows. My architect friends tell me the main house defies all the rules of architecture, yet it has stood for more than seventy years, even though it is built on sand.

It is surprising how the same people kept reappearing at important points in my life. About this time my best friend, John Bradshaw, whom I have already mentioned, having completed his book and a tour as a ship's surgeon, obtained a free passage to Port Elizabeth as supernumerary surgeon with the Blue Funnel Line. He stayed with us and helped me prepare a paper on disseminated sclerosis for the *British Medical Journal*. If I had had a few more patients, life would have been perfect.

In September 1948 I was sitting in my consulting room at Elizabeth House when Don Craib walked in and said, 'Geoffrey, I've been asked to see a man on a ship in the harbour, the *Mirabouka*. It sounds as if he may have had a heart attack. I am completely booked up. Please take your cardiograph machine and go and see him. Do whatever you think is necessary.'

I collected my bag and took my old Chevrolet down to the docks. The *Mirabouka*, which means the Southern Cross in the Australian aborigine language, was a Swedish ship belonging to the Trans-Line. The patient, Sir Maynard Hedström, was in the best private cabin on the ship. He was seventy-nine years old and had suffered a coronary thrombosis. When I had eased his pain with morphine, I said to him, 'Sir Maynard, you have had a heart attack. I am going to call an ambulance to take you into St Joseph's, a very fine nursing home, and when you are better you can take another ship home.' 'Dr Dean,' he replied, 'I am sailing on this ship at three o'clock this afternoon. I feel that if I don't, I will never get home alive. I am sure you have a very busy practice, but would you leave your practice and accompany me to Fiji? You can name whatever fee you like. I am Governor General of the Fiji Islands, a director of the Standard Oil Company of New Jersey and of a number of shipping companies, and a multi-millionaire.'

I was in a quandary. Could I suddenly leave Nonie, who was six months pregnant, at three hours' notice, even with John Bradshaw in the house to keep her company: although I realised it would be hard on Nonie when she had arrived in South Africa only eight months earlier. Sir Maynard had asked me to name a fee. I remembered that my old professor of medicine, Henry Cohen, used to charge fifty guineas when he went from Liverpool to see a patient in London. I decided that I would suggest the same if I were to go, fifty guineas per day until I arrived back in Port Elizabeth. Sir Maynard agreed immediately and I realised this would solve our financial problems.

I returned home and told Nonie and John Bradshaw that I was invited to go to the Fiji Islands that afternoon. Nonie agreed that I should go. I then thought that I should find a nurse to come with me and remembered that Rosemary Jackson had just started work at the Provincial Hospital in Port Elizabeth. A New Zealander, Rosemary had spent some years on the island of Samoa after qualifying as a nurse in New Zealand and then some months nursing in London. She and three friends had bought an old London taxi and had driven it from London to South Africa, across the Sahara. By the time they reached Port Elizabeth, Rosemary had run out of money, so she took the nursing post. She was in her late twenties, and besides being a nurse, she was a good storyteller. I went to the hospital, found her, and asked her if she would accompany me to the Fiji Islands that afternoon. With the permission of the medical superintendent, she agreed, packed her few belongings and joined the ship.

I told Don Craib what had happened; he was delighted. By

coincidence, my one patient of that week, a Mrs Jones, a bank manager's wife, was in the waiting room. I asked Don Craib if he would see her. Then I went into the waiting room at two o'clock and said, 'Mrs Jones, I know that you have an appointment to see me, but I am going to the South Sea Islands this afternoon and cannot see you. However, Professor Craib will see you.' She looked at me as if I had taken leave of my senses.

I collected oxygen cylinders and an oxygen mask, Price's *Text Book of Medicine*, my stethoscope and sphygmomanometer, my cardiograph machine, some drugs and a change of clothes. I said goodbye to John Bradshaw, kissed Nonie and my son John and returned to the ship. We immediately set sail for Lourenço Marques (Maputo) in Mozambique, en route for Melbourne.

Sir Maynard proved to be an easy patient. His wife was with him and my duties consisted of little more than drinking a whisky with him before lunch and then another whisky or two in the evening and listening to his stories. It was believed that alcohol helped to dilate the coronary arteries and, in moderation, it certainly does no harm and probably does some good. Rosemary Jackson made Sir Maynard comfortable and kept him amused with her stories about life in Samoa.

Sir Maynard's father had been a Swedish sea captain trading in copra among the Pacific islands. He became prosperous and built up a shipping line and also a monopoly in trading stores on many of the Pacific islands. Sir Maynard, too, had been an extremely successful man. He owned the gold mines in the Fiji Islands and controlled most of the trade between Sydney and San Francisco. His nickname was the 'Octopus of the Pacific'. Although he was, by birth, one hundred per cent Swedish, the British government showed unusually good sense when they made him a knight and appointed him Governor of the Fiji Islands. He had a great loyalty to the British Commonwealth. I asked him if he had any regrets about his life. He replied: 'Only my lost opportunities.' They must have been very few!

When we arrived at Lourenço Marques, after two days' sailing, a telegram was awaiting me from John Bradshaw telling me to return home immediately because, he said, I had been hoodwinked and it was highly improbable that my patient was the Governor of the Fiji Islands. I replied that all was well.

There were twelve other passengers on the *Mirabouka*, a large cargo ship, and an interesting group they were. There was a handsome young Dane whom we christened 'The Prince of Denmark', and an American woman of about thirty, with blonde curly hair. I tried my American slang on her and toasted her: 'Here's how'. She replied, 'I know how. Here's when'. There was also a beautiful New Zealander, who had recently lost her husband in the Rhodesian Air Force and was returning to New Zealand, and a South African wool farmer who owned large sheep farms and was going to Australia to buy rams.

The wool farmer fell in love with the New Zealand widow, but she gave most of her attention to me. One dark night the farmer met me on an empty deck and challenged me to a fight. He weighed about 220 pounds and was about six foot six tall. I realised that not only could I not fight him but that, if he so wished, he could pick me up and throw me overboard. Fortunately, I can think quickly and knew that he was very patriotic; I put my arm around him and said, 'Ons land, Suid Afrika' (Our country, South Africa). The tears rolled down his cheek, he put his arm around me and from then on we were the best of friends.

After a three-week voyage we approached Melbourne harbour in pouring rain. Standing on the dockside were two men in rain-coats turned up at the collar and with slouch hats. One had a cigarette in the corner of his mouth. They reminded me of George Raft, and Rosemary Jackson agreed that they must be detectives. When the gangplank went down, they were first on board and asked to see Sir Maynard. Imagine our surprise to find that one was the Governor of Victoria and the other was his aide.

After a few days at a hotel in Melbourne we went by special train to Sydney and spent two weeks at a hotel on Bondi Beach. Sir Maynard had now recovered and we were able to fly to Fiji where I left him in the care of his own doctors. Rosemary Jackson remained with him.

Sir Maynard said, 'Geoffrey, you have taken me halfway around the world. I want you to do me a favour and go back the other way. It will take you longer, but it will be worth it. I want you to fly from Fiji to Honolulu and spend a few days at the Royal

Hawaiian Hotel; I am a director of the hotel. Then go by plane to San Francisco. My Standard Oil agent will show you the city. You can see Chinatown and something of the west coast of the United States. Make your way slowly across the United States to Washington and New York. Standard Oil will look after you there. Then fly to England so that you can see your parents, and after you have done that you can return to South Africa.' I asked him had he forgotten our agreement, fifty guineas a day from the day I left Port Elizabeth until the day I got back, plus my expenses. He said, 'Geoffrey, this is what I would like you to do and please do it.' What could I do but agree?

I flew to Hawaii, spent a few days at the Royal Hawaiian Hotel and then flew by night from Honolulu to San Francisco. This flight was the most comfortable I have ever taken, although that was all of fifty years ago. We had supper on the plane and then bunks were let down from the ceiling. After eight hours' sleep we were awakened in the morning for breakfast in bed. After a few days in San Francisco, I went by train across the United States, spent a few days in Washington and New York, flew to London and spent five days with my parents, who were thrilled to see me again, and then I flew back to South Africa.

Rosemary Jackson stayed with Sir Maynard until he died three years later. He left her a large sum of money in his will. After visiting her family in New Zealand, she returned to England and bought a hotel on the Isle of Thanet at the mouth of the Thames. A year or two later a South African veterinarian stayed at the hotel and fell in love with her. They married, sold the hotel at a big profit and went to live in Johannesburg.

Three days after returning to Port Elizabeth, I received a cheque from Standard Oil, New York, covering the fifty guineas a day from the time I had left Port Elizabeth until the day of my return. All my expenses had been paid. I had little enough practice before I left and expected, on my return, that I would have none at all. The opposite proved to be the case. The doctors all knew that I had been asked to look after the Governor of the Fiji Islands. Within a few weeks I had an extremely busy consultant practice. On New Year's Eve Nonie gave birth to a beautiful girl who was christened Patricia. Her obstetrician, our friend Langley Gace, arrived too late for the birth. I remember he said to the nurse, 'Ring my wife. I shall be back in time to let in the New Year!'

In my practice for each patient I would allot an hour, during which time I would take a history, examine the patient, do a cardiogram if necessary, check the haemoglobin to make sure the patient was not anaemic, and the sedimentation rate, a test to see if there was any infection, and arrange for any further investigations if they were required. I would then dictate a report to my large Grundig dictating machine, which would be typed by my secretary, Phyllis Basford, and sent to the doctor who had referred the patient to me. If the patient had to return, he or she would be given half-an-hour of my time.

I was appointed one of the honorary, unpaid physicians to non-paying patients at the Provincial Hospital. This included the two medical wards for non-white patients. Later I was appointed honorary physician to the Livingstone Hospital when it was built for black patients.

Life became pleasant. I was seeing most interesting and unusual patients in the Eastern Cape. We had sufficient money and would spend the weekend at Lauries Bay. There we swam in the sea and in the freshwater swimming pool that Douglas Laurie had built. Spring water would flow into the swimming pool at one end and flow out at the other, down to the sea. There was beautiful and wild countryside along the coast for walking and riding. Nearly always we had guests, who would join us for braaivlais – an outdoor barbecue.

Just after returning from Fiji, in December 1948, I was consulting in my office at Elizabeth House when John Lee, a radiologist who had joined Duxie Osler, walked in and said: 'Geoffrey, one of my patients has collapsed. Please come and see him.' By the time we got to the X-ray rooms, a second patient had collapsed and, within a few minutes, three more patients. All five had had an X-ray of the gastro-intestinal tract and had been given a glassful of barium cream, containing about four ounces of a barium salt which showed up on X-ray. We immediately stopped any further X-ray investigations. I asked if anyone else had been given barium that morning and was told that a patient had left for the hospital an hour before to have a bone removed from his throat. Another man had come from the crew of a Russian whaling ship in the harbour to have a barium meal X-ray examination in case he had a peptic ulcer. He had no ulcer and had immediately returned to his ship which had set sail for the Antarctic.

The five patients who had collapsed were sweating and vomiting. They were pale and had weak, slow and irregular pulses. It looked as if they might well die. We suspected that there was something wrong with the barium and phoned the wholesaler who had provided the barium cream the night before. We found that the wrong barium had been sent: soluble barium carbonate, which is used as a rat poison, rather than insoluble barium sulphate. Astonishingly the barium carbonate and barium sulphate had been stored next to each other in drums. A sixteen-year-old boy had been told to fill the large bottles, known as Winchesters, with 'barium'. He had taken the barium carbonate powder by mistake.

The only patient who died was the man who had had a chicken bone in his throat. He had swallowed only a mouthful of barium emulsion, much less than the other six, who had drunk a glassful. He had been immediately transferred by car to hospital, where he was given an anaesthetic so that the bone could be removed. The anaesthetic prevented him from vomiting. He was thirsty and cold and complained of a great heaviness in his limbs. Thirteen hours after swallowing the mouthful of barium, the poor man died.

We never did find out what happened to the Russian who had returned to his ship. A radio message was sent to the captain, saying that the man should be given Epsom Salts (magnesium sulphate). Magnesium sulphate reacts with barium carbonate to convert it to insoluble barium sulphate. There was no reply from the ship.

The symptoms of the five surviving patients were similar: vomiting, diarrhoea, blurred vision, an irregular pulse, and painful and weak muscles in their limbs. The mind remained clear and there was no evidence of any effect on the central nervous system. They were all treated immediately with Epsom Salts. Although they had drunk one thousand times the known fatal dose of barium carbonate, they recovered – probably because of the large amount of barium they had swallowed, which caused severe vomiting.

I wrote in the *British Medical Journal* in 1950 about the patients who had been accidentally given rat poison. This was the first report of what happens when a large overdose of barium carbonate is taken by a human being. Only one person sued the wholesale chemist who had provided the barium: the widow of the man who had died. She was said not to be legally married, although she had lived with the man for many years and they had four children. She lived in a small village and, fearing the publicity that would result from a court case, she settled out of court for a small sum. Patients in South Africa seldom sued for malpractice in those days and not often today.

In 1949 Rosaleen, Nonie's sister, came by ship to Port Elizabeth and stayed with us for a year. I had always got on well with her and she was great company for Nonie. In 1950 she went to Rhodesia and worked there for a year before returning to England. She later qualified as a doctor in Dublin. Shortly after Rosaleen left us, my mother and father came to South Africa and stayed for three months.

My paper on disseminated sclerosis in South Africa, published at the end of 1949, had been well received and had stimulated my interest in neurology. I decided to study for the higher degree of Doctor of Medicine at my old medical school in Liverpool. The paper on disseminated sclerosis was accepted for part of the MD, but I needed to do further study in neurology and become au fait with the current literature and research for the written and clinical examination.

I obtained the necessary books, including the famous textbook on neurology by Russell Brain, and I also got hold of copies of the recent neurological journals from the medical library in Cape Town. I spent my weekends reading in the cottage overlooking the swimming pool at Lauries Bay. I could break my study by going for swim or a walk along the beach.

In May 1951 I flew to England and went to Liverpool to take the MD examination. The chief examiner was Professor Henry Cohen, later Lord Cohen of Birkenhead. He fortunately had a special interest in disseminated sclerosis. I passed the exam.

Back in South Africa, I found that Mr Gibbings wanted to sell Lauries Bay and we decided to buy the house, two cottages, furniture, electricity plant, dairy, workshop and the outhouses for the cattle (although I could not purchase the land because the Lovemore estate had been entailed by the Crown in 1820). I also bought the cows, hens and ducks. The small farm was looked after by Simon Nonzube, who had built Lauries Bay with Douglas Laurie, and by some of Simon's fifteen children. Lauries Bay always required some attention: either a roof was leaking, or the electricity plant was not working properly, or the pump, which pumped the water from the spring to the top of the hill, needed attention. Electricity for lighting was generated by an old Petter diesel engine and a dynamo in the workshop. They had been manufactured in 1901 and for more than thirty years, before Laurie had acquired them, had been used to supply electricity to the village of Redhouse, near Port Elizabeth. The electricity was stored in ex-railway storage batteries, given to Douglas Laurie by some of his patients who had worked on the South African railways. Starting the Petter engine was difficult; it was necessary to make the firing chamber red hot with a blow lamp before the engine could be started with a heavy handle.

These years were the happiest time of my life. Nonie and I loved staying at Lauries Bay. There was a telephone at the Bay, so I could be at the hospital in twenty minutes; it was only thirteen miles away, although two of these miles were over a rough sand road. By 1952 I was a prosperous physician, living at Lauries Bay in the summer and at Park Drive in the winter. My practice was almost too big. I was attending patients from Port Elizabeth and the hinterland, which included an inland area of prosperous sheep farmers, some with farms of 20,000 acres or more. At Elizabeth House we worked together very well. There were two physicians, Professor Don Craib and me, the surgeon Sandy Stewart, the radiologists, Duxie Osler and John Lee, and the gynaecologist, Langley Gace. We had morning coffee together and consulted with each other when the need arose.

The summer of 1952/53 was a particularly happy one. Patricia was four, and could almost swim. She and John would wait for me to come home in the evening and then go running on the sands

74

with me, and we would all go into the sea and the pool together.

On 6 February 1953, Sandy Stewart had a patient at St Joseph's Hospital who had a severe internal haemorrhage after an operation. He asked me to help him with the patient, who required numerous blood transfusions and an emergency operation. We worked through the night and the following Saturday morning. The patient started to improve. It was two o'clock in the afternoon before I felt that it was safe to go home and I returned to Lauries Bay exhausted. Patricia greeted me and said that she wanted to go swimming. I said I was tired and she must wait until I had had a sleep. The swimming pool gate, on a spring, was always carefully closed because Patricia could not yet swim. John could swim. Nonie and I lay on the bed in the front bedroom and fell into a deep sleep. We left the children in the care of their nursemaid, who called us at four o'clock for tea. We had guests staying with us in the house, and two friends arrived for tea, a veterinarian, Kayser Van Der Walt and his wife, Bobby.

We were sitting in the lounge having tea when Simon rushed in saying, 'Doctor, Doctor, Patricia's in the pool!' I ran out and found Patricia face down in the water. I swam in and pulled her out. She appeared to be dead; her heart had stopped. I started artificial respiration. This was before the time when it was realised that mouth to mouth breathing is the most effective way of ventilating the lungs, and I used what today is considered an old-fashioned method. There was not the slightest flicker of a heartbeat. I was desperate. When the heart stops in the operating theatre, the surgeon opens the chest and massages the heart. When there was no response after about twenty minutes, in spite of artificial respiration, I took a knife, and opened my daughter's chest just below the ribs and massaged her heart. It was flaccid; she was beyond any recall.

I started to walk into the sea. Simon ran after me, put his arms around me and brought me back.

CHAPTER 8

Porphyria's Lover

All her hair
In one long yellow string I wound
Three times her little throat around,
And strangled her.
Robert Browning, 'Porphyria's Lover'

Patricia's death devastated me. Before this I had been a good Catholic, firmly believing that God was looking after His children. What was His purpose in allowing Patricia to drown? She was a girl of exceptional intelligence. She gave everyone the impression that she had lived this life before, she had such understanding and sympathy. I found it dreadful when people said how sorry they were. Nonie took Patricia's death much better than I did, or perhaps one's own pain always feels to be the worst. John, who was seven and loved playing with Patricia, missed her very much. There was only one possible salvation for me at this stage and that was work.

Early in my story I related how I had been called to see patients who had become paralysed and had died. At first this looked like an epidemic. One of these patients was a Nurse Van Rooyen at the hospital in Uitenhage, a town about twenty miles from Port Elizabeth. She had had an unhappy love affair and had started taking sleeping tablets from the drug cupboard on her ward to help her sleep. She developed abdominal pain and was seen by a surgeon, who thought she had an intestinal obstruction. He opened her abdomen: the anaesthetic, as was customary at that time, was started with intravenous pentothal, a barbiturate anaesthetic. The surgeon found no abnormality except for 'adhesions'. When nothing else can be found, the surgeon may convince himself that there is evidence of old inflammation, due to tissue adhering together, which are known as adhesions. A few days after the operation, Nurse Van Rooyen became very emotional and appeared to be hysterical. She complained of severe abdominal pain and then developed weakness in her limbs. By the time I was called to see her, her arms and legs were paralysed, her tendon reflexes, the knee and ankle jerks, were absent, and she could barely breathe because of paralysis in her diaphragm and chest muscles. I noticed that her urine was deep purple after it had been left standing for a while. Nurse Van Rooyen died within 24 hours.

Her father was an Afrikaner sheep farmer from Alexandria, about 100 miles from Port Elizabeth, and I asked him to come and see me. He told me that he had had ten children and three of his daughters had died. One had been diagnosed as having blackwater fever because she had 'black' urine, and one had been diagnosed as having acute poliomyelitis because she had become paralysed. I noticed that Mr Van Rooyen had sores on the back of his hands and I asked him about this. He replied in Afrikaans that he had the Van Rooyen skin. His father had had sensitive skin on his hands, as had his grandfather. The exposed skin abraded easily when it was knocked and sometimes it blistered and formed sores. When the sores healed, they left small scars. I scratched the skin on the back of his hand with my fingernail and the superficial layer came away easily.

Nurse Van Rooyen's urine, which became dark purple after it had stood for a few hours, made me think of the possibility that she might be suffering from acute porphyria. This is a condition which had first been described by Professor Jan Waldenström in Sweden in the 1930s but the Swedish patients did not have sensitive skin. I had never, as far as I knew, seen a patient with acute porphyria in England, although in retrospect there was a patient I remembered at Broadgreen Hospital in Liverpool who had become paralysed and died and she may well have had undiagnosed acute porphyria. Outside South Africa and Sweden, it is very uncommon. The name porphyria comes from the Greek porphyros, meaning purple. Porphyrin is the basic chemical of chlorophyll and of the haem of haemoglobin and has the peculiar characteristic of showing a pink fluorescence when exposed to ultraviolet light.

I looked at Nurse Van Rooyen's urine under an ultraviolet lamp, using a filter to exclude the white light, and it gave a strong pink fluorescence. It contained much porphyrin. I realised that she, and probably some of the other patients I had been seeing who had become paralysed, had been suffering from acute porphyria.

I decided to make a special study of the Van Rooyen family. First I saw an uncle of Mr Van Rooyen, then a very old man. He had known the great-great-grandfather of Nurse Van Rooyen, Gerrit Renier Van Rooyen, who had been born in Alexandria in 1814 and lived there until his death in 1884. Gerrit Renier had ten children by two wives. It was usual in Afrikaner families to have a large number of children and he had many grandchildren and great-grandchildren. I decided to draw up a detailed family tree. When it was completed, I found that Gerrit Renier Van Rooyen had 564 descendants and that nineteen of them had died from illnesses that were typical of acute porphyria, although this diagnosis had never been made. Many of the adults, especially the men, had sensitive skin on the backs of the hands. Acute attacks of porphyria did not occur in childhood but most commonly in women between the ages of sixteen and fifty. During my first years in practice as a specialist physician, from 1949 to 1953, I saw 32 patients with attacks of acute porphyria in 32 different families. For each patient with acute porphyria, I drew up a family tree going back as far as they could help me. I managed to trace all these families back to between 1800 and 1820, some six generations before. Skin lesions and acute attacks of porphyria had occurred in all the families.

In the first family I studied, that of Nurse Van Rooyen, I obtained specimens of urine and later faeces from the living members of the family and tested them for porphyrin. I found that the easiest way of detecting porphyria of the type I was seeing in South Africa was by examining the faeces. A small amount, dissolved in a solvent of equal parts of alcohol, glacial acetic acid and ether, would show a brilliant pink fluorescence when exposed to ultraviolet light. Quantitative analysis was undertaken by a biochemist, Hubert Barnes, who had a special interest in porphyrins, at the South African Institute of Medical Research, Johannesburg. On average, about half the children of a parent who had South African porphyria inherited the disease. It was inherited as a dominant genetic characteristic.

In the families, I found that some affected members, usually men, would have sensitive skin on the backs of the hands and sometimes on the face, and others, most often the women, would have attacks of acute prophyria. The acute attacks followed the taking of certain drugs – in particular barbiturate sedatives such as the pentobarbitone 'Nembutal' or a thiopentone (pentothal) barbiturate anaesthetic. A frequent story was that sleeping tablets were taken for a few days and then abdominal pain would develop. The doctor might suspect an abdominal obstruction or perhaps acute appendicitis. Thiopentone would be given intravenously to induce anaesthesia for an exploratory operation. Very little, if anything, abnormal would be found at the operation. The patient recovered well from the operation and a few days later would become agitated and appear to be hysterical, complaining of abdominal and limb pains. Within a few days the legs and arms would become weak and develop paralysis. The urine was usually normal in colour when it was passed. If left to stand for a few hours in sunlight, it became dark purple.

In tracing the 564 descendants of Gerrit Renier Van Rooyen, I had difficulty with one member of the family, a Miss Van Rooyen from Alexandria. In 1920 she had fallen in love with a Fuller Brush salesman. She eloped with him and had not been heard of since. All I could find out was that his name was Duggan and that he had come from Cardiff in Wales. I wrote to the Lord Mayor of Cardiff, told him about porphyria and of the possibility that Miss Van Rooyen could have porphyria; I said that if she took certain drugs she could become paralysed and die. I asked him to see if he could trace her. To my surprise, a month later I received a letter from the Lord Mayor telling me that he had asked the chief constable of the city to trace Duggan. He had reported that Duggan's wife, formerly Miss Van Rooyen, had died of 'blackwater fever' in 1929. This I understood to mean that she had died from an illness in which she had a dark urine and, since she had come from Africa, it had been thought that the dark urine was due to 'blackwater fever', which is caused by malaria. In all probability she had died from acute porphyria.

Mrs Duggan had one daughter. She had married a Frenchman by the name of – let us say – Dubois, and her daughter was now living in Paris with her two children. The Lord Mayor of Cardiff sent me her address. I wrote to Madame Dubois in Paris, telling her of the porphyria in the Van Rooyen family and asking her if she would send me a specimen of her urine and faeces and that of her two children. About three weeks later I received a letter from Madame Dubois in French accompanying the specimens I had requested. Her faecal specimen was strongly positive for porphyrin, as was that of one of her children. She had inherited porphyria from her mother, the Van Rooyen from Alexandria in the Eastern Cape.

On the evening that the letter and specimens arrived, I was going to the cinema with Nonie and a doctor friend, Jan Hanekom, and his wife, Barbara. During the intermission, I took out the letter and showed it to Jan, proudly relating the story of how we had tracked down Miss Van Rooyen. When I got home, I found that the letter was missing. I phoned the manager of the Opera House cinema and asked him if he would look and see if he could find it where we had been sitting. The cinema was crowded and the manager decided to put an advertisement on the screen which read: 'Doctor has lost French letter. Will the finder please return it to the manager.' The letter was found. Fortunately, no one knew who the doctor was!

By this time, specimens of faeces were arriving from various members of porphyric families from all over South Africa. On one occasion a package arrived at my door preceded by a police car with a screeching siren. The parcel was handed to me on a spade! The sender, believing it was urgent to have the parcel delivered quickly, had written on it in red ink. 'Urgent, deliver immediately, highly radioactive.'

My first report about porphyria in South Africa was published in the *British Medical Journal* in 1953 and further reports were published with Hubert Barnes in the *BMJ* and in the *South African Medical Journal*. In 1954, I was invited to lecture on porphyria and multiple sclerosis at the Columbia Medical Center in New York and at the Mayo Clinic at Rochester, Minnesota. About this time the first jet passenger plane, the Comet, was grounded because some of the Comets had exploded in the air. As a temporary measure, the Comet was replaced by the York, a plane converted from the Lancaster bomber. On the way to New York, we flew from London to Keflavik in Iceland, refuelled and started the second leg of the flight to Gander, Newfoundland. I was sitting next to a very beautiful American, Mary Reid, whom I had met in the airport lounge. She was at the time the girlfriend of the pilot. Halfway to Gander I noticed that the outer starboard engine was on fire. Fuel to the engine was cut by the pilot and the fire went out. 'Don't worry,' I said to Mary Reid, 'I know this plane well. It can fly perfectly well on three engines.' Ten minutes later the inner starboard engine spluttered and stopped and we lost height rapidly in a deep drive. Luckily, everyone was asleep and there was no panic. The air hostess rushed to the pilot's cabin and returned, by which time we had levelled out at only a few hundred feet above the waves. She came to Mary and said: 'The Captain says he is jettisoning fuel and hopes we will be able to make it back to Keflavik. He wants you to know he loves you very much!' We made it back to Keflavik on two engines, flying very low to get maximum lift, and were then grounded in the middle of a cod war – a dispute over fishing rights between Iceland and Britain. It was a week before another 'York' could be sent from England.

In New York I stayed in a red stone house in Greenwich Village, and would take the subway each day from 14th Street to 168th Street to go to the Columbia Medical Center. One of the people who influenced me at this time was Evelyn Belov, a news reporter for *Newsweek*. It was through her that I was asked to write a review article on the porphyrias, and later on multiple sclerosis, for *Scientific American*.

Mary Reid was a beautiful woman, and a model by profession. I still have a portrait painting of her, in a red pullover, painted by a Spanish painter. She introduced me to Homer Smith, professor of renal physiology at New York University. He had written a book, *Man and his Gods*, on religious beliefs, which influenced my thinking greatly on the subject. He also introduced me to another fascinating book, *Sinuhe the Egyptian*, by a Finnish archaeologist, Mika Waltari. It tells the story of an Egyptian physician at the time of King Amenhotep IV, who reigned in about 1500 BC. Sinuhe thought like a modern physician. He visited the eastern Mediterranean countries in which I have also undertaken research, he had many problems in life that I have had, some of them with his woman friends, and developed his attitudes to life from his experiences.

At the Columbia Medical Center I spent my time with Professor Franz Kallman. He was undertaking studies on identical twins, who would have the same genes but often grew up in different environments. This made it possible to separate the effects of inheritance and environment, the seed and the soil, in causing disease and has proved a most useful way of studying many diseases, schizophrenia for example.

At that time psychoanalysis was very much the 'in' thing. I was not impressed by the results. However, I was impressed by David Riesman, an American sociologist who wrote *The Lonely Crowd*. This book discusses the social characteristics that determine behaviour and the transition that had occurred in society from the 'tradition directed' individual to the 'inner directed', as I like to think I am, and the 'other directed' who like to follow the crowd. Another American author I first read at this time was Erich Fromm, a psychoanalyst who describes in his books how modern man was alienated and estranged within our consumer-orientated society. I particularly enjoyed his *Man for Himself* (1947) and *The Art of Loving* (1956).

From New York I went to the Mayo Clinic at Rochester, Minnesota, where I delivered a lecture, and there I met the Mayo Clinic physician Walter Alvarez. He had written a book, *Nervousness, Indigestion and Pain*, which helped me greatly in understanding the problems of my many anxious patients. Although today he might be considered old-fashioned, when he wrote the book Alvarez was way ahead of his time in showing the effects of emotion on both personality and health. His account on migraine was particularly prescient.

From 1954 until 1959 I was away from South Africa every year for two or three months, sometimes with Nonie but more often without her, lecturing on porphyria, multiple sclerosis and later lung cancer. I would generally try to go to Europe during the South African winter so that I could spend the summer at Lauries Bay. My practice was still busy when I returned to Port Elizabeth, although other consultant physicians had settled in the city.

In June 1957, I decided that I would go to Europe and compare porphyria of the type I was seeing in South Africa with the porphyria which had been described by Waldenström in Sweden. I suspected that the porphyria I was seeing in South Africa was a different disease to Waldenström porphyria – acute intermittent porphyria (AIP). My paper about the South African porphyria families had been received with incredulity, bordering on rudeness, by such renowned experts as Professor Claude Rimington in London. Rimington had written to me that it was the South African sunshine only that accounted for the skin lesions and that South African porphyria was the same disease as that described by Waldenström. I flew from Copenhagen to Malmö to meet Jan Waldenström, professor of medicine at Lund University. The university's chief hospital was at Malmö, where Jan introduced me to his porphyrin chemist, Birghitta Haeger-Aronsen, a charming lady who later became professor of medicine. She had undertaken a great deal of research on porphyrin and taught me much about porphyrin chemistry.

Jan Waldenström arranged that Birghitta and I should visit a number of porphyric families in central Sweden and we went by car. I quickly realised that the Swedish porphyric families were different to the South African ones. Skin lesions did not occur, acute attacks did follow the use of barbiturates, as in South Africa, but, unlike South African porphyria, the urine test known as the Ehrlich Aldehyde test for a porphyrin precursor was positive in adults, even when they were not in acute attacks. In contrast, in the South African type of porphyria the test was positive only during an acute attack. The faeces in the Swedish porphyria showed no increase in porphyrin. Swedish and South African porphyria are both inherited as a Mendelian dominant disorder, that is from one parent only.

All the families with porphyria that I had seen in South Africa were Afrikaners, or had Afrikaner ancestors. I suspected that the gene responsible for the disorder might have been brought to South

Africa by an early immigrant from Holland, so I went from Sweden to Amsterdam to visit Professor Formijne, a professor of medicine in Amsterdam, who arranged for me to see porphyric families in Holland. I found families with both typical Swedish porphyria and typical South African porphyria. In each family group I studied, the condition ran true to type. I concluded that South African porphyria was a different disease to Waldenström's acute intermittent porphyria and that it had not been described before.

Back in South Africa I discussed porphyria with Hubert Barnes. We also asked the professor of Greek at the University of Witwatersrand for his suggestions about a suitable name. Since the South African porphyria could appear in a variety of ways – as attacks of acute porphyria, as skin lesions, or with both acute attacks and skin lesions, or be symptomless except for a raised stool porphyrin – we decided to call it *porphyria variegata*. We gave it this name in our 1959 paper in the *South African Medical Journal*, when we compared the families in South Africa, Sweden and Holland.

Patricia's younger sister, Jennifer, who was a baby at the time of Patricia's death, was blooming. In September 1953, our son Michael was born.

Between 1953 and 1956 I thought a great deal about whether or not I believed and accepted the teachings of the Catholic Church. In particular, I found it difficult to accept that the bread and wine at consecration in the Mass became truly the body and blood of Christ. I could accept that it represented it, but common sense told me that it was not truly the body and blood of Jesus. Alternatively, one had to think at two levels – a rational level and an irrational or 'spiritual' level. I was taught at school, 'It is a mystery, my child; just accept it. Do you know better than the magisterium of the Church with its two thousand years of tradition?'

I worried about the whole question of faith, in contrast to reason, and became convinced that to accept some of the teachings of the Church, such as that of the Eucharist or that Mary's body was assumed physically into Heaven, required a degree of split mind, which I did not have. It was a difficult matter because I had had a great deal of support from the Church when I had started in practice, particularly from the Catholic Private Nursing Home, St Joseph's, which was run by the Blue Sisters, who were and are delightful people. Nevertheless, I eventually made a firm decision and sent my three children to non-Catholic schools where I knew they would not be indoctrinated. In retrospect, perhaps I was too extreme: I did belong to a Christian tradition and there was little point in upsetting parents and family. Years later, when I visited my parents, I accompanied them to Mass on Sunday without feeling that I was compromising my principles.

I would often discuss these problems with Don Craib, whom I met every day. One day he said to me something like this: 'You know, Geoffrey, when I die, Almighty God will say to me "Don, you were born among the elect in South Africa and therefore much was expected of you. You have not lived a good life; you have been prosperous, successful and lived comfortably. You played tennis when you could have been looking after poor black patients. You could have done more with your life to deserve heaven. I am afraid you must go down below." I shall reply "Yes, what you say is true, Almighty God, and I accept it; but just before I go, so that I can go with a peaceful mind, please just answer me one question. 'How is it that you, the all-merciful and loving God, could allow six million of your own people to be tortured and then the men, women and children gassed to death!' If you can answer this question, I will go to hell with a contented mind."' I had also felt the same way about Patricia's death: that I had not deserved it and God could have prevented it. I realised now that God had nothing to do with it.

After Patricia's death, I had thought of selling Lauries Bay but my other children loved the bay as much as I did. In the summer of 1954/55 my parents and Nonie's came to stay with us there for three months. This was my parents' second visit to see us. My father remembered this time as the happiest in his life. He loved working with Simon on the old Petter engine or mending a leaking roof.

While we were all at Lauries Bay in 1954, two priests from Ampleforth College who were recuperating after sickness came to stay with us. By coincidence, both priests were named Wright.

They slept in one of the cottages, which had been built on a small hill overlooking the swimming pool; there were two bedrooms and bathrooms. One evening my mother attached a black cotton thread to six feet of hosepipe on the slope leading to the cottage. As the priests went up to bed, she pulled the thread and what appeared to be a snake chased them down the path; they had their revenge later! On the same visit a bullock charged my father as he was in his swimming costume by the sea. He twisted the horns of the bullock which, surprised, fell on its side, then got up and walked away. My children's friends were most impressed. My father said: 'We do this regularly on my ranch in Texas!'

At night we would watch beautiful flashes of phosphorescence as the waves hit the beach. Sometimes when there was a sudden fall in the water temperature, the fish, stunned by the sudden cold water, could be picked out of the sea. We, Simon and his children, would fish from the rocks overlooking the bay. We were never short of fish.

John and later Michael attended a preparatory school, St George's, in Park Drive close to our house in the city, and Jennifer, the Holy Rosary Convent. In order to avoid him receiving too much Catholic indoctrination, we decided to send John to St Andrew's Church of England school at Grahamstown, a small, pleasant university town 80 miles from Port Elizabeth, and Jenny to the Church of England Diocesan School for girls, also in Grahamstown. St Andrew's was a public school attended by descendants of the English 1820 settlers, many of whom were farmers in the Eastern Cape.

John was an introspective boy, short-sighted, like his Dean grandfather and my two sisters, and not good at sports, although he was excellent at science. He was unhappy at this school, although I did not appreciate how miserable he was at the time. Jenny, more of an extrovert, was also unhappy at boarding school, and I have realised since that she would have been happier at a day school. Michael, at the age of twelve, won a scholarship to a Methodist school, Kingswood, in Grahamstown and, because John did not enjoy St Andrew's, Michael went to Kingswood. He was later selected, when he was about sixteen, for an exchange scholarship with the Kingswood College sister school in West Hartford,

Connecticut, and had a most interesting life for a year at a major American private school. When he returned, he wondered why his father did not have his own private yacht! He learnt American football, and his time in the United States was a great experience for him.

John studied science at Cape Town University after leaving school and then took a further degree in physics at Rhodes University, in Grahamstown. He then went to Jodrell Bank, near Manchester, to study radioastronomy under Sir Bernard Lovell whom he greatly admired. He was at university for nine years in all and took his doctorate in astronomy. Michael won a scholarship to study medicine at Cape Town University and Jennifer went to Rhodes University to study business, economics and secretarial practice. Although I enjoyed my children's company at weekends, when they were not at boarding school, I realise now that I was away too much and was too bound up in work and research, as I still am. Whenever I was in Port Elizabeth, I would be booked up at my practice for several weeks ahead. In spite of my views about religion, I attended the Sisters at all the convents in the city and was consulted by many of the clergy of all denominations. In South Africa at that time, the clergy and members of religious orders were not charged for medical services.

The Reverend Mother at the Priory Convent had a major heart attack. When I had relieved her pain with morphine, she still had an imperceptible blood pressure. She asked me if she was dying. I replied: 'It is in the hands of God. You have had communion and the last sacraments. Leave the rest to God.' Then I asked, 'Is there anything, Mother, you would like?' 'Yes', she said. 'A cup of tea.' The tea was brought and she held the cup in her hand and said: 'You know, doctor, it is very nice to have a cup of tea when you are dying' – and then she died.

One day in 1954 Archbishop Lucas, the South African Apostolic Delegate, came from Pretoria to consult me. He was a tall, fine-looking man who had been in the Dutch Resistance during the Second World War. We examined his stomach on the fluorescent X-ray screen in a darkened room. John Lee, the radiologist, said to him: 'Archbishop, take a deep breath and hold it.' There was a long silence and then John whispered to me: 'Geoffrey, what do you call an Apostolic Delegate?' 'Your Excellency.' 'Breathe out, your Excellency,' said John.

Shortly after this I had to attend a conference in Rome. Archbishop Lucas asked me to take with me a letter from him requesting a private audience with the Holy Father. In Rome I sent my letter of introduction to the Vatican and received, within 24 hours, an invitation to a private audience with Pope Pius XII, Eugenio Pacelli. He was a thin, aristocratic-looking man who, with some difficulty, said a few words to me in English. Having left the short audience, with my especially blessed medal, I was getting into the lift on the top floor of the Vatican when a Monsignor ran after me. 'Dr Dean, I am Monsignor Trevi. Monsignor Montini wishes to see you.'

I went back to the Pope's apartments and was introduced to Monsignor Giovanni Battista Montini, who invited me to join him for coffee and biscuits. He asked my opinion about the progress of the Catholic Church in South Africa. I told him that I thought it was making little impression with the black people and that more success was being made by the indigenous African churches. These churches appointed black Africans as deacons and so they took an active part in religious services. I also said that the Africans could not understand what was happening at the Mass because the priest, his back to the congregation, mumbled away in Latin.

Monsignor Montini, who spoke good English, said to me: 'You know, doctor, we are beginning to come to the same conclusion here at the Vatican.' He then opened the shutters in the room from where we had a panoramic view across Rome. He pointed out the dome of a building in the distance and told me it was Propaganda Fides. He asked me to come with him to see Cardinal Cenci, the director of Propaganda Fides, and repeat what I had said to him. With rather poor grace I agreed to do this. A car was summoned and Monsignor Montini and I crossed Rome to see Cardinal Cenci and we were entertained with wine and biscuits. I repeated what I had said to Monsignor Montini.

In the car on our way to my hotel, Monsignor Montini said: 'Doctor, you are going to see big changes in the Church. We are delighted that you should give us these views because, from a layman, they mean much more to us than from a member of a religious order.' In November 1954 Pope Pius XII appointed Monsignor Montini Archbishop of Milan, and in 1963 he was elected Pope Paul VI.

CHAPTER 9

The Curse of the Pharaohs

Ex Africa semper aliquid novi.
Pliny

On 2 November 1955, I got a telephone call from Dr Le Roux of Knysna, a town about halfway between Port Elizabeth and Cape Town. He asked me if I would look after a patient, John Wiles, the son of a well-known South African painter. Dr Le Roux told me that the patient was already in an ambulance on the way to Port Elizabeth and asked me to arrange for his urgent admission to hospital because he was desperately ill with bilateral pneumonia.

John Wiles has given me permission to relate his story. He was employed by the Rhodesian Geological Service and told me that, five weeks earlier, he had been exploring a complex of caves in the Urungwe Native Reserve of Rhodesia to see if it was possible to use as fertiliser the large quantities of bat guano that were there. He had entered the cave with the Native Commissioner, a man named Dawson who knew the cave and who acted as a guide, and with a Mr Swartz. They spent the following day underground surveying the caves, which were connected by passages and were each several hundred feet long. The caves were occupied by thousands of bats, the common small variety and a larger bat with a wingspan of over two feet. The guano was very dry and was in places over six feet deep.

Twelve days later Wiles noticed a burning sensation across his chest; this discomfort worsened. He had a headache and thought he was developing an attack of malaria. The next day he took a train back to South Africa; during the four-day journey his

90

symptoms increased. By the time he reached his father's home, at Knysna, he had a fever, his back and head were aching intolerably and he was unable to take a deep breath without pain and coughing. He called Dr Le Roux, who examined his blood for malarial parasites and trypanosomes, the organism that causes sleeping sickness, but no parasites were found in the blood smear. In spite of penicillin injections, Wiles's pain in his chest and his cough increased over the next two weeks.

When I examined Wiles in Port Elizabeth, he was desperately ill. He had a bluish colour, and his breathing was shallow and rapid; he had pneumonia and had lost a great deal of weight. No parasites were found in his blood, and tests for typhoid fever, typhus and undulant fever were negative. There was an increase in the white cells in his blood, evidence of an infection. An X-ray of his chest revealed woolly-looking opacities scattered throughout both lungs. His lymph glands were enlarged. Unable to make a definite diagnosis, I prescribed pethidine to relieve the pain in his chest and chlorpromazine as a tranquilliser. He had not responded to the penicillin given to him by Dr Le Roux, so I prescribed a different antibiotic, tetracycline, and placed him in an oxygen tent.

Two days later I was attending patients when my secretary told me that a Colonel Alexis Surgay insisted on seeing me. He had been the officer in command of the British South African Police at Fort Usher, Rhodesia, but he was now retired. He had heard about John Wiles's illness and wanted to tell me the story of the mysterious deaths of two members of his Fort Usher police staff some thirty years before. At that time the local *njanga*, or witch-doctors, were stirring up trouble among the Africans. They claimed that their magic was more powerful than the white man's magic and that it could even deflect the white man's bullets. The Africans believed that the caves in the area were bewitched. The *njanga* went down into the caves for their ceremonies. It was believed that anyone who was not a *njanga* and who went down into the caves would die.

In order to lessen the power of the *njanga*, one of Colonel Surgay's constables decided to enter the caves. Three weeks later he became breathless and ill, and he was dead in little more than a fortnight. Six months later a London Cockney joined the British

South African Police. He said he was not frightened of *njanga* or *m'tagati* (bewitched caves), and went down into the cave. Three weeks later he became breathless and he too died. Colonel Surgay forbade any of his men to go into the caves. He told me that he thought John Wiles would die.

I remembered an illness, with pneumonia, occurring among cave explorers in the Transvaal; a similar illness had been described in cave explorers in Arkansas and in Venezuela and in workers in hen coops and pigeon lofts in the Mississippi valley. It was caused by a fungus, *Histoplasma capsulatum*, which grew in the birds' manure. When the dried manure was disturbed, the dust was inhaled and the fungus caused a lung and general infection, histoplasmosis. It occurred to me that Wiles might have the disease; I phoned Johannesburg and asked for histoplasmin to be sent to me so that I could do a skin test. The skin test was strongly positive.

During the following month John Wiles's symptoms gradually lessened, although he still complained of feeling exhausted. The X-ray shadows in his lungs slowly diminished, although residual fibrosis persisted at the base of both lungs. Some years later his lungs still showed marked scarring. I learned that Mr Swartz, who had explored the cave with Wiles, had also been very ill at the same time. Dawson had been into the caves on numerous previous occasions and had remained well.

When I next visited the Transvaal, I discussed the story of John Wiles's illness with members of the Transvaal Speleological Society. It was an unfortunate society because many of those who had joined in years gone by had become ill with pneumonia shortly after exploring caves and some had died. Members of the Speleological Society had a positive reaction to the histoplasmin skin test. Although some members of the society had been ill with 'pneumonitis' for several weeks, once they had recovered, they did not suffer further attacks. The severity of the cave illness depended on the degree of exposure to the fungus–laden dust. Following Wiles's illness, Professor J.F. Murray exposed monkeys, rabbits, guinea-pigs, rats and mice for five hours in a dusty bat–infested cave, Johnston's Pothole, in the Transvaal. Two to three weeks later the animals developed pneumonia and, at autopsy, *Histoplasma capsulatum* was recovered from animals of each species.

I went to Rhodesia to discuss the story of the *m'tagati* with two of the witch-doctors. They told me that to be a *njanga* conferred great power and wealth. They were rewarded very well by those who consulted them and usually had several wives and many cattle. If an aspirant to become a *njanga* believed that he had been granted the special powers of perception and healing required by a witch-doctor, he or she applied to the established *njanga* to join their ranks. If considered suitable, the aspirant was invited into the caves to participate in the next important meeting. Following this initiation, some died; this was considered positive proof that they were not true *njanga*. Those who recovered were admitted in due time to full membership of the fraternity of *njanga*, with all the honours, respect and wealth that went with this membership. Aspirants apparently considered the matter at length before becoming convinced that they had truly been chosen to be *njanga*, the ranks of which were select. The established *njanga* could influence who was accepted into their ranks. A long ceremony, with much stamping of feet – stirring up the guano – resulted in a heavy infection and the likely death of the candidate. On the other hand, if it was a short and quiet ceremony – and therefore a mild infection – the candidate would survive!

The story of the bewitched caves fascinated me and put me in mind of the curse that was said to be responsible for the death of Lord Carnarvon following the opening of Tutankhamen's tomb in the Valley of the Kings of Egypt. The story of this curse was given great publicity by the world press. In 1922 Lord Carnarvon, who had had an interest in Egyptology since 1907, had financed Howard Carter, an expert Egyptologist, to search for tombs of the pharaohs in the Valley of the Kings near Luxor. In November 1922, Carter was excavating in the north-east corner of the tomb of Rameses VI. In this area there were a number of roughly constructed workmen's huts, probably used by those labourers who had built the tomb. On 4 November, when the first hut and about three feet of earth, which lay beneath it, had been cleared away, a steep cut in the rock was discovered. Further clearing revealed that there was an entrance in the rock some thirteen feet below the tomb of

Rameses VI and a similar depth from the then bed level of the valley. As the work progressed, a passage was found, and after the twelfth step down the top of a plastered and sealed stone doorway. Carter thought he had probably found the entrance to the tomb of a pharaoh, so he stopped work and sent a cable to Lord Carnarvon. Carnarvon arrived in Cairo from England with his daughter, Lady Evelyn Herbert, on 21 November and reached Luxor two days later.

By the evening of 24 November, the staircase had been cleared, sixteen steps in all. Tutankhamen's seal could be seen in the plaster on the stone door. When the door was removed, a descending passage was found, filled with rubble. During the next two days this rubble was cleared away, revealing a second door, almost an exact replica of the first. The second door had the seal of Tutankhamen on it and also the seal of the Royal Necropolis. A hole was made through the stone and Carter inserted a candle. This is how he reported what happened:

> At first I could see nothing, the hot air escaping from the chamber caused the candle flame to flicker, but presently, as my eyes grew accustomed to the light, details of the room within emerged slowly from the mist. Strange animals, statues and gold, everywhere the glint of gold. For the moment, an eternity it must have seemed for the others standing by, I was struck with amazement and when Lord Carnarvon, unable to stand the suspense any longer, enquired anxiously 'Can you see anything?' it was all I could do to get out the words 'Yes, wonderful things.'

Inside the door was an antechamber, filled with a fantastic variety of gold and other objects which would be useful for a pharaoh in the next world.

Work in the tomb continued until the middle of February 1923. The first room was an antechamber to an inner room which had three successive walls of gold, now in the Cairo Museum. They are of great beauty, one wall within another wall within another. The room of gold was the burial chamber of Tutankhamen. This inner room was opened at a ceremony attended by Lord Carnarvon.

I suspected in 1955 that Lord Carnarvon's death from 'pneumonia of insidious onset' might have been due to histoplasmosis, and that this disease was therefore responsible for the legend of the 'Curse of the Pharaohs', just as it was responsible for the 'bewitched' caves in the Urungwe Reserve of Rhodesia and for the unhappy sickness record of the speleologists in the Transvaal. An Egyptologist like Howard Carter, who had been working for fifteen or sixteen years in the Valley of the Kings, would, like Mr Dawson and the *njanga*, probably have had a previous histoplasmosis infection and have recovered from it: therefore he would be immune to further infection.

What evidence was there that Lord Carnarvon had been exposed to dust containing bat dung? In 1956 I visited Egypt and spent some time with Dr Fam, professor of history at Cairo University. We were able to confirm the insidious nature of Lord Carnarvon's pneumonic illness and also that a number of other people had died from a similar illness after working in the Valley of the Kings.

The passage leading to Tutankhamen's tomb is now sealed at night by a door. No bats can enter, but they do frequent neighbouring underground passages. I recounted my theory that the Curse of the Pharaohs and Lord Carnarvon's death might be due to histoplasmosis in *Paris Match* in April 1956 and also in the *Central African Journal of Medicine* the following March. Eighteen years later, in 1974, Professor R.G. Harrison, professor of anatomy at Liverpool University, whom I had known as a student, was working in Egypt on the anatomy and cause of death of Egyptian mummies. On 9 April 1974 he wrote to me:

After extensive enquiries I have now heard from the Egyptian Antiquities Organisation in Cairo concerning the question of the presence of bats in the Tomb of Tutankhamen at the time when it was opened. Dr Gamal Mokhtar, Chairman of the Egyptian Antiquities Organisation, has just written to me on the matter and I quote herewith a paragraph from his letter:

'Concerning the question you asked about the presence of bats in the Tomb of Tutankhamen, I enquired from old people who were present at that time. They said that a temporary iron door made of bars was used after the discovery of the tomb and Mr Carter used to ask people in charge to get these bats out in the morning. The permanent door was only used six months later. This was mentioned by the old people living in Kurna.'

The legend of the Curse of the Pharaohs was strengthened by the deaths of others who had visited Tutankhamen's tomb shortly after its discovery; for instance, Arthur Mace, the assistant director of the Department of Egyptian Antiquities in New York, and George Benedite of the Department of Egyptian Antiquities of the Louvre.

So what is the evidence? Lord Carnarvon had been working for three months in the underground passage and antechamber of Tutankhamen's tomb and during this time the passage was frequented at night by bats to such an extent that Carter had to give instructions for them to be cleared out in the morning before work could begin. Then after the opening of the inner chamber of the tomb on 17 February 1923, Lord Carnarvon became very tired and breathless; he had enlarged glands and a headache and grew more and more ill. He returned to the Continental Hotel in Cairo where an insidious form of pneumonia developed. His health continued to deteriorate until he died on 6 April. This is not the type of pneumonia caused by the pneumococcus, the usual cause of pneumonia at that time, in which there is a sudden onset and a crisis on the seventh day.

We may never know for certain, but the evidence suggests that Lord Carnvarvon's death was due to inhalation of dust containing the fungus histoplasma from the dried bat droppings in the passage leading to King Tutankhamen's tomb. Although he had visited Thebes before, perhaps he had not been exposed to histoplasma-infected dust from bat dung. His death so soon after opening the burial chamber and the reported unexpected deaths of Arthur Mace and George Benedite associated with the finding of the tomb led to the persisting belief in the legend of the Curse of the Pharaohs.

CHAPTER 10

Lung Cancer

A counter-blaste to tobacco
Treatise by King James I, 1604

Since the end of the Second World War, cancer of the bronchus of the lung had become the commonest cancer to cause death in men in Britain and the United States. Doll and Hill in the United Kingdom and Hammond, Horn, Wynder and Graham in the United States have shown that the risk of developing lung cancer was proportionate to the number of cigarettes smoked, and that the non-smoker has a very small risk. In South Africa, cigarettes were, and still are, cheap. Most white South African men were heavier cigarette smokers than men in Britain. Yet I was seeing more patients with stomach cancer than with lung cancer. Lung cancer was still relatively uncommon in women because in the past they had smoked much less than men.

Because stomach cancer appeared to me to be more common than lung cancer among white South African males, in 1957 I looked at the national mortality statistics for cancer among white men and found that my suspicions were right: death from stomach cancer was considerably more common than from lung cancer. Because my research into multiple sclerosis and into the porphyrias had shown big differences in prevalence between the immigrants and the South African-born, I wondered whether British immigrants might have a different lung cancer mortality than white South African-born.

When I was next in Pretoria, I went to see Dr H.M. Stoker, director of the South African Census Bureau, and asked him if he would obtain for me an analysis of lung cancer deaths by South African-born, immigrants from the United Kingdom, and immigrants from the rest of Europe. He agreed to do this for the previous year. We found that the death rate from lung cancer among British immigrant men was twice as high as among the white South African-born in the same age-groups. Among the British male immigrants, it was the commonest cancer to cause death.

A few months later when I was visiting England, I wrote to Geoff Todd, the director of the Tobacco Research Council (TRC) in London and told him about my findings. Geoff Todd asked me to meet him; we got on well and became good friends. Geoff pointed out that, to confirm my findings, I should look at a ten-year period and calculate rates based on the populations at risk, for the white South African-born and the various immigrant groups. The TRC offered me funds to continue this research.

Back in South Africa, I calculated mortality rates for lung cancer over a ten-year period in each of the main cities, and in the other towns and the rural areas of South Africa. I found that in all areas, the British-born male immigrants between the ages of 45 and 64 had a higher mortality from lung cancer than the white South African-born or the immigrants from other European countries. Lung cancer in the 1950s and 60s was much less common in females. The mortality from chronic bronchitis among immigrants was as low as in the South African-born, and the immigrants lost the high risk of dying from chronic bronchitis that occurred in Britain. The results of the study were published in the *British Medical Journal* in 1959 and a further study was published in the same journal in 1961. These studies caused world-wide interest. In the United States, W. Haenszel, of the National Institute of Health, reported in 1961 that British immigrants had a higher lung cancer rate than those born in the United States, although the latter had smoked more during their lives. He confirmed that there was a 'British factor' besides the smoking factor. D.F. Eastcott had found the same thing in New Zealand.

In 1959, I was asked by the Tobacco Research Council if I would visit Dublin and see if it would be possible to undertake a study of lung cancer in the Republic. In Dublin I called on Pádraig

Ó Cinnéide, the secretary of the Department of Health, whose offices were in the Custom House beside the river Liffey. He introduced me to Donal McCarthy, the director of the Central Statistics Office. Talking to Donal, I realised that a significant proportion of deaths, particularly in the West of Ireland, were not certified by a doctor but had simply been reported by the local registrar of deaths. I also suspected that a number of deaths in the West of Ireland were neither certified nor registered before burial.

Donal showed me a letter in which a registrar of deaths in the West of Ireland, a local solicitor, had registered a death as 'died from heart failure'. The chief coding officer, unable to classify heart failure, had written to him to ask what the cause of the heart failure had been. The local registrar replied, 'his heart stopped'. At this point so did the correspondence. Some of Donal McCarthy's stories were amusing. One woman, he told me, had replied to the question 'sex' on the death registration form of her deceased husband, 'fine until a week before he died'.

Before I left Dublin, the Minister, Seán McEntee, and the secretary of the Department of Health, Pádraig Ó Cinnéide, invited me to dinner at a delightful restaurant, Jammet's, now no more. In Dublin I also met Risteard Mulcahy, a cardiologist, who was to become a great friend. He became Ireland's first professor of preventative cardiology.

My studies in South Africa confirmed that the risk of developing lung cancer was directly proportionate to the number of cigarettes one smoked, and that smoking cigarettes was the main factor associated with lung cancer, but that the risk was greater in those who had grown up in Britain. The British immigrants in South Africa had a lung cancer risk halfway between those who had stayed behind in Britain and the white South African-born. The evidence suggested that the British factor could well be due to urban air pollution, causing damage to the bronchii of the lungs in childhood. It was well known that chronic bronchitis was very common in Britain; indeed, it was often called the 'British disease'. Chronic bronchitis is much less common in Britain today because of the reduction in urban air pollution that followed the Clean Air Act, after the high number of deaths resulting from smog in London in the winter of 1952. When I was a medical registrar in Liverpool

Royal Infirmary in the 1940s, many of the men in the wards had metal sputum cups on the locker beside their beds, into which they would spit a thick yellow sputum. Gobs of such sputum would also be seen on the pavement, and coughing was non-stop in church or at concerts. At the Royal Liverpool Philharmonic Concert Hall, Sir Malcolm Sargent would often stop the orchestra, turn to the audience and say, 'Ladies and gentleman, if you will all give one good cough, we shall then try and continue!'

A strange situation had developed. The tobacco industry, a highly reputable industry, from which many thousands of people were making a living in the United States, United Kingdom and elsewhere, was suddenly under attack and held responsible for the most common of all cancers and also for the high mortality and morbidity from chronic bronchitis. It was later shown that cigarette smoking was also contributing in a major way to the high death rates from heart attacks and strokes. Every study undertaken on levels of cigarette smoking has shown that the risk of developing lung cancer was directly related to the number of cigarettes smoked. Joseph Berkson, a famous statistician, had been employed by the tobacco industry in Britain and the United States to try and refute these findings. All he could do was point out that a statistical association did not prove causation. He said that the lung cancer rate had increased parallel with the increase in wearing silk stockings, but this did not mean that wearing silk stockings causes lung cancer! During the next five years I was to be heavily involved in the study of the effects of smoking and air pollution on health.

Because of this research between 1958 and 1960, I was invited to many meetings in Europe and the United States and was often away from my practice, although I was well remunerated. Nonie generally did not wish to come and, as a result, she and I began to drift apart. I had become used to the international circuit. In 1958/59 I again spent three months in the United States, living in New York, in Chicago, and at the Mayo Clinic in Minnesota. Since I had been a medical student, I had smoked a few cigarettes a day, but my research on smoking had convinced me of its danger, and I had cut down by this time to one or two cigarettes a day. In 1960 I stopped for good.

In 1958 I wondered how best to invest for my retirement because I would have no pension. On the advice of my accountant, Alex Strelitz, I bought a company that owned a block of 15 flats in a working-class district of Port Elizabeth. The cost was £12,000, about two years' practice income; and I was able to borrow most of this money from an insurance company. I gave half the shares in the company to Nonie. Although in the years to come I was to earn a good income, it did not alter my way of life and I later used the money I had saved to buy a house, as an investment, with a large garden in Park Drive for 50,000 Rand, equivalent, at that time, to £25,000. In 1963 I decided to borrow money from the Aegis Insurance Company and built a block of 42 flats on the large area of land on which the Park Drive house stood. The building of the flats was supervised by a white builder; the workers were Coloured or African. The seven floors went up at the rate of one floor a fortnight, and the building was completed exactly according to the estimated costs. If it had not been, I would have been in trouble. Fortunately, the flats were quickly let and have stayed full ever since. They have not only paid back the mortgage but have enabled me to assist my children and build up a capital asset.

In June 1960, I was invited to attend an international congress on cancer in Vienna; I took part in the debate on lung cancer and smoking. During tea one afternoon, I met a beautiful woman in her middle twenties, Maria Von Braunbruck. She was petite, well-dressed, had red hair and was vivacious. I took her out to dinner that night and over two bottles of wine, she told me the story of her life. She was a Yugoslav, born and raised in Belgrade. Having decided to emigrate, she studied English. In 1958 it was not possible to leave Yugoslavia except on a short-term visa and she could bring out no money. Nevertheless, Maria left Belgrade for Rome by train, smuggling with her a painting by a Russian painter, Kolesnikov. She sold the painting and within 48 hours of her arrival had met an Italian Count at a dinner party. She lived with him for some months; he wanted to marry her, but did not because his family strongly objected to his marrying a Yugoslav.

When her Italian visa expired, Maria took a train to Vienna, having obtained, with difficulty, a three-week visa to visit Austria. In Vienna she became friendly with a handsome and talented woman, Bettina Moser, who was designing the costumes for films being made at the Viennese Film Studio. Bettina, who was half-Austrian and half-Hungarian, knew many people in Viennese society and within a few days Maria was introduced to Baron von Braunbruck, a wealthy chemist and the head of one of the oldest Austrian aristocratic families. (I met him on one occasion; he was overweight and drank large amounts of beer.) He married Maria and this provided her with an Austrian passport. I do not think they were in love; he probably liked to be seen in the company of a beautiful woman and she badly needed a passport so that she would not have to return to Yugoslavia.

When I met Maria in Vienna, about a year after she had married von Braunbruck, she had just obtained a divorce from him and was living with Bettina. Maria was excellent company in Vienna and we went to Sacher's restaurant, and Grinsing, and did the usual sightseeing, St Stephen's Cathedral (the Dom) and Schönbrun Palace. When the conference was over, we decided to spend a few days together in the countryside outside Vienna. We went to Semmering and stayed in an enchanting hotel which had been an old Austrian palace. During this time I was falling in love with Maria and apparently she was with me.

I left her in Vienna and went to London where I had been invited to meet the directors of the Tobacco Research Council to describe the results of my research into lung cancer. The TRC consisted of the directors of the main tobacco companies: the Imperial Tobacco Company, the British/American Tobacco Company, and the Rembrandt Group, which owned Rothman's of Pall Mall. The founder of the Rembrandt Group was Anton Rupert, an Afrikaner with a great personality.

At this meeting I told the council that my research confirmed that cigarette smoking was the main factor responsible for lung cancer. I said that the sale of cigarettes, at least in the United Kingdom, would almost inevitably fall and the best advice I could give the tobacco companies would be to diversify. At that time I thought the fall in cigarette consumption would be more rapid than has occurred. It is surprising how slow people have been to give up smoking, in spite of the immense danger of cigarette smoking to their health.

After this meeting, Sir John Partridge, chairman of the TRC, asked me if I would continue my studies in South Africa. He wanted me to send a questionnaire to the widows, or next of kin, of those who had died from lung cancer, enquiring about the past smoking habits of the deceased, place of residence at different times of life and their previous occupation. They offered to pay my expenses and to recompense me well for the loss of practice this research would entail. Sir John told me that I should publish the results of the study and that the TRC would not interfere in the wording of my report. All the studies I subsequently undertook confirmed that the main factor causing lung cancer was cigarette smoking, but there was also a British factor.

When I was in England, I spent time with my parents, who had retired to Eastbourne. They had a pleasant ground floor flat opposite the entrance of Saffron's Cricket Club and my father was able to watch the cricket and play bowls at the club. My parents were also keen bridge players. The New Inn pub was on the corner, opposite the Catholic church, about 40 yards away from my parents' house, and my father always called there on Sundays for a glass of beer. My sister Helen, who at that time was teaching, also lived in Eastbourne and visited my parents regularly. Both my father and mother had a happy retirement in Eastbourne.

CHAPTER 11

The Turkish Epidemic of Porphyria

He bears the seed of ruin in himself
Matthew Arnold, 'Merope'

In 1955, Dr Cihad Çam, a dermatologist in Diyarbakir in eastern Turkey, saw a large number of children with sores and blisters on their faces and on the backs of their hands. They had dark pigmented skins and great hairiness on their arms, hands and faces. They were described by their neighbours in the villages as the 'monkey children' because of their hairiness. Their urine was a reddish-brown. When Dr Çam examined their urine in ultraviolet light, using a 'Woods filter' to block the white light, it showed a brilliant pink fluorescence. He realised then that these children's symptoms had probably been caused by some form of porphyria. Between 1955 and 1960 he had seen many hundreds of affected children and adults.

Dr Çam took the dietary history of the children with porphyria. The peasants in the eastern part of Turkey, many of them Kurds, were, and still are, very poor; bread was their main diet. To obtain good wheat crops in the area, it was necessary to treat the seed-wheat with a fungicide, or else the seed-wheat would be destroyed in the soil by the fungus *Tilletia Tritici*. Before 1953 the seed-wheat had been treated with mercurous chloride, which had not proved to be very effective and the wheat crops were poor. In 1954, seed-wheat was sent by the United States to eastern Turkey, treated for the first time with the fungicide hexachlorobenzene. This seed was distributed for planting in Urfa Province and, in 1955, was also sold in the neighbouring provinces of Diyarbakir and Mardin. Dr Çam found that the affected children had been eating bread made from the seed-wheat. He quite rightly suspected that this wheat, or what had been added to it, was responsible for the epidemic.

The publication of Dr Çam's views caused an outcry. The matter was complicated because the United States was the main support of the Turkish economy and helped to arm one million Turkish troops. The United States also had, at that time, atomic bases in Turkey aimed at the underbelly of the Soviet Union. The Turkish Ministry of Agriculture believed, with good reason, that if the wheat was not treated with hexachlorobenzene, the crops would be very poor and there would be a shortage of bread. The Health Ministry, on the other hand, wished to stop the use of the new fungicide. By 1960, the problem had not been resolved and the hexachlorobenzene-treated wheat was still being issued with due warning, but in English, which the Turks and Kurds did not under-stand, on the sacks of wheat, that it was for planting and should not be made into flour. Each year many more children developed symptoms of porphyria. It was estimated in 1960 that at least 5,000 children were seriously affected and an alarmingly high number had died from the disorder. Many thousands more were mildly affected.

I had been asked, while still in South Africa, if I would go to Turkey and report on this epidemic, suggesting how it could be stopped. After my meetings with the TRC in the summer of 1960, I flew from London to Rome to meet Maria, and we continued together to Ankara.

Some of the children had been admitted for investigation to the Hacettepe Children's Hospital in Ankara under the care of Dr Joseph Wray. I spent two weeks at the hospital with him exami-ning the children. They had developed much greater pigmentation of the skin and hairiness of the face than had occurred in either *porphyria variegata* or in the sporadic cases of symptomatic porphyria sometimes seen in adults in the West. Sporadic symptomatic porphyria in the West was usually caused by the abuse of alcohol. Several members of the same Turkish family were often affected. The children had enlarged livers and an impaired liver function.

The stool, unlike the urine, showed no increase in porphyrin. That the seed-wheat was responsible for the epidemic was proven by Dr Rudi Schmid, of Minneapolis, who had fed rats with the fungicide-treated wheat. The rats had developed cutaneous porphyria and excreted large amounts of porphyrin in their urine. These findings confirmed Professor Çam's observations.

It appeared likely that the symptoms of cutaneous porphyria were made worse in the Turkish children because they were under-nourished. The Ministry of Agriculture would not agree to stop the distribution of the hexachlorobenzene-treated seed-wheat because of the danger of famine, but it was extremely difficult to prevent the wheat from being sold by the merchants and millers. I proposed that methylene blue powder should be added to the wheat. Then, when the wheat was made into flour, the methylene blue powder would stain the flour and turn the bread blue. This made it impossible for the seed-wheat to be used by mistake because blue bread did not look very appetising. The peasants were living on a diet that was extremely low in protein. In South Africa, soya bean flour (which contains protein) and protein from fish were added at that time to the flour used for making cheaper brands of bread popular among the poorer non-white population. I suggested that this should be done in Turkey.

Maria and I left from Ankara to fly to Istanbul with twenty specimens each of urine and faeces from children with Turkish porphyria. We were a little late for the plane and rushed from the taxi with our bags. Only when we reached Istanbul did I realise that the carrier bag containing the specimens had been left behind in the boot of the taxi. I was not going to leave Turkey without the specimens, so I phoned the hotel in Ankara to enquire if the bag had been found. The manager of the hotel told me that the taxi driver had returned to the hotel with the bag and handed it to him. He said it was quite common for taxi drivers to steal a small bag when they discharged passengers who were in a hurry, but this was the first time a bag had ever been returned! I arranged for the hotel manager to send the bag by plane to Istanbul; it arrived about a week later.

Maria wished to return to South Africa with me and I agreed, with considerable misgivings. I wrote and told Nonie about her while I was in Istanbul. I was in a very disturbed state of mind because I knew how unhappy this would make Nonie and our children. Maria and I flew to Nairobi where the plane was grounded because of a technical fault, and we stayed at the New Inn Hotel for three days awaiting another plane.

On our first evening at the hotel there was a show by a conjurer and 'thought reader' called Koran. He asked guests to place small personal objects into envelopes and seal them. Then he would pick up an envelope and say what was inside. When Koran came to Maria's envelope, he said, 'There is nothing inside; you are trying to deceive me.' 'Yes, there is,' said Maria. 'I don't believe it,' said Koran. 'If so, tell me what it is.' 'Three hairs from my head,' said Maria. 'You terrify me,' said Koran. I realise now that the first envelope to be opened was opened by an accomplice in the audience who agreed that it was the correct object. After that Koran reported each time on the envelope he had previously opened. Maria deceived him because he had not seen the hairs.

When we reached Johannesburg I left Maria at a hotel and flew on to Port Elizabeth. Nonie had received my letter and was very upset but agreed immediately to an amicable divorce (though she later changed her mind). She had been advised by her lawyer the previous day. Within three days I returned to Johannesburg. The two months Maria and I then spent in Johannesburg were, except for Patricia's death, the most depressing and anxious weeks of my life. I was full of guilt about Nonie and missed my children whom I loved dearly, yet I was very much in love with Maria. If Nonie, on legal advice, had not agreed so quickly to a divorce and then changed her mind, it might have been easier. I had been away from Port Elizabeth too often and for too long and we had grown apart.

Maria, who had survived by her great charm since leaving Yugoslavia, was astute. She persuaded me to rent a flat in Johannesburg and quickly went about furnishing it, buying, among other things, three expensive Chinese carpets with my money. They have turned out to be good investments, although I was annoyed at the time.

To my surprise, my friend John Bradshaw, to whom I had

written about Maria, decided to fly to Johannesburg to see if he could help. He stayed with us and said that, in his opinion, Maria and I were not suited to each other because there was a great difference in our cultures. He had said much the same before I had married Nonie. I could not make up my mind what to do and had an unhappy conscience. I suffered from the typical symptoms of depression, awakening in the early hours of the morning in deep gloom. An antidepressant drug did not help.

Maria quickly made friends with a number of Yugoslavs in Johannesburg who advised her to see a solicitor named Simler. I found myself under great pressure from Maria and Simler to provide her with some money to give her financial security. This I did, although at the time I felt there was a degree of blackmail about it.

During my life I have learned a great deal from women friends with whom I had fallen in love, but they have also caused me the greatest problems! My mother wrote to me about this time: 'If only you had remained a good Catholic and not been so questioning and adventurous and stayed quietly at home in England, you would have had a much easier and more contented life.' No doubt she was right, but life would have been much more dull.

CHAPTER 12

Smoke

No man is an Island, entire of itself;
every man is a piece of the Continent, a part of the main.
John Donne, 'Devotions'

In January 1961 when Nonie changed her mind and would not agree to a divorce, I asked Maria, who had quite sufficient money at this time, if she would return to Paris, and I left for Port Elizabeth where I stayed at the Beach Hotel. Maria sold most of the furniture from the Johannesburg flat and put the three Chinese carpets into storage, and then followed me to Port Elizabeth where she soon made a number of women friends. She asked a lawyer, Marcus Jacobs, if he could further the divorce proceedings. I had no enthusiasm about this because I could see that the situation was causing great distress to Nonie and the children. Since Maria would not return to Paris, I decided to fly to Australia to undertake a study on the epidemiology of lung cancer similar to that which I had already undertaken in South Africa and which the Tobacco Research Council wanted to see repeated in Australia. Because I was adamant about going to Australia, and since I did not invite Maria to come with me, she flew back to Paris.

I arrived in Melbourne and hired a car and drove to Canberra, the capital. There I went to see Mr S.R. Carver, the Commonwealth statistician, and Mr V. Pickering, the principal of the Australian demography department and other officers in the Commonwealth Bureau of Census and Statistics. I asked them if they would collaborate with me on a study of lung cancer mortality in Australia. I also had the assistance of Sir Edward Ford, the professor of preventative medicine, and of Professor Oliver Lancaster, the professor of mathematical statistics, at Sydney University. We studied all deaths from lung cancer in Australia over a ten-year period and found, when the deaths were analysed by birthplace and age-group, that immigrants from Britain to Australia had a higher mortality from lung cancer than the Australian-born, but a lower mortality than those who had remained in Britain. The British Tobacco Company (in Australia) provided me with estimates of cigarette consumption in Australia. Consumption in adults had changed from being slightly lower than in the United Kingdom before the Second World War, and then higher than in the United Kingdom after the war. The research in Australia confirmed that there was a 'British factor', probably air pollution, besides cigarette smoking associated with lung cancer and also confirmed the findings in South Africa, New Zealand and the United States.

I was still in love with Maria and the next part of the story is perhaps not rational. I was no doubt influenced to some extent by loneliness. I had previously agreed to give a lecture on smoking and lung cancer to the International Statistical Society Congress in Paris and, when the research was completed in Australia, I flew there a few weeks before the congress and joined Maria. We stayed at a flat that belonged to a friend of Maria's, where she was already living, in the Île de la Cité, near Notre Dame. The flat belonged to an artist and on the wall facing the bed was a copy of a painting by Hieronymous Bosch, 'The Temptation of St Anthony'. In the painting St Anthony is beset by an array of grotesque demons, brilliantly visualised amalgamations of human, animal, vegetable and inanimate parts. It was a disturbing painting to wake up and see in the morning!

Paris was in a state of tension in 1961 because of the war in Algeria between the French and the Algerians. There were many Algerian immigrants in Paris who were at that time very unpopular and Algerian bodies were frequently found floating in the Seine. One evening, as we were returning home down a dark lane, two Algerians followed us. One then moved ahead of us, the other stayed behind. I realised that Maria and I were going to be attacked and we nervously started to sing 'Cherie, je t'aime. Cherie, je t'adore', an Algerian song. Just as the two Algerians were closing in on us, two gendarmes, submachine guns over their shoulders, arrived in the lane on motorbikes. The 'flics' quickly had the two Algerians against a wall, kicking one of them badly as they did so. Both Algerians had unpleasant knives up their sleeves. We had had a narrow escape and decided to spend the two weeks before the Paris Congress at Beaulieu-sur-Mer, near Cannes, in the South of France.

After the Paris Congress we flew to London and stayed, as guests of the Tobacco Research Council, at the Westbury Hotel. Geoff Todd was impressed by Maria; he found her interesting and amusing, besides being beautiful, but he also confided privately with me his opinion that since our cultures were so different we might have problems if we stayed together. He asked Professor John Youngman, a well-known sculptor, to portray Maria in bronze and she agreed. We still have the sculpture; it is about thirty inches high.

On that visit to London, the TRC asked me if I would undertake a study of lung cancer in the Channel Islands. They pointed out that the research I was undertaking on lung cancer and smoking was of the greatest epidemiological importance. They did appreciate how difficult it was to leave my children and my medical practice in South Africa and promised to fund well any study I carried out. I was also influenced in agreeing by my love for Maria. I did not want to leave her, but nor did I want to take her back to South Africa.

Dr Averil Dowling was the Medical Officer of Health in Jersey. He had reported to the Jersey public health committee that the island had the highest lung cancer rates in the world and that the Jersey residents were also the world's heaviest smokers. Cigarettes are cheap in the Channel Islands because they are not taxed. In 1961 Jersey had a population of 63,000. Mortality from cirrhosis of the liver and suicide was also high, largely because alcohol was also very cheap in the Channel Islands.

Maria and I went to Jersey. I secured the approval of the Greffe, or Parliament, and with their permission noted from the Register of Births and Deaths the names and addresses of all those who had died from lung cancer between 1952 and 1961. In order to make a comparison between those who had died from lung cancer and those who had died from other diseases, I needed controls. Therefore I obtained records about the next death in the Death Register that was not from lung cancer but was in the same sex, age-group and birthplace group – born in Jersey or in Britain – as the lung cancer death.

I then called on the widow, or next of kin, of those who had died from lung cancer and of the controls, in order to obtain information about the smoking habits of the deceased. I traced the next of kin of all 222 people who had died of lung cancer in Jersey during the decade I was studying. One in eight of the men who had died, aged 45 to 64, had died from lung cancer and by 1961 this ratio had increased to one in five deaths. In a further study in Guernsey, Alderney and Sark, one in seven deaths among the men, aged 45 to 64 years, was from lung cancer. In the ten-year period of the study, only two male lung cancer deaths in Jersey and four in Guernsey, Alderney and Sark had occurred in those who did not smoke. During the later years, the lung cancer mortality rate of British immigrants had exceeded that of locally born men, although they had smoked less than the locally born men before they had migrated to Jersey. This study in the Channel Islands confirmed the findings in South Africa, the United States, New Zealand and Australia and pointed again to a 'British' factor besides a smoking factor.

In Jersey we stayed with a French-speaking family and they had a ten-year-old son. He was interested in biology and one day I explained to him Darwin's theory of evolution. I asked him if he thought that mankind and the higher apes, such as chimpanzees, had a common ape-like ancestor? He looked me in the eye and said: 'I think some of us did!'

On the smallest of the Channel Islands, Sark, with a population of just over 500 at that time and no cars, we stayed with the Dame of Sark. She told us that it was the established custom that she paid the King or Queen of England every year 'one knight's fee'. She was a fine old lady who went about in an electric wheelchair.

Tourism was, and is, a major industry in Jersey and it was thought that it depended to a great extent on the low cost of cigarettes and alcohol. Unfortunately, Dr Averil Dowling, who had drawn attention to the very high lung cancer rates on the island, found his views very unpopular and soon afterwards retired as Medical Officer of Health. His chief clerk, Tim Simon, still sends me a calendar of Jersey every Christmas.

In 1961, I was asked to attend a neurological congress in Rome and talk about the research I had undertaken on the epidemiology of multiple sclerosis. After the congress I agreed to accompany Maria by train from Rome to Belgrade to meet her parents. They lived in a flat in the centre of Belgrade with her brother, Nicholas, his wife, and their three small children. Fortunately, Maria's father, Stanimir, could speak German, having spent some years in Switzerland where he had been a shoe manufacturer before the Second World War, and I was able to talk to him in the poor German I had learnt as a student in Frankfurt. I was still in love with Maria but greatly missed my children and, realising that our background was so different, I returned without her to Port Elizabeth. Maria went to stay in Paris, where some of her friends were living.

I tried for the last time to make a success of my marriage with Nonie, but found it extremely difficult because I was still in love with Maria. I had been back in Port Elizabeth about ten weeks when Ron Deare, husband of Maria's great friend in Johannesburg, Netta Deare, phoned that they had received a telegram from Maria saying that she would arrive in Johannesburg the following morning. This was a great shock because I had not invited her but it was too late to stop her. A few days later, after telling Nonie what had happened, I went to Johannesburg to meet Maria. I was torn between two women. My relationship with Nonie had grown cold but I knew that she was a very fine, intelligent and good person whom I still loved for the years we had had together. I also greatly loved my three children, although most of the time they were at boarding school and not at home. Maria, in contrast, was exotic, with amusing conversation and was always excellent company. Sexually we were totally compatible. She already had a weakness, which I was only fully to appreciate later, and that was that when she had a drink, she found it difficult to stop. This is often a problem among Slavic people.

The situation had, no doubt, become too much for Nonie and she agreed to an amicable divorce. No custody arrangements were made for the children and none were needed. When the children were at home, they would live with Nonie but often spend the weekend with Maria and me at Lauries Bay. After the divorce Nonie wrote to my father that she thought that if she was divorced I would reconsider and return to live with her. I think that if she had not agreed to a divorce so easily when I had first suggested it, we would have stayed married. Whether or not this would have been a good or a bad thing is difficult to say.

Back in London, and writing the first draft of the report about the Channel Islands for publication in the *British Journal of Cancer*, I was asked by the TRC to organise a major study of lung cancer and bronchitis in Northern Ireland. I knew that a study in a population of one and a half million people would probably take at least three years. I went to Northern Ireland to see if it was practical to undertake the study and to obtain the co-operation of the Northern Ireland Department of Health. The Chief Medical Officer, Frank Maine and his deputy, Sandy Elder, promised their assistance with the study. We obtained a list of all deaths from lung cancer and bronchitis in Northern Ireland between 1960 and 1962. As in the Channel Islands, we selected a control for each lung cancer and bronchitis death. We divided Northern Ireland into six areas: inner Belfast, outer Belfast, the surroundings of Belfast, urban districts, small towns and rural districts. We arranged that a market research company would interview the relatives of the patients and the controls and complete a questionnaire about the deceased's smoking habits, occupation, area of residence and other relevant factors.

Maria and I married in June 1962 and rented a one-bedroomed flat in Port Elizabeth. Shortly afterwards I had to return to Europe to attend the World Cancer Congress in Moscow and then to continue the study in Northern Ireland. Maria, Geoff Todd and I first went to Leningrad, saw the paintings in the Hermitage and the sights of Leningrad and a week later flew to Moscow. There were more than 4,000 delegates at the conference and we were well entertained in the spacious halls of the Kremlin. Maria danced with Yuri Gagarin, the first man to travel in space; he was a small, cheerful, good-looking man. We also met Anastas Mikoyan, the first deputy to Khrushchev. We did not like the Soviet Union; we were watched everywhere we went. There was always a long wait in the restaurants and when we went shopping the shop assistants were not interested in serving customers. All in all, we found Moscow very depressing, although it was a help that Maria could speak some Russian; she had learnt it at school.

Maria and I then went back to South Africa and returned to Northern Ireland for some months in the summer of 1963 and again in 1964. During these visits we got on well with both Catholics and Protestants. There was no doubt that members of the Catholic community had a very raw deal at this time. They were barred from many jobs, for instance in the Belfast ship-building yards. Protestants always had first preference in housing, and the chief posts in the medical services were all held by Protestants.

The lung cancer rates in Northern Ireland were substantially below those in the rest of the United Kingdom. However lung cancer mortality was three times higher in inner Belfast than in the rural areas for light (1–10 a day), medium (11–20 a day) or heavy smoking (21+ a day). I received great assistance in the research from Professor John Pemberton, professor of social medicine at Queen's University, Belfast, and from Sandy Elder, Northern Ireland's deputy Medical Officer of Health. Sandy died shortly after the study was completed, after playing a Chopin prelude at a party for friends. Everybody was clapping loudly when he fell forward, dead. What a lovely way to exit!

We decided to undertake a major study of smoking habits and air pollution in Teesside which included the urban areas of Eston and Stockton municipal boroughs, and the rural districts of Croft, North Allerton, Richmond and Stokesley. The study included environmental factors likely to be associated with lung cancer and bronchitis and also studies of deaths from heart attacks and strokes by area of residence, smoking habits and social class. The study would not have been possible without the collaboration of the

Medical Officers of Health for these districts, in particular Dr Paddy Donaldson. Eston was a heavily polluted area and included an ICI chemical works and a big steelworks.

A similar methodology was used as in Northern Ireland and the Teesside study also showed that cigarette smoking was a major factor associated with lung cancer and bronchitis, but it was also a factor associated with death from heart attacks and strokes. At each level of smoking, the risk of death from lung cancer and bronchitis was higher in the polluted urban areas than in the rural areas. There was a high death rate among the lower socio-economic groups.

The Teesside study confirmed the findings in Northern Ireland and showed that, whereas cigarette smoking was most highly associated with lung cancer, urban air-pollution was as important as cigarette smoking for deaths from bronchitis. We also found that cigarette smoking was an important factor associated with heart attacks and strokes. Both the Northern Ireland study and the Teesside study took three years to complete but they overlapped.

Back in Port Elizabeth, I was seeing patients not only from the city but also from the country areas. Sometimes I would be asked by a doctor in a country town to see a patient who was too ill to move, living perhaps three hundred or more miles away. I would fly by private plane which usually had to land in a makeshift landing place. By flying, I could come back quickly and avoid long car journeys. I was not a 'flying doctor', but I did go by air perhaps four or five times a year to see a patient who lived a good distance from Port Elizabeth. On my way back I would sometimes get the pilot of the small plane to fly low over Lauries Bay and I would drop a note saying that I would be home for tea!

At the instigation of the famous statistician, Joseph Berkson, I decided to undertake a study on all causes of death among the different peoples of South Africa and compare the mortality for different diseases between the white immigrants and the white South African-born. Dr Berkson thought that the reason for the high lung cancer rates in British immigrants might possibly be due to their constitution and not the environment.

Dr H.M. Stoker, the director of the South African Census

Bureau, Pretoria, agreed to decode the Hollerith cards, an information system based on punched cards, for all South African deaths reported during the three years 1957, 1958 and 1959 and for certain causes of death for longer periods. The deaths were analysed by sex, age-group, place of residence and place of birth. At the same time I undertook a study on the causes of death among the white, Coloured, Indian and black South Africans. The long report was published as a special supplement in the *South African Medical Journal* (*SAMJ*) in 1965.

South African-born white men and women, in spite of, or because of, their high standard of living, had a higher death rate up to the age of 65 than men and women in the United Kingdom, the Netherlands, Germany and France. The death rate for the white population was considerably higher in the cities than in the rural parts of South Africa.

Immigrants from the United Kingdom to South Africa had a lower mortality than the white South African-born but not as low as those who had remained in the United Kingdom. In South Africa heart attacks were the major cause of death in white and Indian men. The white South African-born had significantly higher death rates than in the United Kingdom for cancer of the stomach, prostate, uterus and skin, for heart attacks, cirrhosis of the liver, accidents and porphyria. They had lower rates for cancer of the bowel and of the lung, for bronchitis, multiple sclerosis and ulcerative colitis.

The Asian community consisted chiefly of the Indians of Natal. They were often traders and middlemen. Their closely knit family life and strong business sense protected them from many of the hazards of poverty, and their expectation of life was much better than in India. However, many died from raised blood pressure, strokes, heart attacks and diabetes.

The Coloured people, who lived mostly in the Cape, occupied an intermediate position in the social scale between the whites and the blacks. They had largely adopted a western way of life. Like the white population, their mortality statistics were fairly reliable. Many died in infancy, mostly from gastroenteritis. Their birth rate was high, compensating for their raised mortality rates.

I found that the black population had neither the medical

attention nor the necessary level of death certification to make possible detailed comparisons with other South African racial groups. Their death rate at this time was very high. When I first went to Port Elizabeth in 1947, about half the black children died in their first year of life. By the time I left in 1968, it had dropped to 20 per cent, with a resulting big increase in population as the birth rate remained high. I concluded in the 1965 report in the *SAMJ* that Africans should be taught the advantages of limiting the size of their families and that smaller families, among whom most of the children would survive, would result in improved living standards.

My conclusions on the causes of death in South Africans showed that the most important factor affecting their health was the environment. The diseases of the Coloured and African people were mostly the result of poverty and of the white and Indian people their affluent lifestyle.

After completing the study, I thought I would look at the causes of death of my own profession. In 1969 there were only ninety-eight medically qualified black doctors in practice in South Africa. Because of the small number of black doctors, there were few deaths. Perhaps because of their relatively high income and few opportunities to spend it, they appeared to be unduly susceptible to alcohol-related disease. The Coloured doctors had the same pattern of death as occurred among the white doctors, in particular heart attacks. The Indian doctors had a high death rate attributable to heart attacks, high blood pressure, strokes and diabetes. White South African doctors had a considerably lower mortality rate than occurred among the general white South African population. Nevertheless they had a high death rate from heart attacks and lung cancer – at this time most of the South African doctors were still smokers – and from suicide. White, Coloured and Asian dentists had a very similar death pattern to doctors.

I finished my report, published in the *SAMJ* in 1969, by suggesting that doctors should pay more attention to the health of their colleagues, who are often slow to obtain expert advice about their own health. Doctors are more prone than average to alcoholism and to suicide, perhaps because they often work long hours with little time for social relaxation.

It is becoming increasingly possible to identify 'high risk groups' for different causes of death. Those in these groups can often be advised how they should alter their way of life, to lessen their risk of early death. Affluent societies should give much more attention to the effects of our way of life on health – for instance a high calorie diet rich in animal fat, excessive use of the car and a lack of daily exercise, smoking, the abuse of alcohol and air pollution.

In 1976, two doctors, Richard Doll and Richard Peto, showed that doctors in Britain, who by and large had stopped smoking, had a fall in their lung cancer mortality and also in their risk of dying from heart attacks, strokes and chronic bronchitis, strong confirmatory evidence that cigarette smoking was a major factor in causing these diseases.

CHAPTER 13

Porphyria:
The Master Family Tree

The study of things caused must precede the study of the cause of things
Claude Bernard, *Introduction à l'étude de la médecine experimentale*, 1865

Whenever I saw a patient suffering from *porphyria variegata*, I interviewed all the relatives I could find, examined them for porphyria and drew up a family tree. In this way I was able to find out from which side of the family porphyria had been inherited. All the families I studied came from Afrikaner, or Boer, stock. It was possible to trace the ancestors from the family bibles and from the baptismal records of the Dutch Reformed Church. The way the Afrikaners named their children was also a great help; the first son was always given the names of the father's father, the second son those of the mother's father, and the third son the father's own names. The first daughter was given the names of the mother's mother, the second those of the father's mother, and the third the mother's names. This meant that the first-born uncle would have the same names as the great-grandfather. I was able to trace the families on the affected side back about 150 years, to the early part of the nineteenth century. After a great deal of research, I traced 32 family groups to their ancestors back about five or six generations.

Tracing the porphyric families to earlier than the nineteenth century was made easier by research carried out by Christoffel Coetzee de Villiers, the editor of the *Het Volksblad* newspaper, in the 1870s and 1880s. He found the names of the ancestors of his own family and those of most of the old Boer families from their baptismal records back to their ancestors who had come from Europe, many in the latter half of the seventeenth century. When he died in 1884, de Villiers's register of the old Cape families was published in three volumes. Dr J. Hoge studied the families of the early German settlers, while C.G. Botha made a careful examination of French Huguenot refugee families who had come to the Cape about 1688.

Gerrit Jansz came to the Cape in 1685 and was one of the first free citizens or burghers. He was given a grant of land in the Stellenbosch district. In 1687 the Lords Seventeen, a committee of the seventeen directors appointed by the large cities of Holland to direct the Dutch East India Company, decided to send out young orphans from Rotterdam to be wives for the first free burghers at the Cape. The first eight orphans were sent out on the ship *China* in 1688 and four of them had married within a month of their arrival. One of the four was Ariaantje Jacobs. To show how the first group of orphan girls were sent to the Cape, I shall quote a translation of an extract from a letter of December 1687 to Commander Simon van der Stel, Commander at the Cape of Good Hope, and his Council, from the Lords Seventeen:

... Whereas in a Resolution of the Council of Seventeen dated 3rd October 1685 it is already laid down that the Cape Station should be provided with persons who understand agriculture and the soil, both men and women, with a view to establishing in due course an important Colony and place of refreshment for the use of the Company and to the benefit of the inhabitants; we now therefore have favoured the eight young women with a passage to the Cape of Good Hope on the ship *China* (which is a large vessel), proceeding from this Chamber, and they are to remain at the Cape for the above purpose under a five year contract, in accordance with the Resolution of the latest meeting of the Council, whereas prior to this date it was a contract for 15 years, and subject to the Regulations drawn up and laid down for Free Burghers. The names are:

Ariaentgen Jansz van Son van Rotterdam
Willemtgen Arijens de Wit v.   do.

Arijaentgen Jacobs van den Berg   do.
Judith Jansz Verbeecq   do.
Petronelle Cornelis van Capelle   do.
Jongetgen Cornelis van den bout   do.

Catharina Jane van der Zee and Anna Eltrap van Kleef conversant with (farm work and) the cultivation of the soil. And it is the intention of the Lords 17 to employ these and other young women as agriculturists. We therefore request and earnestly recommend to you that you see that they are suitably placed, or if they marry, see that they do so with honest, capable and industrious men engaged in farming or of definite intention to undertake such work, and with whom these young women may be able to make a living, while (at the same time) as far as possible dissuading them from marriage with military men, as this is not within the intention of the Lords Seventeen. In the meantime, and until the marriage of these young women, it is incumbent upon you to provide them with the necessary sustenance and housing, maintaining such discipline you may deem suitable, and providing them with appropriate handiwork or honest employment, so that their occupations and deportment may further their own advancement; and the management and conducting of this recommendation we entrust to your 'Honours' discretion …

The van Rooyen families with porphyria go back to five of the eleven children of Cornelis van Rooyen, who came from Gorkum in Holland and married Jacomijntje Gerritsz, the daughter of Gerrit, in 1720. Other porphyric families go back to a sister of Jacomijntje, Aletta Gerritsz, who married Pieter Willem Nel in 1725. Yet other families go back to Johanna Margrieta Gerritsz, who married twice and had porphyric descendants from both marriages. Lastly, there was a brother, Jacobus Gerritsz, who had twelve children; his seventh and twelfth child are ancestors of porphyric families. Since Gerrit was the son of Jan, he was known as Gerrit Jansz. Gerrit Jansz came from Deventer in Holland and the male side of the family is now known by the name van Deventer.

It can thus be seen that four of the eight children of Gerrit inherited porphyria from him or from his wife Ariaantje. Gerrit Jansz (the son of Jan) married Ariaantje Jacobs (the daughter of Jacob) in Cape Town in 1688. She was also called Ariaantje Adriaansse, after her mother, Adriana. Gerrit's eighth child, a son, was not by his wife but probably by a slave girl. He acknowledged the child and christened him Jan Gerritsz. The family trees are shown in my book, *The Porphyrias: A Study of Inheritance and Environment* (London, Pitman Medical, 2nd edn, 1971).

It would have been very difficult to trace all these early families without the help of an expert archivist. I was fortunate in having the assistance of the Cape archivist, Margaret Jeffreys, who perhaps knew more than anyone else about the old Cape families. With her assistance, we were able to trace the ancestors of the porphyric families which I had not myself found. For each porphyric family, a family tree was drawn up, showing the antecedents back to the seventeenth century. Tracing these families required a great deal of detective work and Miss Jeffreys proved to be a genius in this type of research. In our voluminous correspondence I always referred to her as 'Mycroft', after Mycroft Holmes, who alone could find the missing clue when Sherlock Holmes was baffled. She addressed me as 'Maigret'.

Besides the birth registers and marriage registers which are kept by the Dutch Reformed Church 'Scribas', or church record keepers, a great deal of help was obtained from the wills and inventories of the early settlers which were filed in the archives in Cape Town. The inventory of Gerrit Jansz names his children in order, and his few possessions are also listed. His debts exceed his assets. His son-in-law, Cornelius van Rooyen, died a very much more prosperous man. Cornelius signed his name 'Cornelis van Roye'; Ariaantje was only able to make a cross.

I have attempted in a few words to describe an intensive genealogical search which occupied me for ten years. Thousands of letters were written and I employed a research secretary. Nonie and I also spent many hours searching the records in the various Church and State archives. Nonie was of great assistance with this research during the 1950s.

A master family tree was drawn up, showing how the forebears of 32 large porphyric groups in the early part of the nineteenth century all go back to Gerrit and Ariaantje. The drawing of the master family tree for publication was carried out by Margaret Hitge, a Pretoria artist. The family tree shows the first six generations of this family. Today the family is in the thirteenth to eighteenth generations. I saw only two families in South Africa with porphyria of Swedish type, acute intermittent porphyria (AIP), and they were recent immigrants. AIP does occur, however, among black South Africans.

In one *porphyria variegata* family in the Transvaal, I could not trace the family back further than to the middle of the nineteenth century. It was only when I was able to obtain the complete confidence of the older members of the family that the difficulty was made clear. The forebear of this particular group of porphyric families had fallen in love with an English schoolmaster on her father's farm and had become pregnant. The father was an elder of the Church and, in order to prevent a family scandal, she had been sent to a distant part of the country and had taken the name of the people with whom she had stayed. It was only when this alteration in name was revealed that it was possible to join her to the original porphyric main stem.

In the seventeenth and early eighteenth centuries there was no strong colour bar at the Cape and many of the early burghers had children by half-caste slave girls. *Porphyria variegata* is also relatively common among the Coloured people in the Cape and among them it also traced back to Gerrit or Ariaantje.

Until relatively recently, *porphyria variegata* was not a deleterious gene because the porphyric families had, on average, as large a number of children as did other families. A girl would marry when she was thirteen or fourteen years of age and would often have twelve to sixteen children; living on scattered farms, with abundant food and few infectious diseases most of them survived.

It is interesting to consider how the small number of free burghers in South Africa in the seventeenth century have now become a race. More than a million of the five million white population in 1995 hold the names of twenty original settlers and the men among them have inherited their Y-chromosome, which determines their male sex, from twenty original settlers. The commonest surnames in South Africa in 1964 were Botha (80,000) and Van der Merwe (65,000). There were 28,000 men with the name Van Rooyen in 1964 (and there must be more than 50,000 today). The increase of the first twenty original settlers, and their wives, to a million of the present population, can be contrasted with the increase of the population in Britain or the Netherlands. Three hundred years ago the population of Britain was eight million and today it is approximately 60 million, an increase of sevenfold.

Gerrit Jansz van Deventer or his wife, Ariaantje Jacobs van Rotterdam, carried the gene for *porphyria variegata* and carriers of the gene multiplied in the same way as the number of men holding the name Van Rooyen or Van Deventer. This increase in a gene frequency in a small population that becomes a larger one is known as 'founder-effect'. A small number of fish were placed in a very large fish pond with no natural enemies and were able to multiply like the children of Jacob in Goshen. There are at least 25,000 white and Coloured South Africans who have inherited *porphyria variegata* from Gerrit Jansz or from Ariaantje, the orphan from Rotterdam. Many of them are still children and have no symptoms of porphyria.

I found that *porphyria variegata* was more common among the members of the staff of the large psychiatric hospital in Grahamstown than it was among the patients at the hospital. *Porphyria variegata* in South Africa did not cause long-standing insanity.

In September 1963 the first world congress on the porphyrias was held in Cape Town, under the chairmanship of Professor Don Craib. The world's porphyria experts were invited. Because the delegates were particularly interested in the story of *porphyria variegata*, I made a special arrangement with Pitmans, the medical publishing company, to send me twelve advance copies of my book, *The Porphyrias: A Story of Inheritance and Environment*, so that I could present a copy to the most distinguished of the guests.

When copies of the book arrived at the customs department in Cape Town, I was sent a letter from the chief censor telling me that the books could not be released nor could the book be sold in South Africa. I went to see him and asked why I could not have my books. He pointed out that in the book I stated that *porphyria variegata*, besides being common among the white people of South Africa, occurred among the Coloured at the Cape, and that the Coloured people had inherited porphyria from a white ancestor, Gerrit Jansz, or his wife, Ariaantje Jacobs. He said that this could not be true because the Coloured people were descendants of Hottentot and Malay slaves and British seamen off the ships, that the early Dutch settlers were extremely moral, church-going people and would not have had sexual relations with their slaves. I mentioned to him that most of the Coloured people had good Afrikaner names, which suggested that they had Dutch ancestors.

About this time the private secretary of the Prime Minister, Dr Hendrik Verwoerd, was lying paralysed from acute porphyria in Pretoria General Hospital and this had been reported in the South African newspapers. The secretary's name was Christian Barnard, the same name as that of South Africa's famous heart surgeon. After about a minute's silence, the chief censor said to me: 'Is this the same disease that is paralysing Chris Barnard in Pretoria?' I said: 'Yes, it is.' He replied, 'If it is affecting Chris Barnard, it must be all right. You can have your books.'

CHAPTER 14

King George III
and the Royal Malady

Throughout the greater part of his life
George III was a kind of consecrated obstructionist.
Walter Bagehot

On 8 January 1966, the *British Medical Journal* published a paper by Doctors Ida MacAlpine and her son, Richard Hunter, entitled 'The Insanity of King George III: A Classic Case of Porphyria'. This dramatic paper claimed that the king had suffered from attacks of intermittent acute porphyria, the Swedish type. In their case history the MacAlpines described five attacks between 1765 and George III's death in his 82nd year. A full account of the story is published in the second edition of my book *The Porphyrias: A Story of Inheritance and Environment* (1971). The MacAlpines were unable to find anyone among the many living descendants of George III who had acute intermittent porphyria but, in spite of this, they claimed in the paper: 'The study allows the certain conclusion that George III's malady was not "mental" in the accepted sense, in whatever old or modern terms it may be couched. His long sorrowful illness, in which he suffered severely from his affliction, pitifully from his treatment and miserably from his management, takes on a new importance in the annals of medical history as the first description of a rare metabolic disorder not even today fully understood.'

When I was in England in December 1967, I called on the famous porphyrin biochemist Professor Claude Rimington who had collaborated with Ida MacAlpine and Richard Hunter on a second paper. The paper claimed that not only did George III suffer from porphyria, it was now *porphyria variegata*, but made the astonishing (and, if it were confirmed, epoch-breaking) claim that many members of the royal families of Europe from the time of Mary Queen of Scots had suffered from acute attacks of *porphyria variegata*. I asked Professor Rimington how many living descendants of Mary Queen of Scots had been found to have *porphyria variegata*, pointing out that at that time we had at least 10,000 porphyrics in South Africa who had inherited the disease from one ancestor who had come to the country 300 years before. He said there were only two possible cases: one had been reported to him by a doctor on the Continent who was interested in porphyria, and there was another possible case where there was a slight increase in porphyrin excretion in the stool. I strongly advised against publication of the second paper without stronger evidence that members of the British royal family had suffered from symptoms of porphyria. I reminded him that, just as acute porphyria could mimic other disorders, the reverse was also true. Furthermore, the drugs that had precipitated acute porphyria had not been in use until the last one hundred years. I was so anxious to avoid a major and embarrassing error that I telephoned Dr Ida MacAlpine, whom I did not know, and warned her of the great risk she was taking in publishing this article without proper evidence from living descendants. She told me that she was sick and unable to see me but that she would go ahead and publish.

This second paper was published in the *British Medical Journal* in 1968, entitled 'Porphyria in the Royal Houses of Stuart, Hanover, and Prussia – A follow-up Study of George III's Illness'. It was accompanied by an editorial and was found to be of such importance that the *British Medical Journal* published a supplement (backed in royal purple) entitled 'Porphyria, A Royal Malady'.

In the 'House of Stuart', Ida MacAlpine claimed that James VI of Scotland, who became James I of England (1566–1625), had *porphyria variegata*. He had suffered from repeated attacks of abdominal colic and nausea, vomiting and diarrhoea, a fast and at times irregular pulse, and weakness and spasms of his limbs, which left him with a foot drop. He also suffered from irritability, sadness and fits of unconsciousness. Sometimes he would pass a 'bloody' urine, which he himself likened to his favourite port wine. Once an attack had begun with uncontrollable weeping. Mayerne, the king's physician, diagnosed the mental symptoms as melancholia. Mayerne called the painful weakness 'arthritis'; the attacks of pain in the abdomen and passing red urine he attributed to kidney stones. When James I died, there was an autopsy and stones were found in his kidney. The diagnosis of melancholia and renal colic attributable to kidney stones appears to be the most likely diagnosis.

A voluminous and acrimonious correspondence followed these articles in the *British Medical Journal* and in *Scientific American*, in which I gave my opinion that it was most unlikely that the illness reported in the British royal family was due to attacks of acute porphyria. Professor Charles Dent, a porphyria expert from University College Hospital, London, came to my support. He pointed out that in acute porphyria the urine is generally a normal colour when it is freshly passed and then darkens when left standing. This was not what had happened with George III: his urine had been dark when it was passed. Dent pointed out that it was unlikely that the *porphyria variegata* gene had passed directly down the royal line from Mary Queen of Scots to George IV – in other words through nine generations. If so, the gene must have had an uncanny knack, defying scientific explanation, for picking out the subjects in the direct line of succession: the first son when available, otherwise whoever came next according to the particular rules in this complicated game.

In December 1969, a letter of mine was published in *Scientific American*; it said in summary that it was unlikely that members of the British royal family back to Mary Queen of Scots had inherited porphyria, because if this had been the case, there would be many hundreds if not thousands of descendants, legitimate and illegitimate, alive today who had inherited the disorder. I pointed out that it was very surprising that the royal line back to Mary Queen of Scots should have the gene for porphyria because, on average, only half the children of a porphyric parent would inherit the gene, so that the odds against the gene persisting over so many generations in the royal line were very remote. There was no increase in porphyria among those who were treated in psychiatric hospitals in South Africa. Families with *porphyria variegata* had, on average, as many children as the rest of the population and, before the introduction of modern drugs, they had survived to a normal old age. The illness of James I, with pain in his left lumbar region and the passing of a red urine after riding a horse, was most likely due to a stone in the kidney. His doctor at the time had attributed his symptoms as due to 'gravel', and stones in the kidney were found at autopsy. Mary Queen of Scots had pain in her side made worse by breathing; she could well have been suffering from pleurisy. Others in the royal family had attacks of diarrhoea, whereas in acute porphyria there is usually constipation. Most important of all, the drugs that precipitate acute *porphyria variegata* did not exist until about the last hundred years.

Dr Ida MacAlpine replied to my letter in the same journal and followed it up with a beautifully produced book, *George the Third and the Mad Business*, giving a well-documented account of the illnesses and mental breakdown of George III and various illnesses of his ancestors back to the time of Mary Queen of Scots.

In 1996, Peter Meissner and his colleagues at the Liver Research Centre, Cape Town were the first to locate the gene for South African *porphyria variegata* in a mutation on the IQ23 gene. Independently, Steve Breuning, Teepu Siddique and I were searching for the gene and confirmed that the IQ23 gene was responsible. Nevertheless, the Meissner group beat us to the post.

Now that the gene for South African *porphyria variegata* has been located, it should be possible to detect the gene, if it is present, by examining the DNA of descendants of George III. Dr Martin Warren and his colleagues in the Department of Molecular Genetics, University College, London, are following this trail by obtaining specimens of tissue from ancestral members of the royal families of Europe. DNA can be obtained from bone and other tissue of people who have long since died, although this may mean exhuming the body if no tissue was left behind – for instance, in a pathology laboratory following an operation.

Dr Warren told me that they had heard from an ex-RAF physician, Dr Henry Bellringer, then in his nineties, that the late Prince William of Gloucester, the son of HRH the Duchess of Gloucester (now Princess Alice), had developed a rash on the back of his hands and on his face which Dr Bellringer had diagnosed as being due to *porphyria variegata*. The prince's history was interesting. In 1965, as he was going to Nigeria, he started a course of chloroquine as a prophylactic against malaria. When he arrived in Lagos he developed jaundice due to hepatitis and was unwell for about a year. About this time he first noticed blisters on the back of his hands and on his face, particularly on the forehead. Unfortunately the prince was killed when the plane he was flying in the Goodyear International Trophy competition crashed at Halfpenny Green airport in Staffordshire in August 1972. He appears to have been an outstanding and adventurous young man. He showed the symptoms of porphyria following the use of chloroquine. This strongly suggests that the prince may in fact have had idiopathic porphyria because chloroquine is known to cause disturbances of the porphyrin metabolism due to liver damage, and the prince had hepatitis.

In their book *Purple Secret* (1998), John Rohl, Martin Warren and David Hunt reported on a detailed historical study on the illnesses of members of the royal families of Europe, following up the work of MacAlpine and Hunter. They proposed that many of the illnesses were due to *porphyria variegata*. Members of the European royal family do appear to have had a remarkably bad sickness record, but most of the illnesses described were not typical of *porphyria variegata* as it occurs in South Africa. The authors also decided to try and obtain bone from deceased descendants of George III to study the DNA and with a little luck find a porphyria gene. They succeeded in obtaining permission to disinter Princess Charlotte of Saxe-Meiningen, a grand-daughter of Queen Victoria, and examine her bones. She had been buried in the grounds of her favourite castle, Schloss Altenstein. They found an abnormality in a part of the protoporphorinigen oxidase gene. This was not the same gene that has been implicated in South African porphyria. The three authors wondered if the abnormal gene might be responsible for a form of porphyria, but this will be confirmed only if it is found in other members of the extended royal family.

Thirty years ago, during the controversy with MacAlpine and Hunter, I stated that if members of the British royal family had *porphyria variegata*, I would 'eat my hat'! Perhaps MacAlpine and

Hunter were at least partly right if Warren and his colleagues can prove their case, although, to use the Scottish verdict, 'it is unproven'. If a form of porphyria has occurred in many members of the royal families of Europe during the last 400 years, it is certainly not the same disease that affected the descendants of Gerrit Jansz and Ariaantje Jacobs. Whether or not I shall have to eat my hat is still uncertain; if I do, it will certainly be a paper one!

Manor House, Upholland, Lancashire, where my father Richard was born in 1887. The present-day photograph below shows how little the exterior of the house has changed over 120 years.

My mother's grandfather, John Murphy (above left), who owned the Vauxhall Chemical Works in Liverpool.

Ann Dean, my grandmother (above right), with my Uncle Josiah and my aunts Susannah and Ann at the Manor House around 1905.

John Dean, my grandfather (left), a prosperous landowner of Manor House Upholland.

*My father, Richard Dean,
who was the manager of
the Westminster Bank in
Cressington, Liverpool.*

*Irene Lloyd, my mother,
who married my father in
February 1918.*

Geoffrey Dean,
aged two.

My sisters, Pauline
and Helen, and
myself in the garden
of Eskdale, our house
in Cressington Park,
Liverpool.

A formal portrait of me in the uniform of my hated preparatory school, Bishop's Court, around 1928.

My friend John Bradshaw (left) and me hiking in 1937.

Flying Officer Geoffrey Dean, 1943

My first wife, Nonie Devlin, whom I met and married during the war.

David Gillott, my best friend from Ampleforth College, who was killed during the allied invasion of Sicily in 1943.

David Stafford-Clark, who served with me at RAF Waterbeach and went on to become a famous psychiatrist and television broadcaster.

My consulting rooms in Port Elizabeth, South Africa. I lived with Nonie and John in the house next door but one.

Lauries Bay, South Africa, where we spent the summer months.

Douglas Laurie, physician and inventor, who built the house, cottages and dairy at Lauries Bay

Simon Nonzube, who helped Douglas Laurie to build Lauries Bay and looked after the farm, pictured with my eldest son John.

Patricia, my daughter who drowned tragically at the age of four in 1953.

John, Jennifer and Michael, my children from my first marriage.

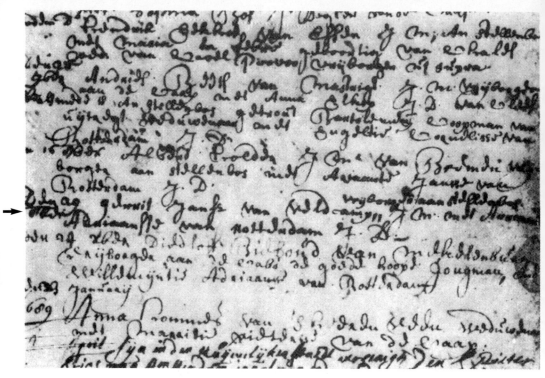

The Cape Town marriage register for 1688 showing the marriage lines of Ariaantje Adriansse (Jacobs) and Gerrit Jansz, from whom all the porphyria families I studied in South Africa are descended.

Myself, Nonie, my father Richard and my cousin Geoffrey Donnelly at Lauries Bay.

With Maria, who was to become my second wife, in Rome in 1960.

Don Craib, who was a consultant physician in Port Elizabeth when I arrived in South Africa and helped me to become established in medical practice there.

Sir Richard Doll, the famous epidemiologist, and a friend of mine for more than forty years.

Marta Elian, a Hungarian neurologist whom I first met in 1970, who has become a close friend and worked with me on more than a dozen research projects.

Teng Chia-Tung – CT to his friends – formerly vice-president of the Chinese Academy of Medical Sciences, who led the visit of five Chinese doctors to Ireland in 1980.

In my office at the Medico-Social Research Board with my personal assistant, Hilda McLoughlin.

With Rauf Denktaş, who as president of Turkish-speaking Cyprus greatly facilitated my research into MS on the island in the early 1990s.

My daughter, Elizabeth, with her son, Zack.
Elizabeth was a make-up artist for Andrew
Lloyd Webber's successful musical the Phantom
of the Opera, here sketched applying the
Phantom's make-up which was created by
Christopher Tucker.

My youngest son, Gordon, who is a solicitor in
Norwich and a county councillor, and his
children Lily and Rose.

My father, Richard, with his children, grandchildren and great-grandchildren on his 100th birthday.

My daughter, Jennifer, with her husband Erik and son Andrew outside the house Erik designed and built for them at Hout Bay, South Africa.

Maria and myself at my 83rd birthday party, December 2001

My sisters Helen and Pauline with me in Dun Laoghaire, Dublin, 2001.

CHAPTER 15

Multiple Sclerosis

What have we done, oh! Zeus!
to deserve this destiny?
Our fathers were wanting, but we,
what have we done?
often quoted by Jean-Martin Charcot, 1825–93

I have already described how my interest in the cause of multiple sclerosis (MS) arose when I first emigrated to South Africa. MS is the most common disabling neurological disorder of young adults in the western world. It seldom occurs before the age of fifteen or sixteen and reaches its peak prevalence in persons in their early thirties. The disorder is more common in women than men, afflicting about three females for every two males, and it is typically a disease of exacerbations and remissions. The nineteenth-century neurologist Jean-Martin Charcot, of the Salpêtrière Hospital in Paris, first gave a good medical account of the disorder in 1857 when he showed that its victims had plaques, or patches of hardening, scattered throughout their brains and spinal cords. He called the disorder *sclerose en plaques*. The plaques are caused by the loss of myelin, the fatty material that makes up the sheath covering the nerve fibre. When the myelin sheath breaks down, conduction along the nerve fibre is disrupted. It can be compared to the insulation around a telephone wire.

Often the first symptoms of MS are caused by patches of demyelination in the optic nerves, resulting in a blurring of vision in one or both eyes (known as optic neuritis). This visual distur-bance may last for a few days or up to six weeks, after which the person's vision generally returns to normal. 35 per cent of men and 75 per cent of women who have an attack of optic neuritis will then go on to develop MS during the ensuing fifteen years. Because the plaques of MS occur anywhere in the central nervous system, they can cause sensory symptoms, such as loss of sensation in any part of the body, loss of muscle power, or ataxia – uncoordination of movement. When the ataxia is severe, it may result in what is known as 'scanning speech', a slow enunciation, with a tendency to hesitate at the beginning of a syllable or word.

Those with MS often tire easily. A minority may have some problem in controlling urination. Mental functions are generally normal. Even after MS has been diagnosed, the majority of those affected are able to live a normal or near-normal life. The common stereotype of the MS patient in a wheelchair is incorrect; less than 5 per cent of those who have the disorder are so seriously disabled. Sexual function, except in those who are severely impaired, is usually normal.

Life expectancy is generally more than thirty years after MS has been diagnosed. It is not much shorter than life expectancy in the general population and many of those with MS live to be over seventy. People suffering from MS do not die of the disorder itself, although the complications, such as immobility, may lead to events that shorten life.

In the early stage, the diagnosis is often in doubt, and the suspicious illness can only be called 'possible MS'. Typically, there is a delay sometimes of several years after the first symptoms appear before a firm diagnosis can be made. In autopsy studies, it has been shown that plaques characteristic of MS are found in the brains of about one in 500 of the general population over forty years of age who have had no recognisable symptoms of MS during their lifetime. This means that there are many of those undiagnosed with the plaques of MS in their central nervous systems who have not experienced any obvious neurological illness.

Although its clinical history, the symptoms and signs, and the characteristic scarring of the brain and spinal cord it produces have long been well known, the cause of multiple sclerosis has remained a mystery. My old teacher, Professor Henry Cohen, asked a student during a ward round what was the cause of disseminated sclerosis, as the disease was then called in the United Kingdom and Ireland. The student scratched his head, looked up and down and replied 'Oh, sir, if you had only asked me ten minutes ago, I could have told you.' The professor replied: 'What a catastrophe. Ten minutes ago you knew and now no one knows.'

On 1 May 1945 a New York woman, Sylvia Lawry, whose brother had developed multiple sclerosis, inserted a small advertisement in the *New York Times* asking for information from anyone who had recovered from the disease. She received replies from hundreds of multiple sclerosis patients and their families seeking the same information. From this very small beginning grew the American National Multiple Sclerosis Society which today has more than 200 chapters throughout the United States. The International Federation of Multiple Sclerosis Societies has member societies in most of the developed countries of the world. When I emigrated to South Africa in 1947, the neurologists and physicians told me that the disease was very uncommon in South Africa, although many of them had been trained in Europe and knew the disease well. I indeed found that MS was uncommon, compared with Britain, among white people who had been born in South Africa, particularly those who spoke Afrikaans, the descendants of the Boers.

Among the great advances in medical science since the Second World War has been the growth of geographical medicine – studies of diseases in populations, particularly populations that have migrated from one country or environment to another. By such studies it is often possible to discover what are the environmental factors that are responsible for a particular disease. With this in mind, I undertook, over a period of twenty years from 1947, a study of multiple sclerosis in South Africa. I required the co-operation of many doctors and lay organisations, such as the Red Cross Society, the press and radio, to tell people about the research. In 1963 I founded the South African Multiple Sclerosis Society with Isobel Henderson, my secretarial assistant for MS research, as its secretary. The office of the MS Society was in her home at Port Elizabeth and many of the MS patients and their relatives joined the society and helped with the research.

The result of the study showed that MS was relatively common in South Africa among immigrants from the United Kingdom and Northern Europe – more than 50 per 100,000 of the population. In contrast, among the English-speaking white South African-born it was only one-quarter, and among the Afrikaans-speaking white South African-born only one-eleventh as frequent as occurred among the immigrants from Europe. Multiple sclerosis does occur, but it is very uncommon among the Coloured people of the Cape and among the Asians, of Indian descent, of Natal. Until 1987 no patients with MS had been reported among South Africa's 35 million black population, although in the country's major cities there were good hospitals for black patients, with neurologists well trained to diagnose the disease. Multiple sclerosis, as we later confirmed, does occasionally occur in the black people of Southern Africa and an intensive search from 1991 to 1994 found seven black people with MS in South Africa and five in Zimbabwe. Nevertheless, MS is undoubtedly very uncommon in the indigenous black African population in South Africa and in the African continent.

The eleven-fold difference in the prevalence of MS in 1967 between the immigrants from the United Kingdom and Northern Europe and the Afrikaans-speaking white South African-born, who are also of Northern European stock, showed that there must be an environmental factor that caused multiple sclerosis. There is good evidence that a genetic predisposition to MS is also a factor. For instance, MS occurs in two or more members of a family more frequently than would be expected by chance, and if one identical twin develops MS, there is a 25 per cent probability that the second will too.

In 1962 Milton Alter reported that Jews who emigrated from Northern Europe to Israel had a high prevalence of MS; those who were born in Israel had a lower prevalence, and those who came to Israel from North Africa also had a low prevalence – a similar pattern to that occurring in South Africa. In both South Africa and Israel, immigrants who emigrated to these countries from Europe before the age of fifteen or sixteen had a lower prevalence of MS, in comparison to those who arrived after that age.

What environmental factor best fits this phenomenon? The first hypothesis was that MS must be related to climate, since it is more common in the colder climates of the developed countries of Europe and North America. Against this is the fact that MS is very uncommon in northern Japan which has a cold climate. R.L. Swank has suggested that the disease may be caused by a diet that is rich in animal fats, but this hypothesis is not likely to be the explanation because the South African-born white population, particularly the Afrikaners, have a diet that is high in animal fat, yet they have a low risk of developing multiple sclerosis.

There is an interesting parallel between the epidemiology of MS and that of poliomyelitis. This was first pointed out in 1963 by David Poskanzer of the Massachusetts General Hospital. Like MS, poliomyelitis in its paralytic form, before the advent of the Salk and Sabin vaccines, was a disease of the more advanced nations, for instance of Europe and North America, and of economically better off people.

I studied the prevalence of paralysis from poliomyelitis among immigrants to South Africa from Northern Europe and found that they had twice the risk of contracting paralytic poliomyelitis than the South African-born white. The South African-born white had in turn a much greater risk of paralysis from polio than the non-white, and paralytic poliomyelitis hardly ever occurred in adult black South Africans.

During the Second World War paralytic poliomyelitis in North Africa was more common among officers of the British and American forces than among men in other ranks. At the time, various wild hypotheses for the difference were proposed; it was even suggested that it arose because the officers drank whisky, whereas men in the other ranks drank beer!

We now understand the reason for the strange distribution of poliomyelitis causing paralysis. Until the twentieth century, poliomyelitis was a universal infection of infancy, and infants seldom suffered paralysis from it. That they occasionally did so gave the disease the name 'infantile paralysis'. With the improvement of hygiene in the economically advanced countries of the world, more and more people missed infection in early infancy or childhood and contracted the disease for the first time as adults, when the risk that the infection would cause paralysis is much greater.

This explains why the big epidemics of poliomyelitis did not occur until the twentieth century and then in adults in economically advanced countries. In South Africa, the black people are universally infected with the poliomyelitis viruses in infancy, as can be shown by antibodies to the virus in their blood, because of poor living conditions and a lack of running water. Most white people who, in South Africa, were cared for as infants by black or Coloured servants were infected by the poliomyelitis virus from their 'nannies' early in life and were, therefore, immune to the virus. Among the white immigrants, a number had missed early childhood infection and were infected for the first time as adults in South Africa – at an age when they were more likely to develop paralysis from the infection. Today we do what nature once did for us: deliberately infect our children with a living poliomyelitis virus in a modified form, the Sabin vaccine.

In my practice in Port Elizabeth I saw a number of immigrants who had developed acute poliomyelitis and paralysis. In 1955 I was looking after a child, Naomi Dalrymple, at St Joseph's Nursing Home, who was paralysed by acute poliomyelitis. At the time, we were staying down at Lauries Bay. My son John developed a headache and neck rigidity and I was certain that he was suffering from the early symptoms of poliomyelitis. I had brought the virus with me from Naomi, the patient I was seeing every day. The next few days were very anxious. Would John become paralysed? I knew that I was immune to the virus, having, no doubt, been infected many years before. It was likely that John, coming to South Africa as an immigrant, had missed this early infection and was now in grave danger of becoming paralysed. He was kept very quiet and, to our great relief, the fever subsided and no paralysis occurred.

The level of hygiene until the twentieth century was not good and children caught nearly all their infections early, as happened with poliomyelitis. Could the same thing be happening in multiple sclerosis, and did an early childhood infection protect against the syndrome found in adults? The characteristics of MS suggests that there is a precarious balance between 'allergy' and 'immunity' to an agent, probably a virus, resulting in exacerbations and remissions of the disease which we call MS. In Australia and New

Zealand there is no significant difference in the prevalence of MS between white immigrants from Northern Europe and the white native-born. White children there are, unlike in South Africa, not attended by servants who are infected by many viruses early in life.

It is now known that a mutated normal protein, known as a prion protein, PrP, can cause normal prion proteins to mutate and become abnormal. A mutated prion, for instance, is probably the causative agent of scrapie, a disease of the nervous system found in sheep, which has now spread to cattle that were fed feed made from affected sheep's brains and spinal cords. The disease in cattle, bovine spongiform encephalopathy (BSE), is known as 'mad cow disease'. In the 1990s, this mutated prion had spread to humans who had eaten affected beef or beef offal. In humans it causes a new variety of Creutzfeldt Jakob disease (CJD) which affects young people.

Another example of prion disease is the agent responsible for kuru, a disease that once brought death from general paralysis to about 10 per cent of the members of the Fore tribe in New Guinea. Originally this was thought to be the result of genetic factors, but kuru has now been transmitted from human patients to chimpanzees and subsequently been passed on from one chimpanzee to another. The incubation period is initially very long. In New Guinea the disease was spread because of the tribal ritual of eating human brains, which were already affected with the kuru prion.

It may be significant that four out of seven veterinary research workers carrying out research in the late 1930s on Bradwell Moor in Yorkshire into a demyelinating disease of sheep, swayback disease, developed an MS-like disease. This could well have been a virus or prion infection caught from the sheep's brains. The recent epidemic of Human Immunodeficiency Virus (HIV) responsible for AIDS is another example of an agent, in this case a virus, which can cause neurological symptoms after remaining latent in the nervous system for a long time.

Later in my life I was able to study whether immigrants to Britain from areas of the world where MS is uncommon – the Indian subcontinent, the Caribbean and Africa – brought with them their low risk of developing MS or whether they had the high risk that occurs in the United Kingdom.

CHAPTER 16

Arrested!

Prisons are built with stones of law.
William Blake, *The Marriage of Heaven and Hell*

Every year I was seeing more and more patients suffering from *porphyria variegata*. In 1963 I thought it might be a good idea to examine the records of patients who had died at the Provincial Hospital in Port Elizabeth (which at that time treated white patients only) to see if some of the deaths had been due to acute porphyria and that perhaps the correct diagnosis had been missed. There were 40 to 50 deaths at the hospital every year and a few deaths, in retrospect, were indeed attributable to acute porphyria, although the diagnosis had not been made at the time.

I also found four deaths among men who had been admitted to hospital from jail and who had died from injuries that looked suspiciously like assault. One man had been admitted to hospital in 1959 with bruising all over his body. The government doctor (known as a district surgeon) who attended prisoners had, accidentally, left his record. This had been included in the patient's folder and stated 'Fibrositis – lin.meth.sal'. 'Lin.meth.sal.' is oil of wintergreen. Apparently the district surgeon had seen the patient covered in bruises and used the term 'fibrositis' to disguise his findings. When he was examined by the doctor on admission to hospital, he realised that the patient was desperately ill and wrote on the patient's record sheet on 17 September 1959, 'Multiple abrasions, intraperitoneal injury, BP 90/50'. The patient had very low blood pressure, evidence that he was in shock. He was given a blood transfusion and taken to the operating theatre. When his abdomen was opened

140

by the surgeon, it was found that part of his intestine, his duodenum, was ruptured. He died twenty-four hours later. No comment was made about the death at the time; it was not referred to the coroner and there was no inquest.

Following my accidental findings of patients admitted to hospital from prisons, with what appeared to be multiple injuries, in 1963 I wrote to Dr Peter Blignault, the editor of the *South African Medical Journal* (*SAMJ*), suggesting that he should write an editorial pointing out the moral duty of government medical officers – that is the district surgeons – to use their power and influence to prevent assaults and cruelty in the prisons and police stations. He did not reply, and no editorial was published.

There were repeated reports in the South African newspapers of cruelty to prisoners. I did nothing further about the matter until I read accounts by a man called Strachan, in the *Rand Daily Mail*, about his ill-treatment in prison in 1965. These reports had the ring of truth and prompted me to write again to Dr Blignault. Once more I suggested that he should write an editorial, adding that if he did not wish to do so, he could print my letter.

About the same time Jack Brock, Professor of Medicine at the University of Cape Town, wrote independently to Dr Blignault describing the condition in which prisoners were often found when they had been admitted to Groote Schuur Hospital. Dr Blignault published my letter in an abridged form in the *South African Medical Journal* on 14 August 1965. After I had sent my letter to Dr Blignault, I phoned him to make sure that my letter was free from libel. I asked him to check with his legal advisers.

Assaults in Gaols

To the Editor: You will remember that I wrote to you two years ago when I found that, over a 10-year period, a number of the deaths among White men between the ages of 15 and 60 occurring each year at the Provincial Hospital, Port Elizabeth, followed assaults in our local gaols and police stations, and that I felt sure from logic, that this only represented a small proportion of the total assaults that were taking place. Assaults on non-whites possibly exceeded assaults on Whites. I suggested to you at the time that you might consider writing an editorial pointing out the moral duty of Government Medical Officers, for instance district surgeons, to use their power and influence as doctors to prevent assaults and cruelty in our prisons and police stations by seeing that, when they occurred, suitable action was taken against those concerned.

The articles in the *Rand Daily Mail* by Strachan and the repeated accounts in our newspapers, both English and Afrikaans, United Party and Nationalist, of assaults by the police and warders must, I am sure, have convinced you that assaults and deliberate cruelty are really taking place. I spent a year in Germany at Frankfurt University in 1937 and 1938 and, at that time, decent men and women were aware of the atrocities that were being perpetrated against the Jews and no one, including the medical profession, had the courage to speak up about it. I can't help feeling that we as a profession in South Africa are becoming guilty of a similar sin of omission and that, unless we do something about it now, the world of the future will always remember it against us.

Geoffrey Dean, 21 July 1965

> The results of a departmental enquiry have been submitted to the Attorney General by the Minister of Justice. It is expected that the facts will in due course be revealed in the courts and/or by a commission of enquiry – Editor.

Unfortunately, my letter had become garbled because the editor had cut out my explanation of why I had gone through the records to find deaths from porphyria that had been 'occurring each year'. The phrase 'occurring each year' had been transposed to the assaults. In fact, there had been four such deaths among prisoners over the ten years I had studied.

After the letter appeared, three members of the security branch raided the office of the *South African Medical Journal* and seized correspondence and all unissued copies of the *Journal*. A Lieutenant Cellier of the security police flew from Johannesburg to Port Elizabeth and interviewed me with a Sergeant Smith. They first telephoned my office and told me to send away all my patients because they wished to see me immediately. I described to them how in searching the hospital records for deaths from porphyria where the correct diagnosis had been missed, I had found four deaths from multiple injuries among men admitted from prison. They demanded that I should give them all the evidence I had. I told them that I would have to go through the records at the hospital once again if they wanted the evidence.

Lieutenant Cellier told me that I had broken the law because it was a criminal offence to make any comment about the prisons, for which the penalty was three years' imprisonment. When he arrived at my office, he searched it, I think to make sure that I had no tape recorder, although I noticed that Sergeant Smith had in his hand a briefcase that very likely contained a tape recorder! During the course of the interview, Lieutenant Cellier produced two photographs from his pocket, gave me one of them and said: 'What does this photograph show?' I replied, 'Well, there are some batteries and an electrical machine and two terminals.' 'Yes', he said, 'that is the electric treatment machine at Boksburg Jail.' He then produced a second photograph and said, 'What does this show?' I looked at it and said, 'It contains a box and a plug that plugs into the mains and ends up in two leads. It is another electric machine.' He said, 'Yes, it is our second electric treatment machine at Boksburg Jail.' He said, 'I want to repeat that these are treatment machines and not torture machines. We treat prisoners with them.'

Unfortunately, Dr Blignault decided not to publish Professor Brock's letter following the publication of my letter, because he feared that all copies of the *Journal* would be confiscated prior to publication.

Following my interview with the police officers, I thought I would write to a very influential Afrikaner friend, Dr Anton Rupert, one of South Africa's leading businessmen, the founder of a South African and international tobacco empire and a great philanthropist. I had first met Dr Rupert during my researches on lung cancer and I sent him the following letter.

Confidential

My Dear Anton,

I thought I would send you a personal note about my letter to the *SAMJ* that has caused such a furore.

More than two years ago I spent some months going through all the records at the Provincial Hospital, Port Elizabeth, looking for men and women who might have died from acute porphyria and in whom the diagnosis had been missed at the time. I found, quite by accident, a number of deaths in men admitted from jail or police stations with multiple bruising injuries, who had died. There was no evidence that the injuries had been committed by jailers but the suspicion was so strong in my mind that I wrote a personal letter to Doctor Blignault, the editor of the *SAMJ*, suggesting that he should write an editorial pointing out and reminding government medical officers of their duty and power to prevent cruelty in our prisons. I was also prompted to do this because when I was the Senior Physician at the Livingstone [non-European] hospital I used to be shocked by the deplorable condition in which non-Europeans were admitted to hospital after being in prison. I did not ask that my letter be published.

The editor was away at the time and no action was taken. Since then, May 1963, there have been repeated reports in the newspapers about cruelties in our prisons but I did nothing further until I read the accounts by Strachan of his experiences in prison which had about them the ring of truth. (If you have not read them you should do so.) This account so shocked me that I wrote again to Doctor Blignault and again suggested he should write an Editorial, adding that if he did not wish to do so he could print my letter. About the same time Professor Brock, the Professor of Medicine, Cape Town, wrote describing the condition in which prisoners were often found when admitted under his care.

After I had sent my letter to the *Medical Journal* suggesting once again an editorial on the responsibility of government medical officers, raids took place on the *Rand Daily Mail*. I was in Pretoria at the time doing research and read about this. When I returned to Port Elizabeth, I telephoned Doctor Blignault to make sure my letter was free from offence as Dr Blignault decided to publish it rather than write an editorial. Unfortunately, as a result, it appeared slightly garbled and I asked Doctor Blignault to check with his legal advisers that it was in order. Doctor Blignault is, I know, a true Afrikaans-speaking Afrikaner and a very loyal South African. His only interest was to prevent cruelty and remind medical officers of their duty towards prisoners. Immediately the letter appears three members of the Security Branch raid the offices of the *Journal* with search warrants and seize the correspondence and all unissued copies of the *Journal*. Lieutenant Cellier of Marshall Square flew down to Port Elizabeth and I was subjected to repeated police inter- rogation and was given to understand that I am in jeopardy for contravening the very wide arms of the prison regulations. Professor Brock's letter cannot be published because Doctor Blignault fears the *Medical Journal* will be confiscated prior to issue.

It is a dreadful situation we are reaching when one cannot protest against cruelty without such government reaction. I fully realise that against the overwhelming power of the State the individual is powerless but as Burke once said: 'For evil to succeed it only requires enough good men to keep silent'.

As you have always been my good friend I thought I would write you this personal report.

Yours ever,

Copy of hand-written letter to Doctor A. Rupert, 13 Thibault Street, Mostersdrift, Stellenbosch, Cape, on 10 September 1965 (not posted, but given by hand).

Anton Rupert did not reply to my letter, or if he did I did not receive it.

About this time the Argentine government had invited me to fly to Buenos Aires to give a lecture on lung cancer and smoking to a very large audience which would include the President of the Argentine, Dr Arturo Illia, who was a medical doctor, and also the Lord Mayor of Buenos Aires. I flew from Johannesburg to Senegal and then by special plane of Aerolineas Argentinas from Senegal to Rio de Janeiro and on to Buenos Aires. I arrived at Buenos Aires having been travelling for 48 hours, desperately tired, to be met at the airport by the president of the Argentine Medical Association and four or five of his henchmen. They all kissed me on both cheeks and explained that I must not change my money at the ordinary rate of exchange, which was 550 pesos to the English pound; they would change my money at the black market rate, which was 750 pesos to the pound! I thought I would be taken straight to my hotel, but instead I was taken to a shooting range, where at least one hundred men could shoot at once, and asked to 'shoot for South Africa'. They told me that a short time before they had had a delegation from West Point Military Academy in the United States and that it was a great honour to be asked to shoot. I explained that I was not a particularly good shot, but did as I was told and fired some rounds at a target. What I hit I cannot remember. I was then taken to the dinner in the same building as the shooting range, attended by many of the country's senior doctors.

During the dinner I had two Italian-Argentinean ladies seated on either side who fanned me and talked non-stop. I was so tired; I could hardly keep my eyes open. Dinner was followed by a series of toasts – 'to the President of the Argentine', 'to the President of South Africa', 'to the President of the Argentine Medical Association', 'to the President of the South African Medical Association', etc. etc.

Following my talk the next day, I was received as a guest of honour at a reception at the South African Embassy. The South African ambassador made a speech telling me that I was an outstanding ambassador for his country and how proud they were to have me in the Argentine. This was all reported in the Argentinean and South African newspapers.

After spending a further three weeks in Buenos Aires, because of an air strike, I flew to Rio de Janeiro. Having delayed my return and cancelled my appointments in Port Elizabeth, I felt that a further week seeing Rio de Janeiro would be a good idea and I spent a very pleasant week at a hotel on Copacabana Beach. I kept my promise to Maria and bought her aquamarine stones in Rio de Janeiro.

Back in Port Elizabeth, I found my waiting room crowded with patients. About five minutes after I arrived at my office, a telephone message came from the security police. Would I empty my office of patients because they were coming to arrest me? I told my patients that I could not see them and ten minutes later Sergeant Smith came into my office and arrested me. I was driven in the police van to Port Elizabeth Jail, had my fingerprints taken, teeth counted, earlobes measured and was photographed. I was then told that I was to be tried in the Supreme Court in Cape Town for breaking the regulations about the prisons. My passport was taken and I was freed on bail. I was told that I must have all my evidence and witnesses available when I appeared in court.

I had to appear in a preliminary hearing a few days later and so I contacted a good firm of solicitors in Port Elizabeth, Pagden & Christian, and saw a Mr Kit Bell of that firm. He advised me to have a senior barrister and suggested Advocate Patrick Tebbutt SC (later to become a Supreme Court Judge in Cape Town). At the preliminary hearing, the trial was set for 3 February 1966. My arrest was reported as the main news in the South African newspapers. The South African Ambassador in the Argentine, who had spoken so enthusiastically at the dinner in Buenos Aires a few days earlier, must have been embarrassed!

About this time a patient of mine, who had inherited porphyria and who worked in the post office, called to see me and warned me that my telephone was being tapped and my letters opened. When I went to see Mr Tebbutt in Cape Town, he asked me to tell him the whole story and I suggested the easiest plan would be for me to use a dictaphone and recount what had happened. This I did.

Back in Port Elizabeth in mid-December 1965, I went to see Dr John McLean, the Medical Superintendent at the Provincial Hospital, and told him that I would need to obtain the records of those who had been admitted from the jails. I also contacted the lady who had assisted me in the hospital records department where

I had done the research to find the porphyria patients. She told me that she had been called on by the security police and she was too frightened to help me further. I started to go through the records myself. Shortly afterwards, John McLean told me he had received instructions from the security police that I was not to be allowed to see any hospital records. Fortunately, I had been able to obtain the record of the patient whom I described earlier, a photocopy of which I passed on to Mr Tebbutt. It was not missed by the hospital.

In December and January Maria and I went, as usual, to stay at Lauries Bay. She had invited her best friend, Bettina Tessler, who lived in Vienna, to stay with us. Lord Platt, the president at the time of the Royal College of Physicians, telephoned me from London to say that he was coming to South Africa to speak at the trial in my defence. He also telephoned a number of other South African physicians soliciting their support. He told me that a committee had been formed in England, which included Geoff Todd of the Tobacco Research Council, Sir Richard Doll, and some of my old masters from Ampleforth, to speak in my defence at the forthcoming trial, because it appeared likely that I would be sent to prison.

My medical friends in South Africa, including many nationalist Afrikaner doctors, were also concerned about what was happening. It was well known by this time that many prisoners were being ill-treated and that the prison doctor, the district surgeon, was in a unique position to protect prisoners from torture or serious ill-treatment.

Two or three days before my trial, in February 1966, Pat Tebbutt phoned to say that he had seen John Vorster, at that time the Minister for Justice (later to become the Prime Minister and, still later, State President). Vorster had decided that the charge would be dropped if I would make an agreed statement. Tebbutt told me that Mr Vorster had accepted that I was motivated by my concern for prisoners and that I had no political axe to grind; he requested that I fly to Cape Town to see him. Pat Tebbutt told me that this was by far the best solution because I had undoubtedly broken the law. It was against the law to make any comment about the prisons; even, for instance, to say that the prison walls were grey, or that the prison governor was a very nice man. Any comment was illegal and so both the editor of the *South African Medical Journal* and I had broken the law; I by writing, the editor by publishing, the letter. I had no wish to be a martyr and accepted this proposal as long as I agreed with the statement that would be made in court.

I was walking into the Supreme Court in Cape Town on 3 February 1966 with Pat Tebbutt when he said: 'Geoffrey, it is a cardinal rule of law that you do not "hire a dog and do your own barking". Please do not open your mouth. Leave the talking to me.'

The statement in court was published in the *Cape Argus* and the other South African newspapers and said:

> Dr Dean has asked me to say that the letter he wrote to the *South African Medical Journal* was written with no political intention whatsoever, nor with malice. It was not meant as an attack on the police, the prison administration or officials or district surgeons. If this letter is capable of being construed as such, Dr Dean expresses his regret.
>
> Dr Dean is not only a physician but also a research worker in the field of lung cancer, multiple sclerosis and porphyria. On these he has done extensive research and written widely. During the course of his researches into the latter disease, Dr Dean came across certain suspicious deaths and it was this which prompted him to suggest that district surgeons should maintain their alertness and not relax their vigilance. His letter was written solely with this in mind and for no other purpose whatsoever.

The reports of cruelty in prisons diminished following my trial and I like to think that it had done some good. Nevertheless, it was in Port Elizabeth that the senior district surgeon, Benjamin Tucker, examined on a number of occasions Steve Biko, the founder of the South African black consciousness movement when he was held in police custody in 1977. Biko had been kept naked and manacled for twenty-four days and had suffered brain lesions caused, according to the post mortem, by application of force to the head. He died after being trucked in an unconscious state 740 miles to Pretoria on 11 September. An inquest absolved the police of any wrongdoing. Biko became an international martyr for South African black nationalism. Only a number of years later did Benjamin Tucker, the senior of the two Port Elizabeth district surgeons, appear before the Medical Council for his negligence.

In July 1995, the Medical Association of South Africa apologised for its lack of action over the negligence of the two Port Elizabeth district surgeons who had attended Steve Biko after his injuries, and for its silence about the ill-treatment of prisoners during the years of apartheid (*British Medical Journal*, 15 July 1995).

CHAPTER 17

Ireland

Bíonn siúlach scéalach.
The traveller has many stories.
Old Gaelic proverb

In 1965, after completing the study on lung cancer and bronchitis in Northern Ireland, I was invited to report the results of the study at a joint meeting of the Ulster Medical Society and the British Medical Association at the Whitla Hall in Belfast. Before the meeting I was the guest of honour at a dinner attended by about 200 Irish and British doctors. Just before the dinner, Graham Bull, professor of medicine at Queen's University, Belfast, announced without warning to the assembled guests: 'Geoffrey Dean, our distinguished guest speaker, will now say grace for us in Afrikaans.' Fortunately, when I was first in South Africa in 1947 and staying with Detective Sergeant Ferreira, we used to say grace in High Dutch and I remembered the prayer: 'Lieve Here, laat ons ete en nimmer U verhete' – 'Dear Lord, let us eat and never forget thee.'

After completing the Northern Ireland and Teesside studies, I returned to my practice in Port Elizabeth. Maria and I now rented a house in town. My eldest son, John, had started to study physics at Rhodes University, while Jenny and Michael were still at boarding school in Grahamstown.

In October 1964 the first child of my marriage to Maria was born. He was a fine boy and we named him Gordon Richard, Gordon after my cousin, who had been killed flying in Bomber Command in 1943, and Richard after my father. Eighteen months later we had a baby daughter, whom we named Elizabeth for many reasons: Port Elizabeth, Elizabeth House, my mother's favourite aunt, Elizabeth Murphy, and Maria's best friend, Elizabeth (Bettina) Tessler.

During the long school summer holidays John, Jennifer and Michael spent some of the time with us at Lauries Bay, where there was a large house and two cottages. We had rented one of the cottages to a wild Irishman, Michael Davern, and his very beautiful wife, Eithne. Eithne wrote 'Aisling' on the outer wall of the cottage with large seashells. Aisling means a 'dream' in the Irish language. Eithne and Michael were excellent company and there was often a party at Lauries Bay at the weekends at which we would boisterously sing Irish songs. The one thing that worried me was that the amount of wine consumed by Maria, myself and the Daverns was sometimes excessive.

Shortly after returning to South Africa, in March 1966, I received a letter from Graham Bull asking me whether I would be interested in heading an epidemiological research organisation in Northern Ireland. I would be able to hold a clinical appointment and see patients both in hospital and privately and would almost certainly receive a high-grade 'merit award', which would mean that I would earn a good income. Graham followed up this letter with a second telling me that he was resigning as professor of medicine at Queen's University, Belfast, because he had been appointed director of research at Northwick Park, a new research hospital that had just been opened in London. Graham suggested that I should apply for the post of professor at Queen's, that he would support my application and that I would probably be appointed. I considered applying for the post but was not very attracted to living in Belfast because at that time I felt that Northern Ireland was a very unjust society and so I decided not to put my name forward.

Life in Port Elizabeth was very pleasant. I would do ward rounds at the Provincial Hospital on Monday and Wednesday mornings and on Wednesday afternoons would work on multiple sclerosis and porphyria research with Isobel Henderson, my research secretary. The rest of my time was spent in private practice. Saturdays and Sundays Maria and I would generally spend with the children at Lauries Bay. In retrospect, even at Lauries Bay, I did not give my children as much time as I should have. I was generally reading or preparing research papers. At least we went for walks and swam together.

One of the patients I was to look after about this time was a wealthy Johannesburg businessman, a multi-millionaire, who had been injured in a car accident. He was not wearing a seat belt and crushed his chest against the steering wheel. I had called Murray Satchwell, a thoracic surgeon, to see him. We decided that he would need a tube in his trachea, a tracheostomy, to help breathing. When he was being wheeled on a trolley to the operating theatre, his heart stopped. Murray immediately started cardiac massage and the anaesthetist provided artificial respiration. After ten minutes the heart started again and the tracheostomy was done. Unfortunately, the blood supply to the brain had been cut off for too long when the heart had stopped and the patient did not regain consciousness or the ability to breathe without the aid of a respirator. The best thoracic physician and anaesthetist were called from Johannesburg but they could do nothing to help. It was quite clear that the patient's brain had been damaged and that he was being kept 'alive' only by artificial respiration. This raised the very difficult question: should we or should we not turn off the respirator? To put it another way, was the patient dead?

This problem is much more difficult than it sounds because death does not take place suddenly. It is a gradual process; we die by degrees. We start to die from the moment we are born, perhaps from the moment we are conceived. There have been many occasions when a patient's heart and respiration have stopped and then, when the heart has been started again, the patient has regained consciousness. For instance, in a drowning accident in icy water, the brain can stay alive for a long time without access to oxygen, perhaps for as long as half an hour. The answer to the moral question at the time, and still today, is that when the vital brain functions are permanently destroyed, the person is no longer alive as a human being, even though the tissues of the body, like the heart and the kidneys, are functioning normally. There are neurological aids, such as a fixed dilated pupil and a flat electroencephalograph, the electric waves produced by the brain, which confirm brain death.

A doctor would not switch off a respirator without obtaining a second opinion. In the last resort, a decision has to be made that the brain is dead and cannot recover. The man or woman may have a good colour, a normal blood pressure and a strongly beating heart and perhaps may start breathing on his or her own, but the brain can no longer function. So is he or she alive or dead? There is no simple answer to this problem and the rule that I have always followed (it sounds arbitrary but it is good sense) is that a person is dead when the doctor, having taken all due measures to be sure that the brain is dead, says that he is dead. Occasionally, of course, the doctor could be wrong, but this has not happened in my own experience.

Whether or not a person is dead is a decision that must be made by doctors and not by lawyers. The doctor, after consultation with other doctors and the patient's family, must take the responsibility for switching off the life-support machine. In the case of the patient from Johannesburg, we did this.

Shortly after my invitation to apply for the professorship of medicine in Belfast, John Bradshaw, my friend since university days, sent me a cutting from the *British Medical Journal* advertising the post of director of a newly founded Medico-Social Research Board in the Republic of Ireland. Without much conviction, I wrote to the chairman of the board, Professor Patrick Lynch, and asked for further information. He replied that, on the advice of Professor Henning Friis of Copenhagen, the Irish government had decided to found a research board to study the country's major medical and social problems. The Department of Health had appointed a board consisting of twelve members. Besides Patrick Lynch, professor of economics at University College, Dublin, they were: Ivor Browne, professor of psychiatry, University College, Dublin; William Jessop, professor of social medicine, Trinity College, Dublin; Cyril Joyce, chief Medical Officer of Health of Ireland; Donal McCarthy, director of the Central Statistics Office; Risteard Mulcahy, a cardiologist; Michael Flynn, the Medical Officer of Health in County Westmeath; Tom Murphy, professor of social medicine, University College, Dublin; Brian McNicholl, professor of paediatrics,

University College, Galway; John Nash, director of Limerick Hospital; Kieran O'Driscoll, master of the National Maternity Hospital, Holles Street; and Monsignor Newman, the principal of St Patrick's College, Maynooth. These men represented medicine, social affairs and the Church in the Republic of Ireland. The first woman was appointed to the board in 1978. She was Dr Barbara Stokes, the director of St Michael's House, Dublin, which provides services for people with learning difficulties.

Following my visit to Dublin in 1965, I was convinced that Ireland presented a great opportunity for the study of the interaction of inheritance and environment in the causation of disease, and this was the main reason why I decided to apply for the post. I was invited to come to Dublin to meet the board. At this time I had to go to England and it was easy for me to spend a day in Dublin. I phoned Professor Lynch from South Africa and arranged to meet the board in Dublin. There were a number of other candidates for the post.

Maria and I stayed at the Gresham Hotel in O'Connell Street. The next day I was brought to a meeting of the Medico-Social Research Board at Liberty Hall on the banks of the Liffey. Paddy Lynch impressed me; he was a man with whom I could collaborate. I later realised that he was an *éminence grise* of Irish politics. I was asked by different members of the board about my past life and the various research projects I had undertaken. Tom Murphy asked me did I consider it right to use research funds from the Tobacco Research Council, a body that had a vested interest in encouraging smoking. I told him that all my studies on smoking and health had shown that cigarette smoking was the primary cause of lung cancer and bronchitis and an important cause of heart attacks and strokes. It may well have been because studies had shown that cigarette smoking was the main factor causing these diseases that the Tobacco Research Council was disbanded in 1978.

Two weeks after returning to Port Elizabeth, I received a letter from Paddy Lynch inviting me to become the first director of the board on, to begin with, a five-year contract at an initial salary of £5,000 per year plus a 10 per cent contribution towards a pension scheme. This was much less than I was earning at that time in South Africa. My contract laid down that I should spend four-fifths of my time on the work of the board. The remaining one-fifth I could use for consultant practice or personal research not directly relevant to Ireland.

In deciding to come to Ireland I was motivated to some extent by Michael winning an exchange scholarship to spend a year at West Hartford, Connecticut, so he would be in the United States. John was still at university and went to Jodrell Bank in Cheshire to study astronomy in 1969, so I would be quite close. Jennifer would continue to live in South Africa. I knew it would be difficult to leave South Africa because I had many friends there and also because of my research interest in MS and the porphyrias. I also enjoyed greatly the weekends and summers at Lauries Bay. It is difficult in retrospect to know what influences important decisions in life. It was perhaps because I thought, like Picasso, that we live our lives in 'periods' and that it was time for me to make a change. I had lived for twenty years in South Africa, so, perhaps for five years, which was my original contract, I should return to Europe? It was a great challenge to be asked to start from nothing a research board for Ireland. The population of the Republic at the time was small, about three million people, and Ireland offered unique opportunities for research. I liked the Irish people and loved what I knew of Dublin and the Irish countryside.

There was another reason that made me decide to go to Ireland – and decisions like this are usually compounded of many reasons. The Daverns were living in the cottage at Lauries Bay while we used the large house where there was plenty of room. I found that in visiting the Bay at the weekends, I was beginning to fall in love with Eithne Davern, a beautiful and intelligent woman, and thought for this reason also it would be a good idea if I was to take the offer of director of the newly founded board in Ireland.

Another factor that made me reassess my life was that I almost drowned about this time. The sea at Lauries Bay was very safe for swimming within the barrier reef and this reef went across the bay except for a ten-yard gap. One day I was trying Michael's snorkel – I had not used a snorkel before – and I was amazed to see the fish under the water while breathing comfortably. I watched the fish, fascinated, for about ten minutes and then, when I looked up, I saw that the tide had taken me out a few yards beyond the barrier reef. I quickly got rid of the snorkel and goggles and started to swim for the shore, but soon realised that the tide was taking me out more rapidly than I could swim back. Nobody was aware that I had gone for a swim and I also realised that it was beyond my capacity to swim against the tide and that I was probably going to be swept out to sea. There was a rock at the side of the bay and I decided, since I could not swim back, that I would swim sideways and try and reach the rock before the tide took me beyond it. I did reach the rock or this book would never have been written.

When faced with drowning, or imminent death, a good Catholic should think of the four last things: death, judgement, hell and heaven (or at least think of his pining wife and children). I must admit that my only thought was that I was going to die before my latest paper on multiple sclerosis in South Africa had been sent for publication! Only *I* had all the data at my fingertips. It was a conceit to think that this mattered.

The Medico-Social Research Board would have liked me to take up my post as its first director in late 1967 or early 1968. I had to delay my arrival in Ireland because Harry Weaver, the scientific advisor to the Multiple Sclerosis Society of New York, wanted to spend some time in South Africa studying the results of my research. Weaver had been the inspiration behind the 'March of Dimes' which had provided the means to fund the scientific research of Salk and Sabin, who solved the problem of poliomyelitis. He spent some weeks in South Africa, part of the time at Lauries Bay. He told me about the new research that was being undertaken on the newly discovered slow viruses, which could be latent in the nervous system for years before they caused symptoms of illness and that possibly such a virus might be behind MS.

Harry was an outstanding research organiser and a fine man but he had one problem: he smoked thirty cigarettes a day. I warned him of the grave danger he was running of developing lung cancer or a heart attack, but he continued to smoke and died of lung cancer a few years later.

Phyllis Basford had been my private secretary in Port Elizabeth since 1948 and it was very hard for us to break our twenty-year partnership. She had been an excellent secretary. Phyllis knew the patients' histories and stories because she typed all the medical reports. She would remind me like this: 'The next lady, Mrs Van Rooyen, from the farm Kopfontein, Somerset East, is a sister of Willem Schalk Van der Mervwe, whom you saw two years ago. You remember, he had severe headaches and it was only when you found out about his money troubles that you were able to get rid of his headaches for him.' These snippets of association were very useful in remembering the patients' various backgrounds. Phyllis was also always able to locate the past record of a patient, even if I had not seen him or her for twenty years.

Fortunately another physician in the town, Victor Solomon, needed a private secretary and Phyllis went to work for him. Isobel Henderson, the secretary of the Multiple Sclerosis Society who undertook MS research with me, continued as secretary of the MS Society.

Maria had never taken a sea voyage between South Africa and England and she wanted to return to England by sea with her great friend Gladys Firebrace, who intended to have a holiday in Europe. They sailed on the S.A. *Vaal* from Port Elizabeth and I stayed on for a further four weeks, saying goodbye to my friends and arranging for my books and some of our furniture to go by freight to Ireland.

Leaving South Africa and my many friends proved very difficult and I wondered at the time if I was making the right decision. I was particularly concerned at leaving behind my eighteen-year-old daughter Jennifer. Fortunately a few years later, after she married, she came to live in Bristol and I was able to see her frequently. My friends invited me to farewell parties and I said goodbye to Nonie and arranged for Jenny to make a visit to Europe the following year. I then flew to London and joined Maria, Gordon and Liz. We went to Eastbourne to see my parents for a few days. They were delighted that I would be able to see them more often. We then flew to Dublin.

We found it hard to leave our many friends in South Africa. Fortunately it has been possible for me, often accompanied by Maria, to return every year, usually for three weeks at Christmastime.

CHAPTER 18

The Medico-Social Research Board

There is a laboratory greater even than the Cavendish, the streets,
the factories, the houses, where the common people live their lives.
Major Greenwood, on a plaque in the Department of
Social Medicine, Belfast and at the Medico-Social
Research Board, now Health Research Board, Dublin.

We flew to Dublin on 27 October 1968. Rooms had been booked at the Montrose Hotel, on the main road from Dublin to Stillorgan. Paddy Lynch met us there, and advised me to organise where I was going to live, to buy a car, get to know my way around Dublin and only then should I begin work. I bought a map of Dublin and an Opel Kadett and within a few days had found a house to rent in Woodbine Road, adjacent to the Montrose. Maria was fully occupied in looking after Gordon, now five, and Elizabeth, just two, and appeared to be adjusting well to life in Dublin, although she greatly missed her friends in Port Elizabeth and was lonely while I was at work.

During our first few weeks we were greatly helped by Michael Fogarty, the director, and Maura Dempsey, the secretary, of the Economic and Social Research Institute of Ireland, who took the newly founded Medico-Social Research Board under their wing. As an office, I rented a room at 65 Merrion Square, a beautiful Georgian house, and bought a desk, chairs and a filing cabinet. My first task was to find a good secretary and, after interviewing a number of applicants, I found a capable personal assistant, Hilda McLoughlin.

In these early days, Shaun Trant, assistant secretary at the Department of Health, acted as the official secretary to the board. He arranged a board meeting at which I was asked what I considered to be the priorities for the board. I had consulted Cyril Joyce, the chief Medical Officer of Health, and Donal McCarthy, the director of the Central Statistics Office, and said that in order to study health we first needed to know what brought people in Ireland to consult their general practitioners, for what illnesses people were admitted to the general and to the psychiatric hospitals and, lastly, what were the major causes of death in Ireland.

I knew nothing about the practice of medicine in Ireland and I thought it would be a good idea to work as a 'locum' for doctors in a number of practices as soon as possible. I enquired from the Irish Medical Association about possible locums and undertook four in general practice and also worked for a fortnight as a physician at Our Lady's Hospital in Drogheda, a major hospital and the mother house of the Medical Missionaries of Mary, while their physician was on vacation. I was particularly welcomed by the missionary sisters in Drogheda because my sister Pauline had joined the order while studying paediatrics in the United States. When we came to live in Ireland, she was working at a mission hospital at Anua Uyo in Nigeria. Later I was twice able to visit her there.

The first locum in general practice I undertook was in Ballyhaunis, County Mayo, in the West of Ireland. At that time the population of Ballyhaunis was 1,300 and there were about the same number living nearby. I acted as locum for Dr Eamon Waldron while he was on holidays. I lived in the doctor's house and was looked after by his housekeeper. Medical practice in Ballyhaunis was very informal: patients would walk into the house at any time of the day, or even late at night, to tell me their problems. They often arrived in the middle of breakfast or during the evening 'fry'. Half the patients belonged to the 'panel', that is, they were patients for whom the doctor was paid an annual capitation fee. The other half were private patients.

As well as seeing patients during morning and evening surgery, I would visit others in their homes in the town or on neighbouring farms. When I visited a patient on a farm – if they were panel patients, they were not paying for the visit – the man of the house would always insist on pushing two or three pounds into my hand, saying 'something for your petrol, doctor'. I visited private patients [...] arms. After I had trudged through [...] een the patient, I would be asked [...] embarrassed about this and would [...] wo or three occasions the farmer [...] ouser pocket a wad of £20 notes [...], but I have nothing smaller than [...] hers, particularly those who were [...] al of ready cash.

[...] uld hear all that was being said in [...] those in the waiting room could [...] One day I overheard two older [...] about me. One said: 'You know, [...] hasn't his own practice by now.' [...] he drink, God bless him.'

[...] d to find that almost all the shops [...] decided to count them. Of the 82 [...] or licence. The elite of the town [...] k of the bicycle shop, particularly [...] nd Friday evening of my stay in [...] s of beer at about one o'clock in [...] nd talking about life in the country [...] eat surprise, in walked the Minister for Health, Seán Flanagan, whom I had already visited. I did not know it but Seán's father, who had been a schoolteacher, lived quite close to the town. He appeared very surprised to see me and asked me what I was doing in Ballyhaunis. It was only with some difficulty that I prevented him from telling everybody that I was the newly appointed director of the Medico-Social Research Board. Nobody in Ballyhaunis knew this.

At about four in the morning, after the local sergeant had spent an hour drinking with us (licensing laws were very easy-going in Ballyhaunis), I persuaded the Minister that we should be going to our beds and took him to Dr Waldron's house. I also arranged for a bed for his driver. The Minister left at midday the following day; as he got into his car, he said: 'Geoffrey, we are having a cabinet meeting this evening. I shall tell the cabinet that we have appointed

---

[Overlaid newspaper racing clipping:]

Danny Mullins 15

g Bay by Passing Glance - Spirit To Earth

Colours: YELLOW, emerald green striped sleeves, red cap
Bred by: John Jiggens
Owned by: J C Jiggens

Garrett James Power
KILKENNY

Career record 2 runs, 1 wins, 1 places Strike-Rate 50 % Prize-money earned 66,344
Pass Hymn (GB) 1 N.H. win €6,160.00
7/2 Mr J.C. Barry 11.9 10L 5th of 8 to Kala Minstrel 10.9 TIPP 23 JUL Bumper 2m Gd
16/1 Mr D.L Queally 11.11 won 2 3/4L from Allardyce (GB) 12.0 and Chateauneuf Du Pap (GB) 12.0 WEX 21 JUN 14m Bumper 2m Gd
RACING POST VERDICT: Won a Wexford bumper first time out, unplaced at Tipperary, interesting on hurdling debut. Probable SP. 10/1

5 Paulie C (Ire) 42   5 11-12

g Bay by Arcadio - Get On With It

Colours: ROYAL BLUE & YELLOW CHECK, red sleeves, emerald green cap
Bred by: Mrs Kathleen Clifford
Owned by: Mrs Kathleen Clifford

Mrs Maureen Danagher
LIMERICK

Career record 2 runs Prize-money earned €160
Lenny Flynn (3) 50
RACING POST VERDICT: First of two bumper runs was satisfactory but not a likely contender as first-time hurdler. Probable SP. 25/1
Paulie C
40/1 Mr R. Deegan 11.7 9ZL 12th of 15 to Awbeg Prince 11.7 0KY AUG Bumper 2m 3f Yld
9/2 Mr D. O'Connor 12.0 14L 5th of 9 to Stage Summit 11.5 LIM 27 JUL Bumper 2m Yld

the right man to be director of the Medico-Social Research Board'!

I became friendly with the parish priest, Canon Garry. On Sundays the men would be on one side of the church and the women on the other, but many men stayed just outside the door where they could smoke a cigarette. Everyone attended Mass on Sunday.

It was in Ballyhaunis that I went to my first dance in Ireland. The girls sat on chairs down one side of the hall while most of the men would be at the bar having a drink. They danced only when the bar closed. The young men would then walk along the line of girls and choose someone for a dance and, no doubt, would walk her home. For me it was a very strange ritual and I was pleased not to be a girl waiting to be chosen.

The four locums I did in different parts of Ireland gave me a bird's-eye view of life in general practice. Most of the illnesses were minor, but I was surprised at the large number of people, particularly women, who, in spite of living in relaxed rural communities, were taking tranquillisers, usually librium or valium, three times a day. Most of them were hooked on these drugs and it was difficult to get them to stop taking them. When the doctor had first prescribed these tranquillisers, he had not appreciated how addictive they were.

The Economic and Social Research Institute's offices were at 73 Lower Baggot Street, a handsome Georgian house built in the late eighteenth century near the Grand Canal. Early in 1969, when I had been in Ireland for about three months, I heard that the ESRI was moving to larger premises close by and 73 Lower Baggot Street would become vacant. I quickly persuaded the Department of Health to rent the house to the Medico-Social Research Board and we moved there in July 1969. My office and my secretary's room had murals painted on the walls depicting Ireland in the eighteenth century. Shaun Trant thought it would be a good idea to have a turnstone as a symbol of the board; this is a bird that turns over stones on beaches looking for what is underneath. A sculpture of the turnstone, turning over a stone, was designed by Gerrit Van Geldern and placed in the wall outside the office of the board at 73 Lower Baggot Street. 'The turnstone' also became the board's logo.

A few days after our move to Baggot Street, we had a reception attended by Erskine H. Childers, the newly appointed Minister for Health. He was the son of Robert Erskine Childers, the author of *The Riddle of the Sands*, an adventure story first published in May 1903. The story is about a voyage by yacht to Friesland on the German coast and the discovery of preparations for a possible invasion of England. The British government shortly afterwards decided to start a peacetime civilian army – the territorial army.

Robert Erskine Childers, although coming from an English civil service family, was a strong supporter of Irish independence and in 1914 smuggled arms into Ireland in his yacht *The Asgard*, to help the Irish Volunteers. During the Civil War that followed the founding of the Irish Free State, the newly formed government of Ireland passed a law that anyone found with a gun would be shot. Erskine Childers's house was searched and a small revolver was found; with the approval of General Richard Mulcahy, he was shot.

I became a great admirer of the new Minister for Health, who had been so free of rancour against General Mulcahy that he had approved Risteard Mulcahy, a cardiologist and General Mulcahy's son, as a member of my board. At our inaugural reception Erskine Childers enjoyed discussing future plans for research which the board might undertake. By protocol, nobody could leave before the Minister and after midnight, Paddy Lynch said to me: 'Geoffrey, no more whiskey for the Minister or we shall never get home'.

When Erskine Childers became President of Ireland in 1973, he still maintained his interest in the work of the board. He invited Maria and me to dine with him on two occasions at Aras an Uachtaráin ('the house of the Chief'), the former residence of the Viceroy of Ireland, in Phoenix Park. Erskine Childers was the best Minister for Health I knew in Ireland. Unfortunately, he died from a heart attack in 1974, while addressing the Irish division of the Royal College of Psychiatrists at their annual dinner on the need to cultivate calm and avoid the use of tranquillisers.

During the twenty years I worked with the board, I was most fortunate in having outstanding men as chairmen. First, Paddy Lynch, and then, in 1971, Tom Murphy. When Tom Murphy became president of University College, Dublin, Michael

McCormack, professor of business administration at the same university, became chairman. My last chairman was Brendan Hensey, a Doctor of Philosophy, who had been the secretary of the Department of Health before his retirement.

It was very difficult to find men or women trained in social medicine to undertake the relatively poorly paid medico-social research of the board. We therefore subsidised young doctors to study epidemiology and social medicine at the London School of Hygiene, hoping that they would return to work in Ireland. The first to go to the London School was Peadar Kirke.

In the past, tuberculosis had been a major cause of death in Ireland, but this had largely been controlled with better living conditions and by the use of the new antibiotics for tuberculosis, the first of which was streptomycin. I knew from my discussions with Donal McCarthy that death certification was unreliable; a number of deaths were merely registered and not medically certified and an unknown number of deaths were neither registered nor certified. I decided to obtain lists of people who had been buried by the parish priests in 21 parishes over a four-year period in the West of Ireland, and ascertained from the Registrar of Births and Deaths in Dublin whether the deaths had been certified and registered, just registered, or not reported. We found that 6 per cent of deaths had been registered but not certified and that a further 8 per cent of deaths were neither registered nor certified and the people concerned were, therefore, still officially alive! When I told the Minister about this, he replied: 'What a pity I did not know this sooner. All those who are not officially dead could have voted for me at the last election'! We published the findings of the study and, in collaboration with the Registrar of Births and Deaths, started a campaign to improve the certification and registration of deaths. After this the Registrar instituted a rule that nobody could be buried by an undertaker unless evidence of the registration of death was first produced. Sometimes when the cause of death was not known, the death would be reported to the local coroner. He could either order an autopsy by a pathologist or ask a doctor to undertake an examination of the body without an autopsy.

Suicide as a cause of death appeared to be very uncommon in Ireland in comparison with England, Wales and other European countries, but it was not as uncommon as was thought. The Catholic Church regarded suicide as a mortal sin and the body of anyone who had deliberately taken their own life could not, in theory, be buried in consecrated ground. If at all possible, the coroner would certify a death, which might have been due to suicide, as 'accidental' or as 'cause unknown'. Following later studies and the resultant publicity, suicide today is much more accurately recorded than it had been; though it is still true that suicide in Ireland is less common than in all other European countries.

One of the main reasons why the Irish government and the Department of Health had decided to develop a quango (quasi autonomous non-governmental organisation) to be called the Medico-Social Research Board was to look at the medical and social problems of the country and the need to obtain much more detailed information about why people were admitted to hospital in Ireland, the nature of the illness, the length of stay, and so on. The information was required for hospital administration and would be invaluable in medical research. It was difficult to obtain this information in Ireland because most of the hospitals were independent of the state and many were owned and run by religious orders, although they obtained financial support from the government. Moreover the hospital consultants did not always like too much enquiry into their workload, the length of stay of patients and the results of treatment; for instance, the mortality of their patients compared with other hospitals.

A hospital in-patient enquiry (HIPE) scheme was already in existence in England, Wales and Scotland. This was a scheme whereby, on a patient's discharge from hospital, a form would be completed providing general information: name, address, date of birth, place of residence, date of admission, date of discharge, diagnosis, operations, and so on. This form would be sent to a central office for coding and the information would be analysed. In Ireland we thought we might learn a great deal by seeing how the HIPE scheme was functioning in Scotland, which had a population size roughly similar to Ireland; the population of Scotland at that time was five million and the Republic of Ireland three million. Shaun

Trant and I flew to Edinburgh to meet the director of the Scottish Central Statistics Office and his staff and learn how they ran their scheme. We were offered every encouragement and were given full information about their methods and copies of the forms they used. The results of the analysis of the hospital discharges were reported back to each consultant and hospital, in addition to national analysis. They also loaned us one of their staff for a few weeks to help us start the scheme.

The board by now required a full-time secretary. We appointed John O'Gorman and he took charge of the hospital in-patient enquiry scheme. We had to tell the consultants and hospital administrators about the scheme and ask them to collaborate. In some hospitals the record-keeping was very poor and much of the information we required – for instance the diagnosis – was not recorded. This meant extra work for the hospitals, although we did subsidise their records departments and, in many cases, provided an additional member of staff to deal with the HIPE. John O'Gorman and I visited the main hospitals in Ireland and told the consultants about the scheme. We provided the consultants with detailed reports about the patients under their care and national information was also provided. Consultants could then compare the results of their treatment with those of other hospitals and of the country as a whole.

When the scheme was up and running, we were able to find the HIPE records of those who had been admitted for any particular condition, and the result of their treatment. If necessary, we could go back to the consultants and obtain more information about a patient. In the years to come, between fifty and seventy research projects were undertaken each year based on the scheme, many of course by doctors who were not working for the board. The consultants who did not like the scheme often used confidentiality as an argument for not participating. It was impressed on them that the scheme was under my personal supervision as a doctor and that confidential information, such as the name of any patient, was never forwarded to the Department of Health.

Ireland had a high level of hospitalisation for psychiatric illness in the 1960s and earlier. Records of admissions and discharges to psychiatric hospitals in Ireland had been kept for some years by a good psychiatrist, Dermot Walsh. We invited him to join the staff and take charge of studies on psychiatric illness, including schizophrenia, alcoholism and drug abuse. He was assisted by an able sociologist, Aileen O'Hare. In 1969 more than 20,000 people were resident in psychiatric hospitals in Ireland, more men than women, the reverse of the situation in psychiatric hospitals in England and Wales. Fourteen per cent of the patients in these psychiatric hospitals were there not because of mental illness but because of mental subnormality, whereas in England and Wales, the respective figure was five per cent. The Irish patients were much younger, on average, than in England and Wales. In the age-group 25–34, there were six times as many males and four times as many females, per 100,000 of the population, in the psychiatric hospitals in Ireland as there were in England and Wales.

The reason for this was not known. It was suspected that it might be because in each generation about half the young people had emigrated, generally to Britain, and perhaps those who emigrated were less likely to have suffered a psychiatric breakdown. Loneliness was also considered to be a factor because many of the people, especially the men, in the West of Ireland did not marry. There were high rates of admission to psychiatric hospitals in Ireland for schizophrenia and for alcohol-related disorders.

The population of all Ireland, by 1968 about five million, can be compared with the nine million population of Ireland before the Great Famine of the 1840s. Since then the population has remained low for three reasons: celibacy, late marriage of those who did marry (the average age of men marrying in 1968 was thirty-two); and, perhaps most important of all, emigration. The recent economic boom in Ireland – the Celtic Tiger – has led to a fall in emigration and the return of a number of emigrants, leading to an increase in population.

From the beginning the board took a special interest in the problems resulting from the abuse of alcohol. Although admissions to psychiatric hospitals for alcoholism and alcohol-related problems were very high in Ireland, rates for cirrhosis of the liver were not unduly high. This was probably because the pattern of Irish drinking in the 1960s right up to the 1990s was often binge drinking or 'Friday night drinking', rather than a high daily consumption of alcohol, often starting in the morning, which was frequently the pattern in France and Spain. The highest mortality for cirrhosis of the liver in Europe was in France. The first admission rate for alcoholic psychosis in Ireland in 1969 was 42.5 per 100,000 population, compared with 20.6 in Scotland and 3.6 in England and Wales.

Mental retardation was also unduly common in Ireland and the board asked Michael Mulcahy, the director of Stewart's Hospital, Palmerstown, Dublin, for the mentally handicapped, to study the problem. The high prevalence of mental retardation was due partly to the high prevalence of Down syndrome, now known as trisomy 21 because there are three chromosomes no. 21 in each cell, instead of the usual two. The risk of having a trisomy 21 baby increases with the age of the mother so that, over the age of forty, the risk is high. There were many older mothers in Ireland. Today mothers at high risk, for instance over the age of thirty-five, can be tested for the condition when they become pregnant and can, if they wish – but not in the Republic of Ireland – have an abortion. Over the last twenty years a major effort has been made to take the mentally handicapped out of institutions and place them, whenever possible, in hostels of six to ten people, where they can be helped to integrate with the general population and lead a more normal lifestyle. There has been a change of attitude towards family planning so that the family size has become smaller.

I was beginning to get a good idea of the pattern of illness that brought people in Ireland to see their general practitioners, the pattern of illness that resulted in their being admitted to general and psychiatric hospitals and in the reported causes of death. The most frequent causes of death in Ireland, as in the United Kingdom, were heart attacks and strokes. Following meetings with the World Health Organisation, we decided to support a study on heart attacks and later on strokes in the countries of the European Economic Community, including an adult population of about 150,000 people in Dublin. In order to carry out this study, I asked a doctor who had taken a special interest in cardiology, Alycia Radic, to join our staff.

Alycia's story is interesting. She was born in a village in eastern

Poland and when the Russians invaded Poland in 1939 the population in her village were 'cleansed' and replaced by Ukrainians.
Her family were sent by train to work on a collective farm in
Siberia. In 1941 when the Germans invaded the USSR, the
Russians formed a Polish army to fight the Germans, and Alycia
and her family were brought west by train. There was very little
food and her younger brother and a number of others died on the
way. Her mother heard that there was a Red Cross orphanage
nearby and sent Alycia and her older brother to the orphanage.
The Red Cross evacuated them to Persia where Alycia and her
brother, three years older than her, volunteered to join the Polish
army which was under British command. They were then transported to Palestine. Alycia was ten years old when she joined the
women's section of the army, the ATS, but said that she was thirteen, the youngest age allowed. The British, showing great good
sense, sent the young volunteers to school. In 1947 Alycia and her
brother were evacuated to England and Alycia was sent to a
grammar school. She matriculated and won a college scholarship
to study medicine at the University of Dublin (Trinity College).
When she qualified, she specialised in cardiology. Her father developed tuberculosis and was sent to a sanatorium in India and, because
two of his children had been in the army, he was allowed to settle
in England. Her mother returned to Poland where she lived to be
ninety-one.

The WHO study on heart attacks showed that in Dublin, as elsewhere, a major factor in causing heart attacks was cigarette smoking.
Other factors were uncontrolled raised blood pressure, lack of
regular exercise and a diet high in animal fat; bacon and eggs was
still the usual breakfast meal, followed by a 'fry' in the evening.
These factors, particularly high blood pressure, also contributed to
causing strokes – cerebral haemorrhage and cerebral thrombosis.
At that time many people with a raised blood pressure were not
aware of it and those who knew that their blood pressure was high
were often inadequately treated.

Since the early 1970s there has been a dramatic fall in deaths
from heart attacks and strokes in many countries of the world; for

instance, in the United States and Australia, there was a 40 per cent and a 60 per cent fall respectively by 1995. This has come about because of better control of blood pressure and a change in lifestyle, stopping cigarette smoking and a change in diet, combined with an effort to take more exercise. Cereals and muesli have now to some extent replaced bacon and eggs for breakfast.

Many of the health problems in Ireland were the result of poverty and unemployment. Among the poorest are the itinerants or 'travelling people'. Many still live in caravans and move about the countryside. The women beggars, with infants in their arms, seen frequently on the streets of Dublin and other Irish cities, are generally itinerants. They have a very different lifestyle to the general population: they marry young and within their own group; they have their own slang or argot, 'shelta', derived from the Irish language; and they have large families although many of the children, particularly when I first came to Ireland, died young because of bad living conditions. They are looked down upon by many of the settled population and the support they receive from the social services was, and still is, much less in Ireland than in Britain. The board took a great interest in the problems associated with poverty and in helping the itinerants. Some of my staff and I joined the Simon Community and, for some years, once or twice a week, we would bring soup, bread and stew in the evening to those who were sleeping rough. One of our staff, Dr Joe Barry, who had trained in social medicine in London, later undertook detailed studies on the health and life expectancy of the itinerants, and much has been done since 1970 to improve their lifestyle and to provide better halting sites for them. As a result, their numbers have greatly increased. Houses have been provided for those itinerants who wish to settle, but most do not. Not enough is yet being done to deal with this very difficult problem.

The chairman and board members of the MSRB appointed by the Minister for Health, no doubt with advice from the cabinet, always included a representative of the interests of the Catholic Church. One or two of the board would be members of the Church of Ireland, although only about three per cent of the population were non-Catholic. Before my arrival in Ireland, the first priest who was a member of the board, and then only for a short time, was Monsignor Newman, the principal of St Patrick's College, Maynooth. He later became Bishop of Limerick and was a prolific writer. One day Paddy Lynch asked me if I had heard about Bishop Newman's latest book about whether or not the clergy should marry. I said 'No'. Paddy replied it was *Marriage or Celibacy: the Via Media*, a jocular reference to Cardinal Newman's 'Via Media'.

The Catholic Archbishop of Dublin at that time was Archbishop John Charles McQuaid. He had great influence in Ireland and was the chairman of the main Dublin hospital boards, run by Catholic Sisters. I made an appointment to see him so that I could introduce myself and discuss with him some of the medical and social problems of Ireland. I found him very pleasant, but quite rigid in maintaining the strictest Catholic orthodoxy. He made it clear that he would co-operate with me only as long as I did not question the Catholic teaching on family planning – that is, no artificial contraception and especially no termination of pregnancy under any circumstances. He said to me: 'Dublin is just a village and I know everything that goes on in this village.' I think he probably did.

At that time, in the late 1960s, Ireland had the highest recorded birth rate of any country in Europe and all forms of contraception were illegal. Before the Second World War, even the use of the 'safe period' was frowned upon. As a Catholic country, where over ninety per cent of the population at that time attended Mass on Sundays, most people kept to the teachings of the Church, although attitudes towards contraception were changing and, in spite of Catholic teaching on the use of contraception, the average family size was falling. Since the Famine, most people married late in life and many did not marry at all. The men were compensated for this by the good care they generally received from their mothers. Abortion is not only illegal but, because of public opinion and the heavy penalties involved, it is to all practical purposes non-existent in Ireland. However, a woman in Ireland who becomes pregnant can easily have a legally induced abortion in England.

Each year Dr Dermot Walsh reported on the number of women from the Irish Republic who had had an abortion in England, obtaining most of the information from the reports published by the Office of Population Censuses and Surveys (OPCS) in London.

The OPCS reports were very limited in the information they provided; for instance, they did not say from what part of Ireland the women came, their socio-economic group or social class, or their use of contraception before their pregnancy. The OPCS information referred only to women who gave an Irish address; if they gave an English address, and many women had relatives or friends in England, they would not be included. The women from Ireland generally had their pregnancies terminated in private clinics and not in National Health Service hospitals.

The number of women from the Republic of Ireland who had abortions in Britain increased from about 100 in 1968 to 4,000 in 1984 and slowly rose to 6,000 in 1999. In order to obtain more detailed information about those women who went to England to have their pregnancies terminated, and to ascertain their characteristics, I later undertook studies based on information I had obtained, by personal contact, from the clinics in Britain. At the same time, Aileen O'Hare, the board's senior sociologist, in collaboration with the Federation of Services for Unmarried Parents and their Children, studied the characteristics of unmarried women in Ireland who became pregnant and gave birth to their babies. The number in the two groups, those unmarried mothers who had an abortion and those who had had their babies, was about the same by 1984.

A study based on information from the British clinics could not be undertaken by the Department of Health, because abortion in Ireland is illegal. Not everybody in the Department was pleased that the MSRB was carrying out the study, although I did have strong support and encouragement from the Minister. By far the majority of Irish women who went to England for an abortion were single and lived in County Dublin. Women living in the cities were more likely to have their pregnancy terminated during the first 12 weeks, whereas those living in rural areas often delayed and had a late and much more dangerous abortion. By 1984/85 abortion rates were lower than those in England and Wales as a whole but higher than in England and Wales among residents of Dublin. Irish women in the higher socio-economic groups were much more likely to have their pregnancy terminated than those in the lower socio-economic groups.

Married women resident in Ireland had a much lower abortion rate than residents of England and Wales. Three-quarters of women in the study had never used contraceptives. When contraception was used, the condom was the most popular form of contraception below the age of twenty-five, and over that age the 'pill'. It was illegal to purchase contraceptives, although the law was modified in 1985 and liberated by the Health and Family Planning Act in 1993.

Many single women in Ireland, as elsewhere, become pregnant and then must make a decision either to get married, perhaps to a man who is unsuitable and with whom the marriage is not likely to be a success, or continue with the pregnancy and look after the baby without a husband, have the baby adopted, or have an abortion. Only much better education about interpersonal relationships and family planning can help with this problem – a particularly sensitive one still in Ireland.

CHAPTER 19

Notebook and Shoe Leather Epidemiology

Luck is the residue of design.
Branch Rickey, on baseball

Much of the research I have undertaken has occurred as a result of serendipity, 'the faculty of making happy and unexpected discoveries by accident'. The word was first used by Horace Walpole in 1754 and was taken from the story of the three princes of Serendip, the old name for Sri Lanka. Serendipity in medicine has been beautifully discussed by Richard Asher in his book *Talking Sense*. He defines it as an ability to recognise the Highest Common Factor, or HCF. McFarlane Burnett has remarked that recognition of the HCF involves what he describes as the 'notebook and shoe leather method' or 'shoe leather epidemiology'.

It was by lucky chance that I went as a ship's surgeon to South Africa and found that multiple sclerosis was uncommon there and unknown among the black population. Then it was by serendipity that I should find myself in practice in Port Elizabeth in the Eastern Cape, the area in Southern Africa with the highest prevalence of porphyria.

My greatest personal interest was to further research into the causes of multiple sclerosis. As I have explained, MS had a high prevalence among immigrants from Europe, but is much less common among the white South African-born. Returning to Europe from South Africa gave me an opportunity to study what had happened to those who came from low MS prevalence areas of the world, such as Asia, Africa or the West Indies, to Britain, a high MS prevalence area. I knew that after the Second World War, over two million immigrants had come to Britain from Asia, mostly from the Indian subcontinent, from Africa, particularly Asians from East Africa and from the Caribbean. The majority had settled in Greater London and the West Midlands. I knew that MS was very uncommon among Asians, whether they were born in Asia or in East Africa, and that it was relatively uncommon in the West Indies. I decided, therefore, to study the records of all patients diagnosed as having MS who had been admitted to hospital in Greater London between 1960 and 1972. The first study was undertaken in collaboration with Dr Abraham Adelstein, director of the Office of Population Censuses and Surveys, London. Dr Rosaleen Brady, the sister of my first wife, Nonie, assisted me, together with a London medical student, Joanne Tallett-Williams. The teaching hospitals all cooperated with the study.

We found that admission to hospital for probable MS was high among immigrants from Continental Europe, Ireland, the Soviet Union, Canada, Australia and New Zealand. Just one ethnic Asian immigrant and only sixteen from the Caribbean were found with a definite diagnosis of MS in 1972.

It later became possible to find out, with the help of Marta Elian and Simon Nightingale in Birmingham, if the United Kingdom-born children of immigrants to Britain, who had come in the 1950s from low MS prevalence areas of India and Pakistan, Africa and the West Indies, kept the low risk of developing MS which occurred among their immigrant parents. They did not. In the age-group available for study, 15–34 years, the United Kingdom-born children of these immigrants had the same MS risk as the general British population. This is proof that, besides a genetic predisposing factor, the environment is of major importance in causing MS and the environmental factor is associated with where one's childhood is spent.

Although MS is extremely uncommon among ethnic Indian immigrants, five Parsis out of a population of approximately 5,000 Parsi immigrants have been found in Britain with MS, a similar prevalence to that which occurs among the general population. Parsis – a name derived from 'Persian' – are Zoroastrians, or followers of Zarathustra, a prophet who lived in Persia five hundred years before Christ. The Magi who, by tradition, came to Bethlehem at the birth of Jesus, were probably Zoroastrian priests. When Persia was invaded by the Muslims, some of the Parsis fled to India, especially to Bombay.

Dr Noshir Wadia, a Bombay Parsi doctor, found a high prevalence of MS among the Parsis living in Bombay. The difference in the prevalence of MS between the Parsis and other Indians appears to be due to the environment because Indians born in Britain have as high a risk of MS as the British. The Parsis in India by and large are wealthy and have a western European lifestyle.

The chance of being hospitalised with a diagnosis of MS was high (the same as in the United Kingdom-born) among the immigrants from the countries of Northern Europe and almost as high for immigrants from Italy. Among immigrants from Spain and Cyprus, the latter both Greek and Turkish Cypriots, it occurred one-half to two-thirds as frequently as among the immigrants from Northern Europe. It was strange that there was not a single MS patient among immigrants from Malta, although the expected number, at the England and Wales-born rate, was ten. Emigrating to England from low MS-risk parts of the world did not apparently increase the risk of developing MS after the immigrants had arrived.

We later broadened the study to include the West Midlands (the Birmingham and Wolverhampton area) and included another disease of the nervous system, motor neuron disease (MND). We found that MND had more or less the same prevalence among the immigrants as among the United Kingdom-born, except that it was less common than expected among immigrants from Asia.

I first met Dr Marta Elian in 1970 — she was at that time a neurologist at the Beilinson Hospital in Tel Aviv — when I attended an MS conference in Jerusalem. Her story was an interesting one. She grew up in Oradea in Hungary (in Hungarian 'Nagyvarad') and in 1944, when the Germans and Hungarians were sending the Jews to concentration camps, where most of them died, she and her parents escaped on foot from Hungary to Romania, where the persecution of the Jews was less extreme.

Unlike many of their friends and relations, the family survived the war. After the war they emigrated to Israel where Marta studied medicine at Tel Aviv University and then specialised in neurology. She settled in London in 1972 and later became a consultant neuro-physiologist at the Midland Centre for Neurosurgery and Neurology in Birmingham in 1976. She played a major part in the second study of MS and MND in London and in the West Midlands and was to continue working with me on fourteen subsequent research projects. She is still collaborating with me on MS research today. Since 1970 she has been my greatest personal friend and I love her dearly.

In Ireland I also undertook, with Rosaleen Brady and two medical students, a study of MS and found much the same preva-lence as in Northern Ireland; in 1977 it was calculated at 66 per 100,000 of the population. This was certainly an underestimate because it was based on a study of the total population of the Republic. For a more accurate estimate, small populations of less than 100,000 people are best studied. The prevalence we now know to be at least 100 per 100,000 of the population.

In 1973 I was appointed a member of the Specialised Working Group (SWG) in Epidemiology of the Committee for Medical Research of the European Economic Community; eight years later I was elected chairman of the SWG. This group met four times a year in Brussels to discuss health problems in Europe and organise research. As a result of my membership, Ireland was able to take part in a number of research projects that the Commission finan-cially subvented, including studies on air pollution and respiratory disease.

Marta Elian is the mother of twin boys, Yoram and Amnon. She was very interested in twinning and told me in 1971 that Ireland had a high twinning rate. Twins are of two types: those who develop from two fertilised eggs, dizygotic, and those who develop from one fertilised egg, monozygotic, which after fertili-sation has split in two and the twins are, therefore, genetically the same. A great deal of information about the genetic cause of diseases can be obtained by comparing the prevalence of disease in identical twins with two-egg twins. By this means, the genetic cause of a disease can be often separated from the environmental cause.

The risk of having two-egg twins increases with the age of the mother. In Ireland, because contraceptives until relatively recently were seldom used, there was a higher proportion than elsewhere of older mothers and these mothers were more likely to produce two or sometimes three eggs at ovulation resulting in twins or triplets. Since 1960 there has been a fall in the number of much older mothers which has resulted in the fall in the twinning rate. Down syndrome, trisomy 21, is also much more common in older mothers and women over the age of forty are at a particularly high risk. The monozygotic twinning rate remains the same whatever the age of the mother. Recently it has been found that the age of the father also contributes to the risk that a baby will suffer from Down syndrome.

Two congenital abnormalities, known as neural tube defects – spina bifida, in which the bone of the spine over the spinal cord does not close properly and the child may have spastic legs, and anencephaly, in which the brain of the foetus does not develop – have long been more common in Ireland than in the rest of Europe. The Committee for Medical Research of the EEC agreed to develop a major project, under the direction of Michel Le Chat, the Belgian representative, and myself, to register congenital abnormalities and twins in the European Community. The project, known as EUROCAT (CAT = Congenital Abnormalities and Twins), still continues and has been a great success.

By 1980 there had been a fall in the incidence of anencephaly and spina bifida in the United Kingdom; this was thought to be attributable to improved diet. Professor R.W. Smithells suggested that if additional vitamin B, particularly folic acid, was taken by the mother from the time of conception, the risk of spina bifida and anencephaly would be reduced. Under the direction of one of the board's research workers, Peadar Kirke, we started a randomised clinical trial of folic acid supplementation in mothers at high risk of having a baby with a neural tube defect. Half the mothers were given the folic acid tablets to take daily and half were given a placebo, a harmless substance that looked and tasted the same.

Neither the doctor who prescribed the tablets nor the mothers knew whether they had been given the vitamins or the placebo. It was done in this way so as to avoid bias in deciding whether the folic acid was effective. This type of study, well publicised by Bradford Hill and Archie Cochrane, is known as a 'double blind' trial.

Mothers who had already had a baby with a neural tube defect had a greater risk. Dublin was probably the most suitable city in the world to pursue this question because some 25,000 births took place each year in three hospitals and because of the high incidence of neural tube defects in the population. This research in Ireland, combined with studies by Nick Wald in the United Kingdom, have shown that the administration of folic acid greatly reduces the risk of neural tube defects, if given to mothers as soon as possible after the time of conception, that is when she misses her first menstrual period or, even better, before she becomes pregnant.

A major study in Ireland, funded by the National Institute of Health, in Bethesda, Maryland, has now confirmed these findings and today women are advised to take folic acid tablets before they become pregnant or at least for the first two or three months of pregnancy. This has resulted in a marked fall in the congenital abnormalities anencephaly and spina bifida. Many women still do not take the folic tablets or do not take them early enough. Nick Wald now suggests, and I strongly support the proposal, that the folic acid vitamin should be added to flour so that all mothers would have adequate folic acid before they become pregnant. There are arguments against this – for instance neural complications in relatively rare pernicious anaemia – but the risk of a neural tube defect is much greater.

There is a high admission rate for schizophrenia to the Irish psychiatric hospitals. Ireland therefore appeared to be a good country in which to study the genetic and environmental factors that might be responsible for this common disorder. The Irish often had large families which would make the study easier. I had heard that schizophrenia had occurred in the Rothschild family and that Miriam

Rothschild, who lived near Oxford, supported a schizophrenia foundation which funded research on the disease. I went to see her, hoping to obtain her support for schizophrenia studies in Ireland. Marta Elian accompanied me. Marta and Miriam Rothschild's mother came from the same city in Hungary, Oradea.

We found that Miriam was an expert on fleas and had written a number of books describing her studies on the different varieties. Each of her well-paid staff wore a little box, strapped to their abdomen or arm, in which Miriam bred different varieties of exotic fleas. Miriam was a tall, unassuming lady with a dry sense of humour. I asked her why she thought schizophrenia affected some members of the Rothschild family. She replied: 'Most people have thirty-two great-great-great grandparents, but some of today's Rothschilds have only nine!'

While Miriam's foundation did not give financial support to schizophrenia research in Ireland, I know she used her influence to help us obtain funds. The National Institute of Health in Maryland later strongly supported the research. This made possible a number of important studies by Dermot Walsh into the genetic and environmental factors responsible for the disease. These have confirmed that there is a genetic predisposition to schizophrenia. Recently it has been shown through X-ray that there are changes in the brain of schizophrenics and in the brains of some of their relatives, perhaps suggesting that, in certain circumstances, they are predisposed to developing the disease.

An epidemic of deliberate self-poisoning, usually by tranquillisers, took place in the countries of Western Europe during the 1970s. In England and Wales in 1977, more than 100,000 young people aged 15–34 were admitted to hospital with deliberate self-poisoning. Although this was called 'attempted suicide', it is doubtful if there was a true intent to commit suicide in the majority of these cases. It was usually a cry for help. Self-poisoning occurred twice as often in women as in men. Successful suicide, on the other hand, was more common among men and more common in older age-groups. In 1973/74 we organised a study of the prevalence of attempted suicide and how it could be prevented in Ireland, England, Wales and Denmark; the results of the study were published in 1975. We found that an overdose of tranquillisers seldom caused death. As this became better known, the use of tranquillisers, usually librium or valium, in attempted suicides became much less common.

The board undertook a number of studies on alcohol drinking habits in Ireland and the effects of the abuse of alcohol on physical and psychological health. A matter of great personal interest! I knew that the Guinness brewery workers had a reputation for drinking heavily. In 1974 in the United States, Breslow and Enstrom found a high correlation between a life-long heavy consumption of beer and cancer of the bowel (that is of the rectum and, to a lesser extent, of the colon). This was a problem of particular interest to the International Agency for Research on Cancer (IARC) in Lyon, France. It had already been reported that there had been an increase in cancer of the oesophagus and of the mouth among workers in breweries and distilleries in Copenhagen. I wondered if there might be an increased mortality from rectal cancers among the workers in the large Guinness brewery in Dublin, which then employed more than 4,000 workers. I therefore suggested to Calum Muir, the deputy director of IARC, that the agency should support a study comparing the mortality from different disorders among the men working in the breweries in Copenhagen with those in Dublin. We found that the male Guinness workers who had died between 1954 and 1973 had on average a better expectation of life than all Dublin males, but they did have twice the expected number of deaths from cancer of the rectum and more deaths than expected from diabetes mellitus.

There was a free allowance of two pints of porter or (later) of stout for everyone in the brewery. Some workers did not drink and they gave their allowance to their friends. For special duties, workers could receive additional stout, sometimes as many as six or eight pints. In addition, there were also points in the brewery where stout could be illicitly obtained, known colloquially as 'Lourdes' because of the miraculous recovery that would occur at these 'taps' on a Monday morning. Guinness is nutritious and the brewery provided a glass of Guinness free to mothers in Dublin maternity hospitals.

Wages at Guinness's brewery were good, the standard of living of the Guinness workers was relatively high, and the level of medical care by the medical officers of the brewery was, and is, excellent. Unlike brewery workers in Copenhagen, who drank more spirits, Guinness workers did not have an increased number of deaths from cancer of the oesophagus or cirrhosis of the liver, disorders often associated with the consumption of spirits and wine.

In England and Wales, the lower socio-economic groups had and still have the highest mortality. This is partly because of cigarette smoking, which is more common among lower socio-economic groups. Other contributing factors may be a poorer diet, overcrowding, lack of sufficient exercise and the psychological effects of unemployment. In Ireland deaths are classified by occupation and not specifically by social class. We found that in Ireland, especially in Dublin, there was a similar relationship between social class, as judged by occupation, or lack of it, and mortality – the poor had a considerably higher mortality rate. The expectation of life in Ireland was better in the rural areas than in Dublin, largely because of the higher consumption of cigarettes among the Dublin population, resulting in a higher mortality rate from heart attacks, strokes, lung cancer and bronchitis. Air pollution in the past also contributed to the higher urban mortality, as was clearly shown in Northern Ireland.

Heart attacks and strokes rank as the major causes of death in Ireland. There has not been the big fall in deaths from these causes that has occurred elsewhere, for instance in the United States, Australia and Finland. In the 1980s the Finns had the highest mortality rate from coronary heart disease but, as a result of an active programme of community health promotion, the rate had fallen by 1999 to a lower level than in Ireland.

One of the outstanding research workers in the Medico-Social Research Board was Dr Emer Shelley. In consultation with Risteard Mulcahy, at that time director of the Irish Heart Foundation, we decided in 1985 to organise a community health programme in County Kilkenny, based on the Finnish model, to try and modify the behaviour of a defined population and so reduce the risk of heart attacks. Emer Shelley opened an office in Kilkenny and employed social workers and an expert in publicity to assist her. The adult population of the county was screened for heart disease risk factors such as raised blood pressure, obesity, cigarette smoking and lack of exercise. There was continued publicity about the scheme in the newspapers and on television and the Kilkenny Health Project started its own newspaper. The restaurants in County Kilkenny put up 'no smoking' signs and provided meals with low levels of animal fat. The Project went well, but the fall in heart attack rates was slow. However, partly as a result of the Kilkenny Project, people in Ireland have become much more aware of the risk factors for heart attacks and strokes, and the mortality from these two conditions is now slowly falling throughout the country.

I had been very surprised that I had found no patients with MS among the Maltese immigrants to Greater London and the West Midlands, although, at English rates, ten was the calculated 'expected' number. In 1976, I went to Malta and spent some weeks working with Luis Vassallo, the Maltese physician with a special interest in neurology. The population of the Maltese islands at the time was approximately 304,000: 279,000 in Malta and 25,000 in the neighbouring island of Gozo. The people of Malta speak an Arabic language and are largely of Semitic origin following the invasion of Habasa in 869-870 AD, although Malta, like nearby Sicily, has been ruled in its time by Phoenicians, Carthaginians, Greeks, Romans, Arabs, Normans and British. Malta, in 1976, had a good health service, largely state-supported, with a teaching hospital and a medical school. There was a strong alliance between the Maltese and the British Medical Association, and many Maltese doctors, including Luis Vassallo, had studied and practised in Britain. They knew MS well. Marta Elian also took part in searching for MS patients, particularly on the island of Gozo.

We looked for all patients who might have MS or other conditions, such as retrobulbar neuritis, which might have been the first symptom of multiple sclerosis. The Maltese government, health administrators and the doctors all collaborated. We held meetings with physicians, ophthalmologists, general practitioners and the medical officers of health. After an intensive three-year search, from 1976 to 1979, we had been able to find only fourteen MS patients. This was a very low prevalence of 4 per 100,000. By the end of the study, we were convinced that we had missed few patients with definite symptoms of MS.

Sicily is only sixty miles from Malta, so after my first visit to Malta I took a ship to Syracuse and visited the senior neurologist in the city. He combined his work as a neurologist with that of psychiatrist and he took me around the Syracuse psychiatric hospital, unlocking and locking doors as we walked through the hospital. The combined neurology and psychiatric hospital was a closed institution. The neurologist was followed by two large men in black suits, who looked well capable of taking care of him. At my hotel I found that my bill had been paid and there was a present of a beautiful Sicilian plate awaiting me – a gift from the neurologist. This doctor had worked in Syracuse for many years; he said he had seen only one MS patient.

I then went to the three university cities of Messina, Catania and Palermo. In Palermo, the capital of Sicily, the population was far too big, over one million people, for a study of MS, although I found there a good neurologist, Giovanni Savettieri. I then went by car to the inland city of Enna, where I had been told that the senior neurologist, Pino Grimaldi, spoke excellent English.

In the beautiful old city of Enna, I was intrigued to find that the men of importance there were often named Grimaldi. The Grimaldi family are said to go back to the second son of Charles Martel, the grandfather of Charlemagne. Prince Rainier of Monaco is a Grimaldi. In the cathedral there was a sarcophagus of an Archbishop Grimaldi who had served there some four hundred years earlier.

Pino Grimaldi and I searched for the MS patients in Enna in a population of 29,000 people and found fourteen. This was a prevalence of 53 per 100,000, a much higher prevalence than had been reported previously in Sicily or Italy.

My most intense memory of Enna was attending, on a moonlit night, a performance of Verdi's opera 'Nabucco' in the grounds of the Castello Lombardia. I still often listen to my tape of this opera as I work at my desk and every time I hear the slaves' chorus, 'Va pensiero', I think of Enna.

Previous studies in Sicily, for instance in Palermo, had reported a low prevalence of MS of between 4 and 12 per 100,000. I knew that I would have difficulty persuading the Italian doctors that the high prevalence of MS I had found in Enna was correct, so I invited Reginald Kelly, chairman of the Medical Advisory Board of the Multiple Sclerosis Society of Great Britain and Northern Ireland, and Dr Lucien Karhausen, the secretary of the EEC epidemiology committee, to join me in Enna and see the patients. They agreed that all fourteen patients definitely had MS.

Lucien Karhausen, who joined me in the MS studies in Sicily and San Marino, was a Renaissance man. He lived at that time in a four-hundred-year-old house on the Île de la Cité in the centre of Paris. He was a great lover of opera and if he wished to attend the Paris Opera on the evening of our Brussels meetings, nothing would delay his bringing the meeting to a close. He married Miss Cohen-Solal, who wrote a book on Jean-Paul Sartre. When I last heard from Lucien in January 1999, he had bought a farm in Italy and was writing a book on the philosophy of medicine. He is a delightful friend.

The Italian neurologists to whom I made the report about the prevalence of MS in Enna told me it must be by pure chance that I had studied the one town in Sicily that had a high MS prevalence. I therefore decided to study the prevalence in another city, Agrigento. This proved a difficult place for MS research because the only neurologist there had seen few MS patients. He had been in prison, where it was said he lived in great luxury! Trays of food were brought to him from a nearby hotel and his secretary kept him in touch with his patients. I do not know the rights or wrongs of the story. We went *en famille* to Agrigento every year for three years and I was generally joined there by Lucien Karhausen. Agrigento, the home of the playwright and Nobel laureate Luigi Pirandello, is a fine city near the sea, and has many Greek temples.

We undertook two further studies on MS in Sicily. Giovanni Savettieri was in charge of a study in Monreale, a city with a cathedral built in the twelfth century by the Arabs, for Roger the Norman, in Arab style with splendid mosaics, and Marta Elian directed a study in the inland city of Caltanisetta. The prevalence of MS in the four cities of Sicily was moderately high, at least 50 per 100,000 – twelve times higher than we had found in Malta.

What was the reason for the sudden fall in MS prevalence between Sicily and Malta? It could be due to genetic or environmental reasons or a combination of both. It was already known that MS was more common in people with certain blood groups, in particular the blood group HLA-DW2. We took blood from the MS patients and from controls, that is, people who did not have MS, in Sicily and in Malta and sent the blood by air to Hilliard Festenstein, professor and head of the Department of Immunology at the London Hospital. He found differences in the blood pattern between Sicily and Malta, but they probably were not enough to account for the large difference in MS prevalence in the two populations. As Marta Elian once remarked, 'the cause of MS must lie in the sea between Malta and Sicily!'

Lucien Karhausen proposed that we should undertake a study of MS in the Republic of San Marino, which in 1979 had a population of 21,000. It had an excellent health service, there was low taxation and the citizens received free health care both at the general practitioner and at the consultant level. In collaboration with the San Marino physicians Giovanni Morganti and Salvatore Naccarato, Lucien Karhausen, Marta Elian and I undertook a study of the prevalence of MS in the Republic of San Marino. We found that there was a high prevalence of MS in San Marino as no doubt there is throughout the Italian peninsula.

We were told about a lady in San Marino known as 'Signora Pappagallo'. She generally had a parrot, a *pappagallo*, on her shoulder when she looked after her stall in the market-square. She had no fingers and we were asked could this possibly be due to multiple sclerosis? We knew this was not MS, but it was a strange story, so we went to visit her. We found that indeed she had no fingers, although there was no sign of scarring; I suspected that she must have been born without fingers. When I asked her what had happened to her hands she told me that her fingers were '*perduto*' and that they had fallen off in bed when she was a child. I went to the next door neighbour and enquired if she had known Signora Pappagallo as a child. She had, so I asked her if she had had fingers. 'Yes', she said, 'she did have fingers but they all fell off.' I asked when this was and she told me that it was about 1944 when Signora Pappagallo was a child of about four. Marta Elian and I were drinking coffee and looking at her remarkable hands when Marta suddenly exclaimed 'Ergot'. Ergot is a fungus that can infect grain, particularly rye, and it causes spasm and thrombosis (clots) in the blood vessels of the fingers, which can result in dry gangrene. We found that in 1944, when grain was very scarce, some ergot-infected rye was used to make bread. It was a strange story.

CHAPTER 20

Alcohol, Heroin and AIDS

Thou hast the keys of Paradise; oh just, subtle, and mighty opium
Thomas de Quincey, *The Pleasures of Opium*

From the inception of the Medico-Social Research Board, we carried out studies of drug taking, including cigarette smoking and alcohol, among children in primary and secondary schools. In the 1970s there was no serious problem of illegal drug taking in Ireland, although about 10 per cent of school children had experimented with marijuana and an even smaller percentage, particularly in the inner city of Dublin, had used 'uppers', the amphetamine group of drugs, and 'downers', generally barbiturate sedatives. By far the commonest drug used by young people was alcohol, cider in particular. We organised a number of programmes to persuade the government to stop all advertising of alcohol and cigarettes in the media and to persuade young people not to start smoking.

In the nineteenth century in Ireland, when alcohol abuse was an even greater problem than today, Father Theobald Mathew introduced the concept of 'taking a pledge' not to drink alcohol. Father James Cullen founded the 'Pioneers' in 1898. Pioneers not only take a very solemn pledge but also wear a pin in their jacket lapel to show that they are total abstainers. While the 'rounds' system was very common in Ireland – a system by which everybody in a group was expected to stand a round of drinks – a pioneer is not persuaded to drink alcohol.

In the late 1970s a number of chemists' shops were burgled and morphine and opium derivatives, such as Diaconal and Palfium, were stolen. From 1980, heroin was being imported into Dublin, and an epidemic of heroin injecting began in the inner city, where over half the population were unemployed. This heroin epidemic particularly affected young people of between fifteen and twenty-four. In 1982, when discussing this problem with Michael Woods, the Minister for Health at the time, I decided to ascertain how common the use of heroin was in Dublin.

According to the superintendent of the Dublin drug squad, Denis Mullins, the abuse of heroin was most common in north-central and south-central Dublin. With the help of my old friend John Bradshaw, who had settled in Ireland, I first decided to take a ward in north-central Dublin where the sex and age distribution of the population was known from the Census. We searched for those who were injecting heroin and at the same time made every effort to build up a profile of the average heroin user. John Bradshaw, Father Paul Lavelle and I also made a preliminary assessment of heroin use in a number of other areas, in particular south-central Dublin, Dun Laoghaire, Cork and Sligo. Paul Lavelle was very popular and, with his help, and the collaboration of a committee of people in north-central and south-central Dublin, those who were known to be injecting heroin were sought out and interviewed about their habit. We visited Mountjoy prison on a number of occasions and also talked to addicts on the steps of the flats where they lived.

In 1982/83, we found that 10 per cent of those aged 15–24 in the area of north-central Dublin who had taken drugs were injecting heroin once or twice a day. In males aged 15-19 it was 12 per cent and among females of the same age-group, 13 per cent. The high proportion of this population injecting heroin was similar to that in a New York black ghetto at about the same time.

The epidemic of heroin and synthetic opiate abuse in Dublin was responsible for a great increase in drug-related crime; it cost as much as £100 per day to buy the heroin. This money could be obtained only by 'pushing' drugs or by theft. Most of the heroin users were heavy cigarette smokers, but relatively few drank alcohol, although one-third of them came from homes where the parents were heavy drinkers. They were generally also taking opiate drugs by mouth; Diaconal and Palfium were selling on the street for £6.50 a tablet. Three-fifths of the heroin-users in north-central

Dublin had been arrested, often more than once, for a range of offences such as theft, assault and drug-pushing. Many of the girls worked as prostitutes.

In 1984/85 we undertook a second similar study in a south-central Dublin ward in collaboration with a local general practitioner, Fergus O'Kelly. There, too, 10 per cent of the young people were injecting heroin daily. We did a similar study with Father Brian Power in an area of flat-dwellers in Dun Laoghaire where there was a similar high abuse of heroin and other opiates. From garda (police) information we knew that at the time in other cities of Ireland there was little heroin abuse, although in Cork there was abuse of synthetic opiates, obtained on prescription.

Analysis of the area of residence of the patients treated by staff at Jervis Street Drug Treatment Centre in Dublin, under the direction of Dr Michael Kelly, showed that there had been a steady increase in the number of patients attending for opiate addiction in the four years of the study (182 in 1979 to 1,028 in 1983). There was no electoral ward in Dublin free of heroin and other opiate-related problems. Drug abuse was, nevertheless, most frequent in north-central and south-central Dublin and in certain wards in Dun Laoghaire.

The two major reasons for the abuse of opiates were the importation and sale of heroin and the sale of synthetic opiates obtained from a small number of doctors. Urgent action was taken by the Minister for Health and the Medical Council to warn the doctors who were responsible for synthetic opiates being freely available that if they did not stop prescribing these drugs in such a heedless way, they would be struck off the medical register. As a result, the quantity of synthetic opiates available rapidly diminished. The Garda Drug Squad was also strengthened and managed to convict some of the major heroin importers. The drug barons did not deal in the sale of drugs themselves, and so were very difficult to convict. Erskine Childers, when he was Minister for Health, had stopped amphetamine abuse in Dublin by the simple expedient of banning all sales of amphetamines by chemists.

There was great concern, particularly among parents, about the heroin epidemic and the crime and illness that resulted, such as infective hepatitis. In north-central and south-central Dublin, 'concerned parents' groups were formed to deal with the heroin pushers in their own areas, and they generally succeeded in forcing them to leave the neighbourhood. While the concerned parents' methods were at the edge of the law, they were certainly effective and probably more effective than the work of the gardaí. It is interesting to note that at this time there was no serious heroin problem in Belfast, probably because the paramilitaries, republican and loyalist, dealt harshly with anyone attempting to sell heroin, usually by 'knee-capping' or by breaking one or more limbs. Other drugs such as cannabis and more recently ecstasy, on the other hand, are easily obtainable.

The sudden growth in the number of heroin users in Dublin was a consequence of the easy availability of heroin in Western Europe – imported from Iran following the fall of the Shah in 1979, and from Pakistan in the 1980s. At the Jervis Street Drug Treatment Centre in the 1980s, opiates were found to be the commonest drug of abuse, followed by barbiturates and cannabis and, to a much lesser extent, LSD.

The vast majority of heroin users had come from the poorest section of the community. Most had left school early, and three-quarters had never passed any examination. Only one in five had any kind of paid employment. The typical progression in drug abuse was from cigarettes to alcohol, to cannabis, to heroin, although once they were taking heroin daily, they spent money on heroin rather than on alcohol. In comparison with the control group, those in the same sex, age-group and area of residence who did not inject heroin, the abusers socialised much less. They were little influenced by family and much more by their friends who were taking drugs; they had a poor educational and employment record, were generally unemployed, smoked heavily, and spent little on alcohol but often had a drinking problem in their families. A high proportion had been arrested for a variety of offences and were found more frequently than the control group to have lost one or both parents through death. There is no doubt that unemployment was a major factor, and an effort was made in central Dublin to start social centres and provide alternative leisure activities for young people.

We publicised our findings on the heroin problem. Perhaps

more was done by the Church than by the state to deal with heroin addiction. The priests in the affected area, particular Paul Lavelle, were able to mix with the heroin users and addicts and knew them by their first names. They did not pose a threat, whereas the state, the gardaí, did because they would arrest those taking illicit drugs. The clergy started social clubs, such as the 'Anna Liffey', and were able to deal with the young people as individuals. When Paul Lavelle met the prisoners and went round the flats, he carried packets of cigarettes and would pass one to the young man or woman with whom he was talking. For all my conviction about the dangers of cigarette smoking, I realised that this was a very good tactic.

In 1984/85, there was evidence of a definite reduction in the number of young people in north-central and south-central Dublin who were starting to use heroin, and there was a fall in the first-time attendance at the Jervis Street Drug Treatment Centre. The gardaí also reported a reduction in the amount of heroin and Diaconal that was available on the streets. Against this good news, a new and dreadful problem arose: infection by the Human Immunodeficiency Virus (HIV), the virus responsible for AIDS. Infective hepatitis had long been a problem among heroin injectors, who generally shared their needles and syringes, but the new problem of infection by HIV made even more urgent the need for education about the danger of infection from sharing 'gear'. In the 1990s there was a big increase in the use of heroin, although there was a change away from injecting to smoking the heroin (chasing the dragon). Among those who still injected heroin a smaller percentage shared their 'gear' as a result of the free distribution of syringes and needles. In Ireland, as elsewhere, a number of haemophiliacs had been infected with the AIDS virus from blood, or blood products, taken to treat their haemorrhagic tendency, before it was realised that these blood products, imported from the United States, were infected by the virus. There was a relatively small number of homosexuals in Ireland, some of whom were infected by the AIDS virus. The majority of those infected by HIV in Ireland were the heroin injectors, and later some of their girl-friends or boyfriends and, very sadly, even their children. Fortunately, the spread of the virus among the heterosexual population in Ireland has been slow to develop, no doubt owing in great measure to the fact that prostitution is today relatively limited.

In 1990 and 1991, after retiring as director of the board, I undertook a study to find out how many of the original patients from north-central, south-central Dublin and Dun Laoghaire were HIV positive. Of those tested, 86 per cent were infected by the AIDS virus and many had died. The realisation that Ireland, like the rest of the world, was threatened with a pandemic of infection by the AIDS virus resulted in the Department of Health instigating publicity campaigns about the danger of spreading infection by sexual contact. The emphasis in Ireland was on no sex before marriage and keeping to one sexual partner. This, of course, was the teaching of the Catholic Church and, if adhered to, is undoubtedly the surest way to avoid infection by the virus. The Church formed a committee, of which I was the chairman and Paul Lavelle was the secretary and the guiding light, to work with the main groups who were liable to be infected by the AIDS virus, including representatives of the haemophiliacs and of the gay movements and, of course, of the drug users themselves. The committee included representatives of the Church and of other organisations that were working in the inner city.

In Britain, there had been much publicity about 'safer sex': while the best protection against infection by the AIDS virus is abstinence, if you did have intercourse outside of marriage, you were advised to use a condom. There is very good evidence that using a condom does greatly reduce the risk of passing on the AIDS virus, but using a condom is against the teaching of the Catholic Church. Fortunately, we now know that, in North America and in the developed countries of Europe, heterosexual intercourse does not present such a high risk of infection with HIV as was previously feared, although the risk is greater for women than it is for men. In the 1990s the majority of those infected in Ireland are the past or present heroin injectors and their children.

The condom question raised a major problem for Ireland. The Catholic Church opposed the use of a condom under any circumstances, because it prevented the primary purpose of sexual intercourse: procreation. I put forward the argument that if one person within a marriage was HIV positive, it should be permissible to use a condom for the primary purpose of preventing HIV infection and not to prevent conception. Paul Lavelle went along with this argument and pamphlets were printed for distribution by Veritas, the Catholic publishers. They emphasised that the sure way not to become infected with the virus was to keep to the Catholic teaching of no sex outside of marriage and sticking to one partner, but that if, for any reason, one person in a marriage was infected by HIV, the condom could be used to prevent the other person becoming infected.

The day before this pamphlet was to be distributed, the Archbishop of Dublin, Desmond O'Connell, forbade its distribution. Shortly afterwards Father Lavelle was transferred to Lusk, a parish outside Dublin. In my opinion, Paul Lavelle has done more to deal with the heroin problem in Ireland, and to help to prevent the spread of AIDS, than anyone else. He has a wonderful ability to mix with people of all social classes. He is a good priest and a good man.

There is no doubt that HIV infection is the plague of our age. In many towns in Africa 30 per cent of those aged 15–34 are already infected with the virus, which means that there is every likelihood, unless some wonder drug is found, that they will die from AIDS. In Africa, sufferers do not survive after infection as long as they do in Ireland. The only good news for Ireland and the developed countries is that heterosexual spread is slower than was feared. This is not true in Africa, in the West Indies, South-East Asia and South America, perhaps because among the populations of these areas other infections, frequently genital infections, are often present, and resistance to infection is low.

CHAPTER 21

China

Serve the people.
Mao Tse-Tung, *The Little Red Book*

In 1975, I was asked to take part in an EEC symposium on multiple sclerosis at the CIBA Foundation, now the Novartis Foundation, named after a drug company, at 41 Portland Place, London. Four doors away, at number 49, I saw the Embassy of the People's Republic of China. The idea suddenly came to me that I should call on the Chinese ambassador to see whether it would be possible to arrange for a visit of Irish doctors to China. I had long been fascinated by what I had read about the Chinese use of traditional and modern medicine, and the widespread use of paramedics to improve the health of their one billion people.

I rang the bell at the Embassy and asked to speak to the ambassador. I was courteously brought to see him. Having introduced myself, I asked him if the Chinese government would consider inviting a group of Irish doctors to visit China so that they might see at first hand how the Chinese looked after the health of their people. Three weeks later I received a letter from the president of the Chinese Academy of Medical Sciences inviting myself and nine other Irish doctors to visit China in May 1976, as guests of the Academy. I was asked to choose the doctors.

Because this was difficult, I wrote to the editor of the *Irish Medical Journal* asking him to publish a notice that those doctors who would like to go should write to me. There were over eighty replies. I chose doctors who represented different medical disciplines. Besides myself, they included: a professor of social medicine, the medical editor of *The Irish Times*, a psychiatrist, a neurologist, two general practitioners, one from Cork and one from the West of Ireland, an expert in mental retardation in children, a micro-biologist and a specialist in diseases of the eye. We were eight men and two women.

The visit was scheduled for May 1976 but in March, while energetically doing the dance from 'Zorba the Greek' at a party, I ruptured my right Achilles tendon. When it was repaired, my leg was in plaster up to my hip. I requested that the visit be postponed until September. Unfortunately in July there was a severe earthquake in north-eastern China, close to Beijing, with up to one million casualties. So the visit was postponed until early October, shortly after the death of Chairman Mao Tse-Tung.

We flew to Beijing, via Addis Ababa, arriving in Ethiopia on a day when there was a revolt against the ruling party, the Dergue. Our plane was delayed, so we moved to a hotel where we had our first meeting with a group of Chinese. They belonged to a dance ensemble, sent to Ethiopia as part of Chinese public relations. They were cheerful company!

We found Beijing airport very small and homely by international standards. We were warmly welcomed by the president of the Chinese Academy of Medicine, Professor Huang, his colleagues and the interpreters. They had been waiting for us at the airport for twelve hours. We then started a routine that was to be with us throughout our stay in China: the tea ceremony. We sat around in a group, had tea poured for us out of thermos flasks and listened to an address of welcome. It was the first of many. I soon realised that at all these addresses, and on some days there were three or four, I, as the so-called 'responsible person', was expected to reply.

We were ushered to six waiting cars. I accompanied President Huang in the front car. This procedure continued throughout our stay. Whoever was the Chinese leader of the particular meeting to which we were going would sit with me in the leading car. I found this embarrassing because I did not wish to take the limelight from my colleagues, but I soon realised that I had no choice. Throughout our stay, we had VIP treatment. We stayed in large rooms with bathrooms at the Peking Hotel, overlooking the Forbidden City. After Beijing we visited Shanghai, Canton and rural areas near Wushih.

We found that in China, following Chairman Mao's teachings, there had been an attempt to combine traditional medicine, which includes the use of herbs and remedies such as acupuncture, with modern medicine. By this means, hundreds of thousands of 'doctors' who used traditional Chinese methods had been incorporated into the medical system. It also meant that in the country and in the factories, it was possible for the peasants and workers to receive treatment largely independent of modern, and often expensive, drugs. For most minor disorders the people received traditional methods of treatment by paramedics, known as the 'barefoot doctors', who had perhaps only eighteen months' training. They were not, in fact, barefoot but wore gym shoes. In all the hospitals we visited, we saw patients treated both by modern methods (the general medical knowledge of the physicians in the chief hospitals was excellent) and by traditional medicine, particularly acupuncture.

In China there did not appear to be the surveillance that I had found in the Soviet Union in 1962. For example, we never saw a policeman except for the traffic police. The State Bureau of Security and the 'neighbourhood system' undoubtedly kept tabs on all that was going on, but the control was much more subtle than in the USSR. On the other hand, there were many meetings for 'self-criticism'. No one was allowed to depart from the party line and there was very little freedom of thought.

One evening we were shown a recent Chinese film, *Spring Sprout*, about a young 'barefoot doctor' who is training at the local hospital. She, the Spring Sprout of the story, endeavours to cure Uncle Han's lumbago with traditional herbs which she collects in the mountains. The head of the hospital – obviously a 'bad guy' – makes life very difficult for Spring Sprout and does not believe that the herbal medicine will work. Nevertheless, she cures Uncle Han's lumbago, to general public rejoicing in the village.

Many of the doctors we met had been sent to work on the land during the Cultural Revolution when the young people and students were 're-educating' the established leaders. Some we talked with were clearly not displeased at Madame Mao's fall from power. She was very radical in her thinking. Perhaps *Spring Sprout* would not have been such a popular film.

When we were in Shanghai, the 'Gang of Four', including Chairman Mao's widow, were arrested. On a portable radio we heard the BBC Overseas Service say that there was rioting in the city. There was no sign of unrest and David Nowlan sent a cable from Shanghai to *The Irish Times*, describing how peaceful everything was. It published the true state of affairs before other newspapers.

We were taken for a trip up the Yangtze on a steamboat. On board was a good conjuror. He had a big trunk and he asked for a volunteer to get in it and he or she would be made to disappear. No one else volunteered, so I climbed in. When the box was opened for the audience, I had disappeared, to the great amusement of my friends. As far as I know, I had stayed in the box.

We visited two schools and I often think of the five-year-old girl in a blue uniform taking me by the hand and showing me around – all the time talking non-stop in Chinese. They were delightful children.

We visited a number of rural communes, where there were numerous 'barefoot' doctors among the workers. Housing was free, and grain, generally rice, was provided by the commune to all the workers, cheaply, on a points system; men had 10 points, women 8 points and those deemed to be 'politically unreliable' 7 points. By European standards personal income was extremely low, but everybody we met appeared to have sufficient food and reasonable comfort. In many ways life in the communes was similar to that in the kibbutzim I had visited in Israel.

Because of my special interest in multiple sclerosis, patients with the disease were admitted for us to examine in hospitals in Beijng, Shanghai and Canton. We found that the MS in China was different from the MS seen in Europe and North America. It more commonly occurred in children; it tended to affect the optic nerve severely, like a form of the disease uncommon in Europe, 'Devic Syndrome'; and it was likely to cause paralysis rather than ataxia or unsteadiness. MS is uncommon in China. It is very similar to the type of MS that had been reported from Japan.

We visited the Shanghai Medical College, which takes in about 600 medical students every year. The students were chosen at that time from the 'peasants, workers and soldiers', in collaboration with the Communist Party. All the candidates had spent at least two years working in factories or on the land since leaving school. The medical course lasted for three years, and it appeared that everyone qualified. Students were allowed to use their books and discuss questions with their colleagues during examination; there was no set time limit. There were more women medical students than men. A proportion of the graduates would be selected for training in special departments of medicine. There was no difference in the title 'doctor' among college graduates, 'barefoot doctors' (who had perhaps only had a few months' training in a communal hospital) and nurses, who also treated patients. In medical training at university level there was a great emphasis on traditional medicine and the use of herbs and fungi. No doubt many of these have effective pharmacological action and a number of important drugs in the West have come from plants, for instance digitalis, atropine and opium.

We were entertained lavishly to meals with many courses. At every one I was expected to make a short speech and propose toasts. There is no doubt that the Chinese show more sensitivity and courtesy than is usual in the West; some of our group were unduly thrusting and sometimes interrupted the Chinese interpreters before they had finished a sentence. Our two interpreters, Dr Wu, aged about forty, and Mrs Han, who was perhaps thirty, had a good sense of humour. Mrs Han told us the story of how when she was describing 'hen soup' to a party of prominent visitors, forgetting the word for hen she said, 'the soup of the wife of the cock'!

We visited health centres which emphasised preventive medicine and the control of the 'four pests' – flies, mosquitoes, bedbugs and rats. A record card was kept for every women and baby. The women were expected to mark on their card the date of the onset of their menses to make sure they were not pregnant. Family planning was the most important part of the health centres' work, and contraceptives were provided free for married women.

At the Hua Sha Hospital in Shanghai, we saw a number of operations in which acupuncture was used to prevent pain, including open heart, thyroid and brain operations. The patients had no anaesthetic or analgesic, except for a very small dose of Dolantin, an opium derivative, equal to about one-twentieth of a grain of morphine. An acupuncture needle was inserted in the patient's face and ear. An electrical stimulus machine, giving a mild electric impulse at a rate of about 120 a minute, was attached to the needle. The patients were fully conscious and appeared completely relaxed. The acupuncture continued for about twenty minutes before the operation started and some of the operations lasted for several hours. The acupuncture needles and the six-volt intermittent current applied to the needle appeared to be causing no pain, nor was the operation. One patient complained that her feet were cold and asked for an additional blanket. It was impressive. How does it work? I suspect it can be used only on a proportion of Chinese and that it is tried out on the patient before a decision is made to use it for the operation. The Chinese are conditioned to expect acupuncture to work and it was used very frequently to relieve pain. I doubt if it would be so effective as an anaesthetic in Western culture because we would not have the same confidence in its success as do the Chinese. In the West it often helps to relieve pain, particularly among those who believe it will help them.

It was interesting to see the difference between China and Europe in the epidemiology of a number of cancers. In south China, cancer of the nose, throat and pharynx was the commonest cancer, followed by cancer of the liver and the stomach and only then by cancer of the lung, the most common cancer in men in Europe and North America. The Chinese doctors thought that there was a genetic predisposition, as well as an environmental factor, responsible for the high naso-pharyngeal cancer rates. Oesophageal cancer was common, perhaps because of the popularity of sour cabbage. Hens fed on this cabbage often also develop cancer of the oesophagus. Lung cancer was four times more common in men than in women and was rapidly increasing in frequency. Little was being done at the time to discourage smoking.

I liked the formal way people addressed each other. Young people were addressed as 'Xiao', pronounced 'Shau' – meaning 'young'; Mrs Han would be called Xiao Han, 'young Han'. On the other hand, if she wanted to talk to an older person respectfully, she would speak to them as 'Lao', which means 'old'. I was 'Lao Dean'.

On our last evening in China, we had a state dinner with the president of the Academy of Medical Sciences. I wanted to say something new because I felt that I was boring my colleagues. I therefore asked the rhetorical question: 'Who are the four men who may most have affected our social thinking?' The four who came to my mind were: Moses, the Lawgiver, translated by Huang as Moshe for Chinese guests who did not understand English; Jesus, who taught us to love one another – translated by Huang as Jehu; and Karl Marx, who spoke for a fair distribution of wealth. It was interesting, I commented, that all three should be Jews. Then, to flatter my Chinese friends, I added Chairman Mao! Professor Huang, immediately asked me publicly, 'What about Confucius?' At this time Confucius was out of favour because he emphasised the importance of the family and respect for older people, rather than that of the state, so this was a courageous intervention.

I realised that in this first visit to China, we were to some extent brainwashed and that the system at that time discouraged initiative and private enterprise. This was to change. The form of communism that had developed in China appeared to me to be much less bureaucratic, and much more human, cheerful and friendly, than the communism I had seen in the Soviet Union. I would not like to live in either country because I am moulded by the freedom and individualism of the West, but, if I had to make a choice, I would choose to live in China because of the general humanity of the people and the atmosphere of enthusiasm and cheerfulness. It reminded me of the descriptions of the communal life of the early Christians: love of neighbour without a belief in God. Three of Chairman Mao's aphorisms particularly impressed me: 'put the emphasis on the rural areas'; 'women hold up half the sky'; and 'serve the people'.

In retrospect, we were so well entertained in China, and shown only the best, that we did not fully appreciate at the time the immense damage to society that had resulted from the Cultural Revolution. At that time the students and young people were encouraged to attack their teachers, and the elite, such as professors in the university, were sent to work in the lowest of occupations in the countryside. Nor did we fully appreciate the inefficiency of a system in which people were chosen for the university by how well they supported Chairman Mao, not by their ability. An excellent account of what life was really like both before and after the establishment of communism was written much later by a Chinese graduate in English literature, Jung Chang, in her book *Wild Swans* (1991).

We returned to Ireland via Addis Ababa. Here David Nowlan and I left the plane and our friends continued on to Dublin. David wished to visit the Irish nurses and priests sent by the Irish relief organisation Trōcaire. The poverty, starvation and disease in Ethiopia were the worst I have ever seen. The country was in civil war, corrupt, and run as a military dictatorship. There were no staff in the two large foreign-built hospitals in Addis Ababa. In the rural areas, we saw Irish nurses in the clinics, working in almost impossible conditions, with little in the way of useful drugs for the patients. Ethiopia was crying out for a system of paramedics, such as we had seen in China. Perhaps the most urgent problem was the very high birth rate and the need for family planning. I left Ethiopia with great admiration for the work the Irish nurses and priests were doing there in caring for the desperately poor. The clinics were generally run by two nurses. With no doctors to advise them, they had to undertake surgery that would normally be done by a doctor, and also teach family planning, the need for clean water and how good hygiene would reduce disease.

One month after returning from China, my pyjamas, which I had left behind by accident in Beijing, arrived by post, having been sewn in a hand-towel into a perfect parcel. It was impossible to lose anything in China!

Following our visit to China, the Chinese opened an embassy in Dublin and, in 1980, I was able to arrange for the Medico-Social Research Board to invite five Chinese doctors to visit Ireland. They were Professor Teng Chia-Tung, the vice-president of the Chinese Academy of Medical Sciences; Feng, professor of neurology in Beijing; Wang, professor of orthopaedics; Zhao, a neurologist; and Wu, our interpreter during our visit to China and then in the Division of Foreign Affairs of the Chinese Academy of Medical Sciences. All five could speak good English. We showed them the work of the Medico-Social Research Board and our hospitals and social services. They were entertained by the board and by the President of Ireland, Dr Patrick Hillery, and his wife, Maeve, at

Aras an Uachtaráin. In Cork, as guests of Dr Dermot Gleeson, they had the unusual experience of staying at a monastery. In the West of Ireland Dr Seán Maguire of Castlebar, a general practitioner, took them to a number of farms and to Ballinrobe races. I think their visits to the farms in the West of Ireland was a highlight of their visit to Ireland. I then arranged for them to visit England, to see the research taking place on multiple sclerosis. Later, during the same visit, as guests of the MS Society, they visited the United States of America. We were able to repay at least some of our Chinese hosts with an unusual visit to the West.

Following the visit of the Chinese doctors, the president of the Chinese Academy of Medical Sciences, now Professor Huang Chia-Tsu, asked me to choose five world experts in MS research to visit China with me for two weeks as guests of the Academy. I chose Barry Arnason, Floyd Davis, Reginald Kelly, John Sever and the scientific advisor of the MS Society of the United States, Byron Waksman. Byron was the son of Selman Waksman, who found that streptomycin, cultured from a soil bacterium, was effective in treating tuberculosis. We went to China for two weeks in 1981 and published the report about demyelinating disease (multiple sclerosis) in China in *The Lancet* in March 1982. As a result of these visits, we were able to involve Chinese neurologists in research into the aetiology of multiple sclerosis with Japanese and Western neurologists. This collaboration continues.

I still receive, written in impeccable English, letters from my Chinese friends, in particular from Professor Chia-Tung, whom I now address, at his request, by his initials 'C.T.' I often think about my fortuitous call on the Chinese ambassador in Portland Place, London, and the speed with which he followed up my suggestion to invite a group of Irish doctors to China.

CHAPTER 22

Retirement and
a Shotgun Marriage

Life is short, the art is long;
The occasion fleeting,
Experience fallacious;
And judgement difficult.
Hippocrates of Kos

Towards the end of 1985, when I was about to retire as director of the Medico-Social Research Board, I was asked by the medical adviser of the Agricultural Institute of Ireland, Dr Alan O'Grady, if I would undertake a study on the cause of death in men in the research and technical staff at the institute, because there appeared to be a high number of deaths from cancer among them before they reached retirement age.

The national agricultural research organisation, now renamed the Agriculture and Food Development Authority, has its head-quarters in Dublin and has seven major centres. The research programme carried out at the centres covers a broad spectrum of activities relevant to the agricultural industry. The director of the institute, Dr Pierce Ryan, through the personnel officers, provided me with a list of the research and technical workers who had died while still working at the institute and a breakdown of the work-force by age. I obtained copies of their death certificates and their hospital records. The work and medical histories of those who had died were also obtained from the personnel officers' records.

There had been, in the previous twenty years, twenty-one

deaths among the research and seven among the technical staff, all men; eleven of the twenty-eight deaths were from cancer. Four of the eleven cancer deaths were from primary brain cancers; three were from leukaemia, and one death was from Hodgkin's disease, a disorder related to leukaemia. There were also two deaths from abdominal cancers of unknown primary source, probably due to cancer of the pancreas, and one from cancer of the stomach. Approximately one in thirty of all cancer deaths, or one per cent of all deaths, would have been the 'expected' number from primary brain tumours in males in the age-group 40–64 years. Leukaemia and lymphatic cancers are relatively uncommon cancers to cause death.

In April 1986 I prepared a report on the high proportional mortality from brain and blood cancers among the research staff of the institute. After reading the report, Dr Pierce Ryan told me to stop the study and that I would have no further access to the institute's records. He would make his own enquiries with an internal committee.

About this time, *The Irish Times* reported that there had been more than the expected number of blood cancer deaths among the research and technical staff at the Pasteur Institute in Paris. I went to see an old friend, Calum Muir, of the International Agency for Research on Cancer in Lyon, and he arranged for me to visit the chairman of the committee that was researching the problem in Paris, Professor Jean Barnard. The number who had died from leukaemia in the Pasteur Institute was less than at Ireland's Agricultural Institute. At another Paris institute, the Orsay Institute, more than the expected number of deaths had been reported as the result of primary brain cancers. I suspected that the small cluster of brain and blood cancers among the research and technical staff in the Agricultural Institute was unlikely to be due to chance and was probably attributable to one of three possible causes: the effect of radiation from radioactive isotopes; a virus infection; or, most likely of all, the absorption of some organic chemical or chemicals used in their research work for the institute. It had been reported, for instance, that the by-products of dioxin, the 'agent orange' of the Vietnam War, could cause cancer. Some of the related products of dioxin had been used as a weedkiller in Ireland.

The small clusters of brain and blood cancers in the staff of the Agricultural Institute and at the Pasteur and Orsay Institutes stimulated the International Agency for Research on Cancer to hold an international symposium on cancer in laboratory research workers in Lyon in January 1989. At this symposium I described my findings among the research workers at the Agricultural Institute. My paper was reported in *The Irish Times*, to the extreme annoyance of Pierce Ryan, who appeared on television that night (I was still in Lyon) and said I had no right to reveal the information and that he had forbidden me to study the problem further.

This was the only research project in which I have been blocked because those who had requested it did not like the results. I had obtained from the hospital records the histories of the patients who had died of cancer and I also had the details of their employment background. I drew up a report for the International Agency for Research on Cancer because they had a particular interest in cancer occurring in laboratory research workers. IARC suggested that I should undertake a study on the cause of death among all farm workers in Ireland and this study was funded by the European Community. I found that farm workers in general in Ireland had an excellent expectation of life, better than that of city-dwellers, and that they did not have any increased mortality from brain and blood cancers, unlike the research staff at the Agricultural Institute. I prepared a paper reporting my studies and it was published in the *Journal of Epidemiology & Community Health* in 1994.

The same year further study was reported by Leslie Daly, Bernadette Herity and Geoffrey Bourke, which included not only men of working age at the Agricultural Institute, but also those who had retired from the institute. This study confirmed my findings that there was a significantly higher than expected mortality in men below the age of retirement from brain and blood cancers. It also showed an increase in cancer of the bladder in older men who had retired and who had previously worked at the Agricultural Institute.

Before the Medico-Social Research Board began its work in Ireland, there was already in existence a Medical Research Council

(MRC). This council, which was similar in many ways to the MRC in the United Kingdom, was a grant-giving body which, in Ireland, largely represented the interests of the consultants at the various teaching hospitals. Besides giving grants to hospital and laboratory research projects, the MRC also ran a research laboratory at Trinity College, Dublin. The Department of Health had long desired to bring the MRC under its control and to close the laboratory at Trinity College. In 1984, Barry Desmond, the Minister for Health, decided that both the MSRB and the MRC should be brought under the management of a single board, whose members would be appointed by the Department. In order to further this change, the Minister had not appointed new members to the board of the MSRB, and in 1985, Dr Brendan Hensey was replaced as chairman by Jerry O'Dwyer, assistant secretary in the Department of Health.

Neither I, as director of the Medico-Social Research Board, nor the Medical Research Council wished to lose independent status for our research institutes and we fought valiantly to prevent a 'shotgun marriage'. Because the Department of Health provided most of the funds for the MSRB and the MRC, agreement was eventually forced and, in August 1986, the Minister for Health announced the establishment of a new board, to be known as the Health Research Board. This new board was to come into effect on 1 January 1987 at the offices of the Medico-Social Research Board in Baggot Street. Barry Desmond promised that, on the foundation of the new board, funds for research would be increased. In the event they were nearly halved!

During the eighteen years I was director of the Medico-Social Research Board, I was able to involve many overseas organisations in supporting research in Ireland and elsewhere. I was also able to continue with my own special interest: research into neurological disorders, in particular multiple sclerosis and motor neuron disease.

I was officially due to retire in 1983 on reaching the age of 65, but because the Minister was hoping to create the new Health Research Board, I was asked to continue in office for a further two years. I was anxious that a director should replace me who was trained in epidemiology and medical and social research and that, preferably, he or she should be someone with experience in community medicine. The Minister for Health decided that my replacement should not be a medical doctor, perhaps because over the years I have been considered to be too independent and because I had undertaken research in Ireland that did not always meet with the approval of the civil servants in the Department. No director was appointed to the new board, but a chief executive officer, Dr Vivian O'Gorman, an able administrator, was appointed from Forbairt, now named Enterprise Ireland.

In order to gain the approval of the members of the Medical Research Council in the formation of the new board, the Minister had agreed that half the members of the newly created board should represent the old interests of the council – that is, in the main, consultant staff of the teaching hospitals. As a result of the down-grading of medico-social research, the morale of the research staff of the old MSRB was low. The trend of the new board has been towards funding research projects in hospitals and laboratories. Medico-social research has taken a very poor second place.

The demise of the Medico-Social Research Board and its forced amalgamation with the Medical Research Council, while it was thought to be politically expedient, I regard as my major failure in Ireland. Perhaps I did not spend sufficient time with the politics of how the board should continue after my retirement. If I had been able to appoint a strong assistant director who could have taken my place, it might have been more difficult to appoint a chief executive officer as administrator. It was difficult to find a doctor of medicine of the right calibre to act as assistant director because the salaries offered were low, compared with those in medical prac-tice. I had been able to maintain a reasonable income because, owing to the terms of the agreement when I was appointed, I could spend one-fifth of my time working on my own account and receive funds for research projects that I undertook abroad. The political reason for forming the new board was, as far as I could see, so that the Medical Research Council could be brought under the control of a board chosen by the government and would not be too autonomous.

Another board, the Health Education Council, had been summarily disbanded shortly before the forced amalgamation of the MSRB and the MRC. This followed publicity it had prepared about the steps that could be taken to avoid HIV infection in the general population, in which they had included the use of condoms.

Among the Medico-Social Research Board's major projects were the hospital in-patient enquiry scheme, the psychiatric reporting systems, and reporting systems and studies on mental handicap and on the care of unmarried mothers. The board had carried out over 100 research projects into the medical and social problems affecting the people of Ireland. The results of these projects, eventually published in reputable journals, were well publicised; they led to the alleviation of many of Ireland's major social problems. On the inauguration of the new Health Research Board, the most important project of the MSRB, the hospital in-patient enquiry scheme, was brought under the aegis of the Economic and Social Research Institute, and lost most of its research potential. It was no longer directed by a doctor of medicine and was used mainly for hospital management. Within a short time the scheme was receiving reports of only 55 per cent of hospital discharges since it no longer had the support of many of the hospital consultants. However, it has slowly regained its former high level of support.

I often wonder what I could have done to prevent the disbanding of the Medico-Social Research Board. Perhaps I could not have prevented it. My hope is that the wheel will go full-circle and the Health Research Board will return to undertaking more studies on how social conditions and lifestyle affect health in Ireland.

CHAPTER 23

Cyprus, Turkey and Spain

Sana söylerim kizim, sen is it gelinim.
I tell it to you, my daughter, so that
my daughter-in-law may hear it.

Turkish Cypriot saying

I am sometimes teased that I choose beautiful and interesting islands on which to undertake research. There is truth in this and one of the reasons is that island populations can be ascertained fairly accurately since they are relatively closed communities. In 1985 a letter arrived from Dr Ntinos Myrianthopoulos, an advisor to the National Institute of Heath in Bethesda, Maryland. He told me he was a Greek Cypriot and that he considered that Cyprus would be an ideal island in which to undertake a study on the prevalence of multiple sclerosis. He said that he was friendly with one of the neurologists on the island, Dr Lefkos Middleton, who was interested in collaborating with me in such a study.

Recalling the words of well-known detective story writer Edgar Wallace – 'case the joint' – I decided to visit Cyprus before making up my mind. First, I found out the history of Cyprus. Over the centuries Cyprus has been invaded many times. Richard Coeur de Lion, on his way to a Crusade, conquered Cyprus in the thirteenth century and the island was sold to another Norman family, the Lusignans. The Greek-speaking Cypriots belong to the Cypriot Orthodox Church, an independent branch of the Eastern Orthodox Church.

In 1572 Cyprus was conquered by the Turks, who then ruled the country until 1878. The Turks permitted the Orthodox bishops and priests, but not the Roman Catholics, to continue as leaders of the Christians in the country. In 1853, Turkey sold Cyprus for a nominal amount to Britain in return for its support against Russia. After the Second World War there was considerable unrest against British rule and, among many Greek Cypriots, a demand for enosis, or union, with Greece. Enosis was strongly opposed by the Turkish-speaking Cypriots and by the British, who generally used Turkish Cypriots to police the island. In 1960, Cyprus gained independence from Britain and Archbishop Makarios became president of Cyprus. He was overthrown in 1974 and a puppet of the 'Greek Colonels' of mainland Greece, Sampson, was installed as president. When this happened, Turkey invaded the northern part of the island, rather than see Cyprus become part of greater Greece, and the Greeks were forced to leave their orange groves and farms in the north and move south. The Turks in the south moved to the area occupied by the Turkish army in the north of the island. The capital, Nicosia, was divided, the northern half under Turkish-Cypriot and the southern half under Greek-Cypriot control. The line between the Greek and Turkish areas is separated by a no-man's land, policed and controlled since 1974 by the United Nations. The British still retain two military bases in Greek-speaking Cyprus.

I flew to Cyprus in 1985 and found that Paphos district, in the east of Greek-speaking Cyprus, appeared to be a good area in which to start studying the prevalence of MS. The population of Paphos district, 30,000, was about right and there was a hospital in the city of Paphos itself. I found the district beautiful and the people charming and helpful.

I met Dr Lefkos Middleton in Paphos and we agreed to collaborate in a study into the prevalence of MS among the Greek-speaking Cypriots, if we had financial support. Lefkos, I found, was an exceptionally good neurologist. He spoke perfect French and had trained at the Salpêtrière Hospital in Paris, a famous hospital for neurological disease, renowned for the pioneer work there of Jean-Martin Charcot. Charcot gave the first full medical description of multiple sclerosis.

Lefkos was an excellent host and raconteur. He was a Greek Cypriot and his father had changed his name to a British one,

Middleton, in the days when Britain ruled Cyprus. He knew all the politicians and everybody of importance among the Greek Cypriots and the senior staff of the United Nations in the island. On returning to Ireland, I asked the National Institute of Health, Bethesda, Maryland, for financial support and received a research grant.

It proved to be 'notebook and shoe leather' research. Each summer I would travel to Paphos with Maria, Gordon and Elizabeth and spend two months searching for patients who had any neurological disorder that might have been MS. In the villages everyone was friendly and many people could speak some English. It was unknown at that time to lock the car and almost impossible to lose anything since the people were honest. The records in the hospitals and the doctors' files were poor and I could only find MS patients by talking to key informants in the villages. When I went to a village, I would go straight to the coffee shop, with Julie Siaelie, a physiotherapist from Paphos Hospital who acted as interpreter. We would talk to the *Muktar*, or mayor of the village, who knew everybody. I visited all the doctors, most of whom lived in Paphos city, and the neurologists in the main Greek-Cypriot cities, Nicosia, Limassol and Larnaca. The director of the Paphos Social Services, Socrates Kleantous, and his staff assisted me.

Socrates told me that in Kathikas and Arodhes, sister villages a mile apart, there were a number of people who were unsteady in their movements or unable to walk and who might have MS. I went to these villages and found, on examination, that these individuals did not have MS but another disease of the nervous system, Friedreich's Ataxia. I was already interested in Friedreich's Ataxia and had seen many patients with the disorder. Starting in the teenage years, it causes unsteadiness in the legs and arms. It is a genetic disorder and the gene responsible must be inherited from both symptomless parents for the symptoms of the disorder to appear. In Kathikas-Arodhes there were eight people with Friedreich's Ataxia in a population of 2,400 and there were also six others affected who had been born in the village but were living elsewhere. They were all related.

Finding the Friedreich's Ataxia extended family in Kathikas-Arodhes is a typical example of the 'lucky chance', which has followed me in research throughout my life. It appeared to be a unique opportunity to trace the responsible gene because the family was so large. I asked Sue Chamberlain, a genetic research worker whom I knew was interested in Friedreich's Ataxia, to join me from St Mary's Hospital in London. We took blood from all members of the family and this helped her to trace the gene responsible for Friedreich's Ataxia to chromosome number 9. Later, the exact location of the DNA gene was found. The abnormal gene affects one of the body's proteins, Frataxin. Tracing the Friedreich's Ataxia gene means that it is now possible to detect those without symptoms who carry the gene and they can ensure that they do not marry another carrier. If two carriers of the gene marry, on average one in four of the children will be affected, two in four will inherit the gene from one parent only and be a 'carrier', and only one in four will not inherit the gene.

I decided in 1988 to extend the MS study to the Greek-speaking Famagusta district at the west of the island and once again I was lucky! In one village, Liopetri, there were seven people with multiple sclerosis who were all members of one extended family. By studying this family, and other large families where several members were affected by MS, it will in the future be possible to find the gene or genes that predispose to MS, but this has not yet been achieved. The prevalence of MS in Greek-speaking Cyprus was at least 44 per 100,000, much the same prevalence as in Sicily and not the low prevalence that occurred in Malta. Lefkos Middleton and I found no higher MS prevalence in the cold Troodhos mountain area, a skiing resort, than in the warm coastal Paphos and Greek Famagusta areas, so climatic temperature was not in itself a contributory factor for MS.

Cyprus is a paradise for research into neurological diseases. In the past the roads between the villages were bad or non-existent and people nearly always married within their own village. There is a Greek-Cypriot proverb: 'Better a shoe from your place even if it is patched.' Because people married within their own village, often a near relative, a number of genetically determined disorders occur from close intermarriage; for example, in one village there would be a certain form of muscular dystrophy, in another village Friedreich's Ataxia, and in yet another multiple sclerosis.

The commonest Mendelian recessive inherited disorder in Cyprus is thalassaemia and the gene for this disorder is inherited by 16 per cent of both Greek and Turkish Cypriots. If the gene is inherited from both parents, the blood cells break easily, causing severe anaemia and poor development. Why, it may be asked, is the gene for thalassaemia, which is potentially so deleterious, common in Cyprus? The reason is that until the twentieth century in Cyprus, and throughout the Mediterranean and in Africa, everyone was infected with malaria by mosquitoes, and many died early in life from malarial fever. Those who inherited the gene for thalassaemia from one parent only do not have the symptoms of thalassaemia but they do have resistance to the malarial parasite. This is because when the parasite invades the red blood cells, the cell wall breaks down before the malarial parasite has a chance to multiply. Those who were resistant to malaria were more likely to survive and have children, who in turn, would inherit the gene for thalassaemia. The carriers of the gene from one parent only, the heterozygote, are better able than average to survive malaria, and outnumbered those who died from the disease.

Because of the serious risk of developing the disease thalassaemia when the gene is inherited from both parents, in both Greek-speaking and Turkish-speaking Cyprus everyone is tested for the thalassaemia gene before they marry. They must show the result of the test to their proposed partner. If two carriers of the thalassaemia gene marry, which sometimes happens even after the warning, they will have a one in four chance of having a child with thalassaemia. Therefore when pregnancy occurs, the fluid around the foetus, which carries cells from the foetus, is examined. If the cells show that the foetus is a homozygote for thalassaemia, and would therefore develop the disease, the foetus is generally aborted. As a result of this policy, the prevalence of the disease has now become much less common.

When I had completed the study on MS in Greek-speaking Cyprus in 1990, the director of the United Nations High Commission for Refugees (UNHCR) in Cyprus, Mrs Dolores Lasan, asked me, no doubt prompted by Lefkos Middleton, if I would direct a bicommunal project on MS, in which both Greek-Cypriot and Turkish–Cypriot neurologists would take part. At that time the Greek and Turkish doctors were cut off from each other. The idea of the bicommunal project was to use a medical research study to foster good relations between the Greek–Cypriot and Turkish–Cypriot doctors and the doctors' patients. Lefkos also had another idea in mind: to obtain support for a neurological institute on the island. It was proposed that the patients would be seen by both Turkish–Cypriot and Greek–Cypriot neurologists. UNHCR provided me with a pass which enabled me to move freely across the buffer zone. The study was undertaken in collaboration with two Greek-speaking neurologists, Lefkos Middleton and Koulis Kyriallis; on the Turkish-speaking side were Hatice Aksoy and Turgay Akalin.

The background of the study is interesting. The 1973 census showed that there were 116,000 Turkish Cypriots and about 450,000 Greek Cypriots, so the Turkish Cypriots represented 20 per cent of the Cypriot population when, in 1974, the Turkish army occupied 37 per cent of the island. The Greek Cypriots, particularly those who had to flee to the south of the island, feel extremely bitter towards the Turkish Cypriots for seizing their homes and possessions (for example, the hotels in Famagusta city, Varosha). The Turkish Cypriots, in turn, feel insecure because they are a minority in Cyprus and do not wish political power to be in the hands of the Greek Cypriots or of Greece. The Turkish Cypriots have their security in the 30,000 strong Turkish army in Turkish-speaking Cyprus. Since 1974, many Turks from mainland Turkey have settled in northern Cyprus, increasing the population to about 170,000 (1997), including the children of Turkish immigrants born in Cyprus. There has been no census in Turkish-speaking Cyprus since 1973. No Greek Cypriots are allowed to visit the Turkish-Cypriot side and vice-versa, except when patients are brought by ambulance, under UNHCR protection, to hospital in the Greek-Cypriot part of Nicosia.

Time appears to be on the side of the provisional Turkish–Cypriot government because the children of the Turkish immigrants, born and educated in Cyprus, consider themselves to be Cypriots, and it will be very difficult, and probably impossible, to persuade them to leave and return to the more impoverished districts of Turkey from which they came. There is little genetic difference between the Greek Cypriots and the Turkish Cypriots or in their way of life. In both communities the men tend to spend much of their time in the coffee shop and the women do most of the work. Historically it appears likely that the Turkish soldiers and followers who came to Cyprus after 1571 took Greek-speaking Cypriot women as wives – they were allowed to have four under Islamic law. This is supported by the fact that the thalassaemia gene is 16 per cent in both the Greek-Cypriot and the Turkish-Cypriot communities. Their blood groups are very similar and are different to the blood group distribution found in Greece and Turkey. They are Cypriots, not Greeks or Turks.

Unfortunately, only the older Turkish Cypriots, who lived with the Greek Cypriots before the 1974 invasion, can speak Greek. It would, in my opinion, be a good thing if in the Greek-Cypriot schools the children learned some Turkish and in the Turkish-Cypriot schools some Greek. I have suggested this to Mr Rauf Denktaş, the president of Turkish-speaking Cyprus. He speaks both Turkish and Greek fluently and also, having studied Law in England, perfect English.

The invasion of Cyprus by Turkey in 1974 was not prevented by Britain and the United States for political reasons. The British, who had given up their sovereignty over Cyprus, still have two large independent military bases in the south of the island. If Greek control of Cyprus became too strong, the British might be forced to leave. The United States, at least in the past, did not wish to offend Turkey because there are American bases in that country, certainly in the past including atomic missile bases, ready to threaten the underside of the USSR. In 1974, neither Britain nor the United States felt obliged to take any action to halt the Turkish invasion of Cyprus.

The Greek Cypriots do all they can to make life difficult for the Turkish Cypriots: electricity, which comes mainly from the Greek-Cypriot side, is frequently switched off at night; tourists are discouraged from crossing the buffer zone to visit the Turkish-Cypriot side. Planes cannot fly directly to the Turkish-Cypriot airport, Ergan, but must first land in Turkey.

Whereas different neurological conditions occurred in villages in Greek-speaking Cyprus, because of marriage within the village, in Turkish-speaking Cyprus genetic disorders often resulted from marriages between cousins, particularly among the Turkish immigrants. If two cousins marry, the risk of the same gene being inherited from both parents is, of course, greatly increased and often it is the effect of a potentially deleterious gene inherited from both parents which causes disease.

An important development from the bicommunal MS project was the funding by the Americans of a Cyprus Institute of Neurology and Genetics, with Lefkos Middleton as director. The institute was built between 1992 and 1995 on the Greek-Cypriot side of the buffer zone. Free entry to the institute for Turkish-speaking patients had been promised, but the Turkish-Cypriot politicians objected to the project because the institute was on the Greek-Cypriot side of the zone and was therefore under the control of the Greek Cypriots. I strongly recommended to UNHCR that it should be built within the wide buffer zone, which includes Nicosia airport, under the control of UNHCR, because this would ensure equal access for both communities. This did not occur.

In 1991 the Turkish-Cypriot politicians, because of the proposal to build the Neurological Institute on the Greek-Cypriot side of the 'Green Line', withdrew all co-operation for the bicommunal MS project and did not allow me to see patients. In desperation I went to see Rauf Denktaş and obtained his support. Only then did the Turkish-Cypriot ministers agree, with great reluctance, that the project might continue. Cyprus could be a Mecca for research into the causes of neurological and other diseases, particularly if there is co-operation between the Greek and Turkish Cypriots. The bicommunal MS project has shown that this will be very difficult to achieve.

We found that there was a reverse of the usual male to female MS ratio among the Turkish Cypriots. In men, MS was as frequent as in northern Europe, but in women the prevalence was the same in Turkish-speaking and in Greek-speaking Cypriots. The reason for the high prevalence in men is not known. Turkish-speaking women are as likely, or more likely, to visit a doctor as men, according to the Turkish Cypriots and neurologists and also in my own experience. The neurological services in the hospitals are free.

During the study we found five patients with MS in an extended Turkish family who had come to Cyprus in 1974 from the village of Ayvocik in northern Turkey, about sixty miles from Samsun on the Black Sea. During 1993/94, Hatice Aksoy, her husband Huda, Maria and I visited Ayvocik to take blood from members of this family which we then sent to the famous geneticist Teepu Siddique, in Chicago, hoping that he might find the predisposing gene. In Ayvocik we travelled up a dangerous path by tractor ambulance to the top of the high mountain where a number of the related families lived. The founder of this extended family had fled to the top of this mountain in 1860 after committing a murder and fearing revenge. He had four wives, permitted by the Koran, and fathered many children. The MS patients traced back to his marriage to two of his four wives – evidence that he held a genetic trait predisposing to MS.

Hatice Aksoy and I also found and studied a large extended Turkish-Cypriot family with a different disease of the nervous system, amyotrophic lateral sclerosis (ALS), which has an incidence as high as MS in northern Europe. In Britain it is usually called motor neuron disease (MND) and in the United States 'Lou Gehrig's Disease', after a famous baseball player who died from the condition.

ALS affects men more often than women and causes paralysis of the muscles over one to three years, resulting in total paralysis. The muscles twitch – a condition known as fasciculation. Most people experience mild fasciculation of the muscles at some time in their lives and many medical students and doctors, including myself, have wondered if they were developing ALS when they saw their muscles, often in the hand, fasciculate. This condition is known as benign fasciculation. Sometimes, but not often, patients with ALS/MND, or a variant of it, live for a long time. The most famous example is Stephen Hawking, the author of *A Brief History of Time*, but his ALS is not typical. ALS is familial in about 10 per cent of sufferers from the disease and we found that eight members in the particular Turkish-Cypriot family had already died from the disease. We decided to study all the siblings and children of those who had died to ascertain what gene was responsible.

I was particularly interested in this family because reported deaths from ALS in Europe and North America have doubled since 1960. Marta Elian and I had already studied mortality from ALS in England and Wales, Ireland, Australia, New Zealand and South Africa. In each of these countries ALS had greatly increased but, strangely, the reported mortality in white South Africans was only half of that in England and Wales. The low mortality from ALS in white South Africans is interesting because there was also a low mortality from MS among the white South African-born, particularly the Afrikaners. Dr Michael Goldacre, the director of the Oxford Record Linkage Scheme, and I showed that the annual incidence, or new cases each year, of ALS in the Oxford region of England is now the same as the annual incidence of MS; we confirmed that the increase in ALS mortality had really occurred.

In the United States, where there had been a similar rise in reported ALS deaths, the increase was first attributed to the large increase in the number of neurologists in practice there. It was suspected that when there were fewer neurologists, many of the patients with ALS had not been diagnosed. This cannot be the explanation because in England and Wales there has been a big increase in ALS deaths but hardly any increase in the number of neurologists and in its later stages the disease is not difficult to diagnose.

Familial ALS is inherited as a Mendelian dominant disorder, that is, the gene causing the disorder is inherited from one parent only, and half the children of this parent, on average, are likely to develop the disease. The large extended Turkish-Cypriot family with familial ALS was very co-operative because Hatice Aksoy was well known in their village. We were able to take blood from all the related members of the family, except for one lady who refused. It was agreed that none of the family would be told whether or not they carried the gene for ALS. The blood was sent from Larnaca (I had to use my UNHCR pass to bring it across the Green Line) via Air Express to Professor Teepu Siddique in Chicago. He and his staff located a new gene for ALS only once previously reported, the A4T gene on chromosome 9.

We found that ten healthy members of the family in Cyprus had the gene that caused ALS and were therefore going to develop the disease unless they died from some other cause first. Since 1993, three of the carriers of the gene have developed ALS. It is a great responsibility to tell the young and healthy that they are likely to die from ALS, or for that matter from any other serious inherited disorder. Certainly nobody should be told they have the gene unless they wish to know and then only after they have had good counselling and fully understand the nature of their decision. This is a particularly difficult decision because it involves not only the fear of an unpleasant illness and death but questions such as: Should they marry? Should they have children? Will they be able to obtain life insurance? And might the disease affect their employment prospects? On the other hand, if they know that they do not carry the gene for the disease which runs in their family, they can be sure that they and their children are very unlikely to develop it. This will be an important problem in the future as more and more genes predisposing to disease are detected.

Detecting the carrier of the gene for ALS is important because it is hoped that, in the future, by understanding how the abnormal gene affects the body's chemistry, the disorder can be prevented. Fortunately for us, none of the Turkish Cypriots who were tested wished to know the results of the test. We later found that the same ALS gene occurred in a large branch of the same Turkish-Cypriot family that had emigrated to Australia and three members of the Australian branch have since developed the symptoms of ALS and died and two others have symptoms of the disease (May 2001).

A great fear of patients with MND/ALS is that, as their paralysis progresses, they will choke to death. They can be reassured that, with good medical care, this will not happen. A problem arises about whether or not to use a ventilator to provide artificial respiration when normal respiration fails. Artificial respiration is carried out through a tube placed in the trachea; this is attached to a machine that inflates the lungs with air. It requires constant day and night care either at home or in a nursing home or hospital. It is a very expensive treatment: there must be a secure electricity supply, and the cost places a great financial strain on the family.

Total paralysis will develop, but the intellect remains intact and the patient is fully aware of the situation. Personally I would rather die quietly in my sleep and, in the meantime, be kept comfortable by the judicious use of opiates such as pethidine or morphine. The poppy has been one of the greatest gifts to man when properly used in treating and preventing pain and relieving mental anguish. The ALS/MND Association has made a major contribution both to the care of ALS patients and by increasing public awareness of the need to find the cause and treatment of ALS/MND, so that there will be an end to what David Niven, who died from ALS, called 'this bloody disease'.

Perhaps I have said enough about the epidemiology of MS and MND, so I shall just mention for the record that between 1988 and 1996 I took part in three epidemiological studies on MS in Spain. In Vélez-Málaga, near Málaga; in Osona, around the city of Vic in Catalonia; and in Gijon in Asturias. These studies were supported by the Spanish MS Society. It had been thought that MS was uncommon in Spain, but in all three studies we found a relatively high MS prevalence of between 40 and 60 per 100,000 population, a similar MS prevalence to that in Sicily and Cyprus.

Each summer in the late 1980s and in the 1990s Maria and I spent some weeks in Spain while I worked on these studies. We greatly enjoyed getting to know the Spanish doctors, people and way of life. I should mention in particular Oscar Fernandez, Enric Bufill and Dionisio Fernandez Uria.

CHAPTER 24

Inshallah – God Willing

Chaos umpire sits,
And by decision more embroils the fray
By which he reigns; next him high arbiter
Chance governs all.

John Milton, *Paradise Lost*

In 1976 Dr Patricia Sheehan, a Dublin doctor, was talking to a mother who had a Down syndrome child. Down syndrome, a disorder in which there are three chromosomes number 21 instead of the usual two, is also called trisomy 21. It causes changes in appearance which gave the disorder its old name, 'mongolism', and usually causes mental retardation. The mother told Dr Sheehan that there were other girls who had attended her school, St Louis, in Dundalk, Co. Louth, in 1956/57 who also had Down syndrome babies and that the mothers were young when the babies were born.

Patricia Sheehan decided to investigate the story and spent the next eighteen years finding out what had happened to the 178 girls who were attending the school at that time. She was able to trace 159 of them, 89 per cent, and questionnaires were completed by them and returned. She found six of the mothers had given birth to Down syndrome babies. Patricia Sheehan and a microbiologist, Professor Irene Hillary, published an account about this cluster in the *British Medical Journal* in 1983. In a follow-up letter, the number of girls at the school in 1956/57 reported to have had Down syndrome babies increased to eight.

In October 1957 there was a fire at Windscale, now Sellafield, the nuclear power and reprocessing station which is across the Irish Sea from Dundalk. At about the same time as the fire, there was also an influenza epidemic which affected many people in Dundalk, including girls at the school. The question was raised: was radiation from the fire at Windscale responsible for damage to the ova of some of the children attending the school, which had caused them to give birth to a child with an extra chromosome 21.

After the Chernobyl disaster in 1986 there was greatly increased concern about the possible effects of radiation on health. This was made more acute by the reported increase in leukaemia in Cumbria around the Sellafield site. In Ireland it was feared that not only Down syndrome, but various forms of cancer and other disorders might be due to radioactive material escaping from the reprocessing plant in Cumbria.

Sadly Patricia Sheehan was killed in a motor car accident in 1994. She had not published anything further about her research since 1983. In 1996 Sir Richard Doll, whom I knew well, suggested that I should reinvestigate the reported cluster of mothers who had Down syndrome babies. I agreed to do this and also decided to ascertain whether there was an increased number of Down syndrome births in the general population of Dundalk and the surrounding county of Louth or over the border in the Newry/Mourne district of Northern Ireland. It was a difficult and time-consuming study because I had to find all the Down syndrome births, whether they were still alive or had died, for a twenty-year period from 1961 to 1980 in County Louth and in the Newry/Mourne district.

The risk of having a Down syndrome baby increases with the age of the mother. After the age of forty-five there is a very high risk – about one in twenty. What was unusual about the cluster of Down syndrome babies born to mothers who had attended the Dundalk school was that all, except for one, were under the age of thirty, when the risk of having a Down syndrome baby is small, about one in 1800; one woman was aged thirty-one.

During the course of the study we found two mothers who had attended the school at the same time as the Down syndrome mothers with another chromosome abnormality – instead of two 'X', or sex, chromosomes, they had only one. This condition, known as Turner syndrome, affects only women. The usual risk is about one in five thousand, so two out of the small number of female births was indeed remarkable.

Six girls who had attended the school in 1956/57 later had Down syndrome babies, not eight as was first reported. One of the original eight was attending an associated nearby primary school; the child of the second, born in England, did not have Down syndrome. Only three of the six were attending the school at the time of the Windscale fire in 1957; the other three had left and were either in London or Dublin. There was no increase in Down syndrome babies, in the different age-groups of the mothers, in Dundalk nor in County Louth, nor in Newry/Mourne district of Northern Ireland. The pattern of Down syndrome by the age of the mother in all these areas was similar to that occurring in the rest of Ireland.

There was undoubtedly a cluster of Down syndrome babies born to mothers who had attended St Louis School in Dundalk in 1956/57. It is not likely to have been due to the Windscale fire, since three of the mothers were not at the school at the time of the fire but were in Dublin or in London. The influenza epidemic is also unlikely to have been the cause because it affected many people in the town besides those at the school. It may have been due to some as yet unknown cause, perhaps a virus infection, or more likely it was pure chance.

Clusters can appear by chance and have sometimes been described as what happens when a sharpshooter fires his gun at a target and then puts a ring around where the bullets have clustered. In this case the ring was around the girls attending a certain school, at a certain time. Nevertheless it is a fascinating story. It may well end in a major lawsuit involving British Nuclear Fuels plc, which is responsible for Sellafield, a Dundalk action group and the Irish government.

Doctors who collaborated in the study included Professor Norman Nevin, professor of medical genetics, Queen's University, Belfast; Dr Joseph O'Sullivan, a gynaecologist at Our Lady of Lourdes Hospital, Drogheda; Dr Mary Kelly, a psychiatrist at St John of God Hospice for the handicapped in Drumcar, County Louth; and Professor Margareta Mikkelsen and her colleagues, geneticists at the Kennedy Institute in Denmark. Professor Mikkelsen had also worked with Patricia Sheehan. Dr Rosaleen Corcoran, the director of public health of the North Eastern Health Board of Ireland, and her staff collaborated with the study, and her board provided financial assistance.

The Down syndrome study took five years to complete and presented great difficulties because Patricia Sheehan had kept secret the names of the girls who were sent questionnaires, including the names of the eight mothers whom, she reported, had been mothers of Down syndrome babies. Fortunately I had the assistance of Sister Colmcille and Sister Maeve, who were at the school in 1956/57 and also of Mrs Carmel Byrne of Dundalk, who had worked with Patricia Sheehan.

Finding one of the mothers proved particularly difficult. After an extensive search, all we knew were her initials and a date of birth but no one with these initials and date of birth could be found among the school rolls. There was a rumour that she had come from the town of Carrickmacross, in County Monaghan, and I spent some time in the town trying to find who it was. Dr Rory O'Hanlon TD, a general practitioner in Carrickmacross, had been Minister for Health when I was director of the Medico-Research Board and he invited me to have lunch with him at the Dáil, the Irish Parliament, to discuss the problem. With his help we eventually found who it was. She had had a baby in England and the baby had been adopted a year later in Ireland. The child did not have Down syndrome, but a cousin, born about the same time, did. This was probably the reason for Patricia Sheehan's mistake.

The results of our study were released on the Internet in December 2000 and the newspapers in Ireland and England were informed of the release day and time, with the usual embargo on prior publication. One Irish newspaper broke the embargo, to the annoyance of the other papers which then broke it also. The study was widely publicised and was greatly opposed by those who wished to blame the fire at Windscale for the cluster.

Dr Mary Grehan, a Dundalk general practitioner very involved in politics, spoke on the radio and said that I had been a pilot in the RAF during the war and must have a RAF pension and was therefore in the pay of the British government. She said the study was 'flawed', was a 'whitewash' and published to 'muddy the waters'. She gave no reasons. I replied that I was not a pilot but a medical officer in the RAF and, unfortunately, had no British pension, and that in our report we had given the facts.

Representatives of Greenpeace objected to the study, as did Mrs Nuala Ahern, a member of the European Parliament. Our report was clearly unpalatable to those who wished to blame the cluster on radiation from the 1957 fire at Windscale. The director of the Radiological Protection Institute of Ireland (RPII), Dr Tom O'Flaherty, nevertheless issued a press release agreeing with our findings but this did not stop the controversy.

Since atomic bombs were dropped on Hiroshima and Nagasaki in 1945, there has been great interest all over the world in the possibility of an increased risk of cancer resulting from radiation. Between 1982 and 1985, with support from EURATOM, Fontenay-aux-Roses, Paris, the board undertook a study of 8,000 young people who had received X-ray therapy to the skin of the head and neck for various skin conditions. We found that in this group there was an increased risk of cancer of the mouth, but the risk was still small. Radiation to the eye increased the risk of cataracts later in life.

It is understandable that many in Ireland do not like the idea of a large nuclear reprocessing station across the Irish Sea, particularly after the Chernobyl disaster. Claims that radiation from Windscale (Sellafield) not only caused the cluster of Down syndrome at the school but also a big increase in cancer, low levels of vitamin B12 and other disorders in County Louth have continued. Until now these claims have had no scientific foundation.

A new development in the porphyria story began in 1988 when I received a letter from Dr Philip Playford, the director of the Geological Survey of Western Australia, telling me that patients with porphyria in Western Australia had been traced to the area, Murchison Sound, north of Perth, where the Dutch East Indies ship *Zuytdorp* had been shipwrecked in 1712 en route from the Cape to Batavia in the Dutch East Indies. Some of the seamen had managed to get ashore. It was a reasonable assumption that a member of the original South African porphyria family might have joined the *Zuytdorp* at the Cape. The porphyria families I had traced in South Africa had inherited the disorder from four of the children of Ariaantje Jacobs and Gerrit Jansz, who had married in 1688, and all four and their children had stayed at the Cape.

Ariaantje had a half-sister, Willemyntje, who had married Detlef Biebou, the first doctor to settle at the Cape, and she had a son, Hendrik. In 1707, Hendrik Biebou, aged seventeen, with three friends, became very drunk in the mill at Stellenbosch. All four young men were brought before the magistrate, Starrenberg, and were sentenced to be whipped. Hendrik, alone of the four, was ordered to leave the Cape. In the court Hendrik made the dramatic statement in High Dutch: 'Ik will niet loopen, Ik ben een Afrikaner', 'I will not leave, I am an African.' He was the first white South African to say publicly, and have it recorded, that he was an African. Hendrik protested but he had no option and the *Zuytdorp* called at the Cape shortly afterwards on its maiden voyage. Had Hendrik stayed on the ship and brought porphyria to Western Australia?

This exciting story was spoilt in 1998 when Ric Rossi of the Queen Elizabeth Medical Centre, Nedlands, Western Australia, found that the Australian family did not have the same gene mutation for porphyria as the family I had studied in South Africa. A story on which I had been working for ten years was spoilt, but was saved by 'a duck'.

The Western Australian porphyria family traced back to Charles 'Doughboy' Mallard, who had been transported to Australia in about 1840 for stealing stale bread. In 1998, Giles Youngs, a gastroenterologist in Chester, England, published a book, *Dobson's Complaint*, describing the researches he and his colleagues had been making into a family which had inherited a form of porphyria. Many of the family had died from acute porphyria. The family tree published with the book showed that the Chester family were descendants of Elizabeth Mallard (1795–1849). Mallard is an unusual name and it appeared very probable that Elizabeth Mallard and Charles 'Doughboy' Mallard were related. Giles Youngs, Ric Rossi and I hope to see if they have the same porphyria gene by studying their DNA.

Starting in 1999 I undertook a follow-up study on the prevalence of MS in Malta with Marta Elian and the Maltese neurologists. In the 1978 study the prevalence was remarkably low. The MS prevalence is still very low in comparison with Sicily and other Mediterranean countries. In contrast to the Maltese, immigrants to Malta have a high prevalence of MS. We hope to find the reason by studying the genetic differences between the Maltese and the Sicilians.

CHAPTER 25

My Family and Personal Life

The friends thou hast, and their adoption tried,
Grapple them to thy soul with hoops of steel…
William Shakespeare, *Hamlet*

In the account of my work after leaving South Africa, I have said very little about my private life. It is difficult to do so when immediate family and personal friends are alive. It is easy enough to praise and say good things about those we know, but not so easy to be objective. Nor is it easy to be dispassionate about the decisions I have made, good and bad, in my own life.

On coming to Ireland, Maria and I, Gordon and Elizabeth spent a year in a rented house and then, in 1970, bought a house in Donnybrook, very close to St Vincent's Hospital and University College, Dublin. It was within walking distance of Baggot Street and my office. The house cost £9,700, which I obtained by selling some of my South African shares. Gordon and Elizabeth first went to a local convent school and then, when Gordon was about seven, he went to a boys' school, St Michael's, and Elizabeth to Mount Anville Convent.

Maria is Serbian. She is a loving and good wife. Settling in Ireland, where she at first did not know anyone, must have been difficult for her because I was away a great deal attending conferences, undertaking research, and representing Ireland on the EEC committee on epidemiology. Fortunately, she has an outgoing personality and soon made many friends.

In London we often met Maria's friends from her schooldays

in Belgrade. I was told how, during the German occupation, she would steal candles from the Catholic church and sell them; then with some of the money, she and her friends would buy loaves of bread and throw them over the barbed wire to the Yugoslav Jews and gypsies who were kept in an enclosure, open to the sky, in the town square, before being sent to camps where most of them died. From all I heard, Maria was the most popular girl in her class at school.

In Dublin Maria has always kept an open house and friends call almost every day and drink Turkish coffee in our kitchen. Maria and her Yugoslav friend Marina Brbro are often asked to read the cups of their friends after they have finished their coffee. What is read in the cup is usually vague and nearly always positive. Fortune-telling is very popular in Eastern Europe.

I knew that if I was to change my way of life and give up overseas travel and meetings, it would make life easier for Maria but I would not be able to continue with my research into the cause of MS. Maria often accompanied me. Maria has been a very loyal wife and supported me in whatever research I wanted to undertake.

What happened to Nonie and my three children when I came to Ireland? Fortunately, Nonie adjusted well to living alone and we remained good friends. I arranged for her to have a flat at a nominal rent in Elizabeth House, the block of flats I had built in Port Elizabeth. She decided to attend Port Elizabeth University and took two degrees in English Literature there; subsequently she lectured in English at the university. For three or four years she also took part in running a restaurant to collect funds for charity. She took a great interest in the lives of our children and, in due course, of her grandchildren, particularly after Michael returned to live in Port Elizabeth in 1986.

John, my introspective first-born son, took numerous degrees in physics and astronomy. After working with Sir Bernard Lovell at Jodrell Bank, the famous observatory near Manchester, and gaining a doctorate in radioastronomy, he returned to South Africa to work at the observatory in Cape Town. He married Ann, a South African woman, of German-Jewish extraction and they have two children, Geoffrey and Pamela. Because he found that his work meant that he had to be away from home for long periods – it was necessary to go into the country to get away from the light-pollution of Cape Town – he joined the South Africa Electricity Corporation as a physicist and science advisor in Johannesburg. He lives there today in a very pleasant house complete with a swimming pool. John would prefer to live at the Cape because Johannesburg is a tense and rather soulless place. He missed me greatly when I went to live in Ireland and I missed him. He was our first-born child and we were particularly close.

My second child, Jennifer, took as subjects English, French and business economics at Rhodes University in Grahamstown. She then took up nursing at Groote Schuur Hospital in Cape Town. Jennifer fell in love with an architect, Erik Schaug, of Norwegian parents, whom she met at a church meeting. He is a sensible, practical man, and a great lover of music. Nonie and I attended their wedding in Cape Town in 1984. Shortly afterwards, Erik and Jennie came to live in Bristol, and I was able to visit them relatively easily. Their son, Andrew, was born there. There was little work for architects during the building depression in England in 1992 and 1993, so Erik, who had insured himself against being unemployed, did a two-year course in urban design at Oxford Brookes University and was awarded his MA and the Francis Tibbalds Prize for his dissertation on the subject. He and Jennie returned to the new South Africa of President Mandela in 1994. With a little financial help from Nonie and me, they built a house in Hout Bay, a very beautiful suburb of Cape Town.

My son, Michael, did very well at college in Grahamstown, winning a scholarship to spend a year at Kingswood's sister college in West Hartford, Connecticut in 1968. He stayed with a number of families there including a family called Cohen. He can still recite the prayers that are said before the Sabbath meal on a Friday night. He also became good at American football. I spent two happy weeks with him in Connecticut. Michael won a scholarship to study medicine at Cape Town in 1969. I visited him in Cape Town on a number of occasions and had a good idea of Michael's enjoyable life as a medical student. After qualifying as a doctor in 1976, he took a number of 'house jobs' and did his two years' service as a medical officer, with the rank of lieutenant, in the South African army, which at that time was assisting Ian Smith's government in Rhodesia (now Zimbabwe). While in the army, Michael married a sister tutor, Jennifer Meiklereid. Jennifer is a highly competent woman and was awarded the President of South Africa Prize in 1984 as South Africa's top student in nursing education. Michael also learned to fly and got his pilot's licence. He took me on a number of flights and is a skilled pilot. After obtaining his higher medical degree, he came to England and in 1985 passed the difficult examination for membership of the Royal College of Physicians in London.

Michael went into practice as a consultant physician in Port Elizabeth in 1986, where he soon had a thriving practice. After three years there, he decided to specialise in cardiology. He rented his house in Port Elizabeth and obtained a consultant post at Tygerberg Hospital in Belville in 1989, the teaching hospital of Stellenbosch University and Medical School in Cape Town. When he registered as a cardiologist, Michael was offered the opportunity to work for a year at the John Radcliffe Hospital in Oxford, taking the place of the professor of cardiology, Peter Sleight, while he was away on sabbatical leave. Michael, with Jennifer and their three daughters Alison, Deborah and Catherine, lived during this time in Peter Sleight's beautiful sixteenth-century house in the village of Wheatley. On returning to Port Elizabeth, Michael was invited to join in partnership with Steve Spilkin, an exceptionally good cardiologist. Steve is quite uninterested in fame or material reward and he looks after many patients and often forgets to charge them.

Perhaps here I should relate what had happened to Lauries Bay after I left South Africa in 1968. Simon, who had built the house, cottages, and other buildings with Dr Douglas Laurie, continued to look after the property. Nonie visited the bay every week and would bring down food for Simon and his family. I arranged for necessary repairs and repainting to the buildings when I visited South Africa each year in January, and when Michael returned to Port Elizabeth he took my place. Since coming to Ireland, I have become aware that I should have done more to improve Simon and his family's standard of living during the twenty years I was living in Port Elizabeth. In comparison with other black workers in the rural areas, Simon was well looked after, but in retrospect I feel I could have done more for him. He lived with his wife Maria and their twelve children (not all of whom were at home at the same time) on the hill above the bay, without running water or electricity. Although he lived in a more solid two-roomed building than was usual for black workers at that time, I did not, and I should have, rebuild his home and connect it to the electricity supply we had from our Petter engine, dynamo and railway batteries. He had as much milk as he wanted from our cows and kept hens and ducks and he was never short of food. Simon appeared to be, and I am sure was, fond of me and was distressed when I decided to go to Ireland, although he knew he would continue to receive his salary and food. He felt, I think, that I was deserting him. In retrospect, I should have done more to raise his standard of living and that of his children. The Daverns, in particular Eithne Davern, who continued to live for a few years after I left South Africa in one of the cottages at Lauries Bay, looked after Simon and his family. Eithne took a black child, not one of Simon's because this would have caused jealousy, into her home and helped educate him. Today, he is headmaster of a school. When Simon died in 1976 I arranged with his family for a headstone for his grave.

Simon Nonzube: with Douglas Laurie,
he built Laurie's Bay –
A talented and gentle man.

Since 1948, when I first realised that South African porphyria was an inherited disorder, I have had a great interest in diseases that run in families. This interest included my own family and the disorders to which they are liable. I mentioned at the beginning of my story how I had traced my mother's ancestors back to Daniel Murphy, who came to Liverpool from Ireland in 1848; how his son, John Murphy, my mother's grandfather, had four daughters and my mother's mother was one of the four. John Murphy died in 1901 at the age of seventy-one and on his death certificate was written: 'Encephalitis – 14 months'. This I interpret to mean that he had lost his memory for at least the previous fourteen months and probably suffered from what we now call Alzheimer's disease.

When I visited England, I would call regularly to see my parents at Eastbourne. About 1969, I realised that my mother's memory was failing. Over a period of three years she lost her memory completely and undoubtedly had Alzheimer's disease. Alzheimer's is often inherited as a Mendelian dominant characteristic which means that, on average, half the children of someone who has the disease, if they live to a sufficient age, will also develop it. It appears very probable, judging by his death certificate, that my mother's grandfather, John Murphy, had Alzheimer's disease. My mother's mother died, aged twenty-nine, from tuberculosis, so I shall never know if she would have developed it. John Murphy's other three children did not develop Alzheimer's disease, although they all lived to a good age.

If Mendelian-dominant Alzheimer's runs in our family, there is a fifty per cent chance that I may also develop it. It has recently been found that it is possible to ascertain whether or not the genetic trait for one form of Alzheimer's disease has been inherited; the responsible gene has been located on chromosome 21. I have decided not to find out if I may have inherited a gene for the disorder.

It has become possible to detect the genes that are responsible for a number of diseases which develop in the latter part of life and I have already discussed familial amyotrophic lateral sclerosis (FALS). Another good example is Huntington's chorea, which causes dementia and gross unsteadiness of the arms and legs, leading to paralysis. This condition, like some forms of Alzheimer's, can also be detected early in life, long before there are any symptoms. The question arises: 'Do you wish to know whether or not you are going to be affected in the same way as one of your parents, or would you rather not know?' The advantage of knowing is that you can then decide about having children. If the gene is present, the knowledge that the disease will develop in later life must always be at the back of your mind. On the other hand, if you are tested for the disorder and it is found that you are not going to inherit the disease, which will be true of half of those who are tested, you can stop worrying about it. The dilemma has come home to me personally with Alzheimer's disease.

My father's brain remained acute until his death at the age of 101. However, his legs became weak about twenty years before he died, so that he had difficulty walking. This was partly due to Parkinsonism. During the final ten years of his life, he could walk only from room to room. This may also be genetically determined.

My youngest son, and Maria's first-born, Gordon, attended my old school, Ampleforth College, in Yorkshire but only for two years. We share many interests; for instance, in honour of my father, Gordon undertook a study on 'The Oldest Old', in Ireland, people who were reported on their death certificates to be 100 years old or over. Gordon found, by checking the birth and death registrations, that it was quite common for very old people to have exaggerated their age and their families believed that they were 100 or more, when they were in their nineties. He has inherited my interest in genealogy and is also an entrepreneur. When he was a student in Dublin, he made good pocket money by tracing Irish ancestors for Irish-Americans. I had hoped that he would become a doctor, but he decided to study history and economics and later law. In September 1991, he married Charlotte, the head teacher at an English language school. She has a degree in fashion and textiles. They have two beautiful daughters, Elizabeth ('Lily') and Octavia Rose. Gordon and his family love Norwich where they live in a nineteenth-century house. In May 1997 Gordon was elected a Liberal Democrat county councillor for Norfolk and has been much involved in plans to build a new hospital for Norfolk outside Norwich. Charlotte has her own business making personalised christening blankets.

My youngest child, Elizabeth, has a different personality than my other four children. She is beautiful, an extrovert like her mother, and popular. After training in stage and film make-up in London, she got a job applying the complete make-up for the Phantom in the Andrew Lloyd-Webber show 'The Phantom of the Opera'. She spent six years in London and then came back to live in Dublin, where she bought an apartment and continued to work for films and television. It was while working as a make-up artist on a film in Ireland that she met and fell in love with Michael Measimer, an expert in special effects, such as making dinosaurs and monsters. They married and lived first in Los Angeles before returning to Dublin where they started their own special effects business. They now have a fine son, Zack.

My sister, Pauline, qualified as a doctor in 1945 and then trained to be a paediatrician. She is a practical and down-to-earth person. In 1950 she took a post in paediatrics at the children's hospital in Columbus, Ohio, and later obtained the American Medical Board Diploma in Pediatrics. In 1953 she joined the Medical Missionaries of Mary, an Irish-based missionary order. She spent many years working as a paediatrician at a mission hospital at Anua Uyo in eastern Nigeria, where I twice visited her. She was there during the Biafra War in 1968–69. The area surrounding the hospital was controlled by the Biafra forces and the Federal army advanced as far as the nearby river. The staff fled carrying their few possessions on their heads, leaving the very sick patients and a group of four-teen orphan babies to be looked after by four sisters and four visiting priests. They planted maize and ground nuts because no food was available for purchase. One of the priests volunteered to look after the patients and infants during the night and became very adept at changing nappies. One woman kept on complaining of abdominal pain in the middle of the night and the priest, rather annoyed, gave her Panadol every two hours, which did not help. In the morning the sister turned down the bedclothes and delivered a baby! Fortunately the Federal troops stopped at the nearby river.

After my mother died in 1972 and when my father was nearly ninety years old, Pauline was given permission by her Order to look after him in Eastbourne. It was, no doubt, the good care that my father received from her, and from my younger sister Helen, that resulted in his remaining well and living to such an old age. After his death, Pauline was sent to Kenya and has since worked there with sufferers from AIDS. It was a great sacrifice for her to give up her missionary work for eleven years to look after our father, a sacrifice that is, wrongly, expected of a woman but not of a man.

Helen, who trained as an architect, would also have liked to have spent her life working with a religious Order. She taught in a number of convents and, on her retirement in 1985, went to live in Eastbourne. Like Pauline, she is artistic and enjoys making pottery. She is almost as good at crosswords as my late father.

I had three first cousins on my father's side. Gordon, my Uncle Josiah's son, as I have described earlier, was killed as a navigator on a Lancaster bomber in April 1943. Malcolm, Joseph's son, became a successful architect. Unfortunately, probably because during the war he worked in the coalmines and because he smoked cigarettes, he died young of lung cancer. Sonia, Malcolm's sister, was curator of the main art gallery in Melbourne.

And what about my friends? There are, I suppose, no friends like the friends of one's youth and my best friend, after David Gillott, who was killed during the invasion of Sicily, was John Bradshaw. John and I started out as first-year medical students dissecting frogs and rabbits and we continued to work together throughout medical school. Before the war, we went hitch-hiking around England with almost no money. After I went to South Africa, he came to stay with me in Port Elizabeth and then became a government doctor in Rhodesia in 1948. He could not tolerate the whipping of prisoners he had to witness and returned to England a year later. Throughout his life since leaving the army, except for a short time in Rhodesia, he made his living by writing books. Two of his successful published books are *Doctors on Trial* and *The Drugs We Use*. John was a good Catholic but rather rigid in his thinking. His eldest son, David, while still a student, was killed in a car accident. John named another son, Geoffrey, after me and had two further sons, Toby and Simon, and, a daughter, Catherine. On a small income, John somehow managed to give his children a fine education, not only sending them to Belmont College, but also by teaching them country lore.

During his later unhappy days, John lived in Oughterard, County Galway, separated from his wife Sheila. He worked with me and with Father Paul Lavelle on the developing heroin problem in Ireland. He developed cancer of the oesophagus and died in February 1989 at a hospital in Galway, while Maria and I were in South Africa. We flew straight back from South Africa to Shannon to attend his funeral. When we arrived in Oughterard, we found him lying in an open coffin while the men, women and children of the village came to pay their respects. I helped carry his coffin along the street to the church and Father Paul Lavelle came from Dublin and spoke at the service about his life and work. I was the executor of John's will and he left the little he possessed to his only daughter, and my godchild, Catherine, who was then still a student. I wrote his obituary in *The Lancet*: it finished: 'He loved the house where God dwelt and he died poor.'

The women in my life have, almost without exception, remained good friends and I have learned a great deal from them. They include medical colleagues, Eithne Davern, whom I knew in South Africa, and Marta Elian. I have also been fortunate in having exceptionally good secretaries: Phyllis Basford when I lived in South Africa, Hilda McLoughlin in Dublin, and, since my retirement Maureen Moloney and Susan Murray.

It was easier to keep in contact with friends in South Africa than in Ireland. Certainly Maria and I find there is much less house-to-house socialising in Dublin than in South Africa, and many Dublin friendships, unfortunately, revolve around drinking in the pub or club. My life in recent years has been much more lonely than my life in South Africa probably because I spend too much time on various research projects and reading and writing papers.

CHAPTER 26

A Heart Attack:
What Does It All Mean?

It matters not how one dies; but how one has lived.
Boswell's Life of Johnson

After returning from Kenya in January 1992, where I had been visiting my sister Pauline, I noticed that I was unduly tired and my ankles were swollen. I dealt with a large backlog of letters and reports and then decided to complete a study I was undertaking to find out how many of the 202 young people injecting heroin in the central Dublin and Dun Laoghaire study in 1982/83 were positive for the AIDS virus.

On the afternoon of 5 February I went to the Virus Laboratory at University College, Dublin, in Belfield, to obtain reports on the blood tests for HIV infection of those in the study. Helen, the technician whom I wished to see, was out at lunch, so I went for a walk in the university grounds. It was cold and the rain was pouring down. While walking, I developed a severe pain in my chest, just beneath the sternum. I suspected that the pain was caused by angina or perhaps a heart attack. I walked slowly back to the laboratory, sat down, and asked for a glass of water. Over twenty to thirty minutes the pain subsided. I hoped it was perhaps just a severe attack of indigestion and fooled myself that it might have been due to an excess of hot mustard on my dinner the night before.

I considered going to the nearest hospital, St Vincent's, for a cardiograph, but decided against it because the pain had by now subsided and, no doubt, because I did not wish to accept that I had heart trouble. During the following few days, after walking two or three hundred yards, I experienced pain in my chest and a similar pain awoke me two or three times in the middle of the night. On 13 February, I phoned the cardiologist Risteard Mulcahy, a close friend, and asked if he would see me. He arranged an appointment for me five days later. I think I made light of the pain.

On the evening before my appointment, I was invited to a lecture on Free Will by Finola Kennedy, who was undertaking a study on family life in Ireland. After her talk, members of the audience made comments and one lady said that free will must always be subject to the teachings and magisterium of the church. I could not agree with this, stood up to speak, and said that if we had free will, we should have free will to use our reason, even if it went against the teachings of the church. For instance, my reason told me that the host in Communion was not truly and physically the body and blood of Jesus Christ, nor could I believe that Mary's body had gone physically to Heaven. I also said that if I had lived in the Middle Ages I hoped I would not have agreed that heretics should be burned at the stake. Becoming quite tense about this thesis, I developed a severe attack of substernal pain, so I sat down. (If I had dropped dead, I would have lost my argument!) Again, I thought I had better go to hospital. However, since I had an appointment with Risteard Mulcahy the next morning, and the pain had subsided, I returned home to bed. In retrospect, this delay was foolish.

When I went for my consultation the following day, Risteard told me that he would do an exercise test. The electrocardiograph was abnormal. I had a block in a coronary artery. Risteard advised me to take aspirin tablets (Nuseal 300mg) every day and gave me an amyl nitrate inhaler to use if I had another attack of angina. He advised me to lose 20 pounds weight. I was not, in my opinion, significantly overweight. I was five foot seven inches tall and at that time weighed 165 pounds – with increasing age I have grown shorter!

I saw Risteard again a week later and he advised me that I should have an angiogram, an X-ray picture of the heart's blood vessels and, if there was a severe blockage, I would need a bypass, an operation to insert blood vessels to bypass the obstructions in a coronary artery or arteries. He arranged for my admission to the Adelaide Hospital two days later.

That evening, because I thought it was possible that I would not survive the bypass operation, I decided I had better write a few lines to complete my unfinished autobiography. This is what I wrote:

What then are my conclusions from my life of seventy-three years? I had been brought up in the Catholic (Universal) Christian tradition based on teachings developed by the Jewish people. They developed the great concept of only one All Powerful Power, or God, who had no materiality. The Jews also developed practical laws to hold society together, laws sanctified as the 'Word of God.' I believe that Jesus was a great rabbi or teacher, who spoke out against the hypocrisies of his time and emphasised the teachings of Rabbi Hillel, who had lived a century earlier. When Hillel was asked to summarise the Law, standing on one leg, he said: 'Love God above all things and our neighbours as ourselves.'

No doubt Jesus knew Rabbi Hillel's teachings well. Christians, including those like myself who had been brought up with Catholic teaching and tradition, are seldom taught a clear appreciation of the Jewish background to our religion. A complex theology has been built up, first by St Paul, which is far from the simple teachings of Jesus. We are expected to believe in the theology and philosophy based on the thoughts of the early theologians honed by Aquinas. To take the 'heart of the matter', I do not think that Jesus, when he held the bread in his hands at the Passover meal, or 'the Last Supper', and is quoted as saying, 'This is my body', meant that the bread was literally his body, nor when he held the cup with the wine and said, 'This is my blood', did he mean that it was literally his blood. He was surely using a metaphor, as he often did, symbolising his approaching death. He said to his disciples: 'Do this in memory of me', and so we should, but in the right context. The Jews were a realistic and highly practical people. Did the twelve Apostles believe that the bread and wine were 'truly the Body and Blood of Jesus'? They believed that He was the

241

Messiah, the Christos, but could an orthodox Jew of that time believe the blasphemy that a man was God? Did He believe it? 'Eli, Eli, lama Sabachthani?'

Nor is it sufficiently emphasised how the Jewish, Christian and Moslem traditions have so much in common. 'Peace be with you' is the common greeting for Jews, 'shalom aleichem', Muslims, 'salaam aleikum', and Christians, 'pax vobiscum'. When we say the 'Our Father, Hallowed be Thy Name', we refer to the tetragrammaton, the Holy Name of God – 'JHWH' – 'I am what I am' – a name so holy that it cannot be uttered except by the High Priest, who must be a hereditary Cohen, a descendant of Aaron, on one day in the year in the Inner Temple. This is a concept of God I can accept.

Working in Cyprus gave me an understanding of St John's Gospel – the Gospel that was read at every Mass. 'In the beginning was the Word and the Word was with God and the Word was God.' However, when I heard it in Greek, I realised that 'the Word' is from the Greek *logos*, via the Latin *verbum*. *Logos*, if I understand it correctly, shows the subtlety of the Greek mind. It was used by Philo, the Greek-speaking Jewish philosopher of Alexandria, before the birth of Jesus. It best stands for reason or rationality. The word *logos* is etymologically linked to many words in English, such as 'logic', 'theology', 'logarithms'. 'In the beginning was the Logos and the Logos was God' has for me a meaning. The 'word' is also used as a synonym for the second person of the Trinity, for Jesus, but I find this difficult to accept.

You might perhaps ask at this point in my life-story, what do I believe about the possibility of survival after death? On this matter I think like the Jews. At the time of Jesus, the intellectual Jews, the Sadducees who ran the Sanhedrin and ruled Jerusalem, accepted as God's word only the first five books of the Old Testament, the *Torah*, or *Pentateuch*, in which there is no mention of life after death. Life after death was not, therefore, part of their original tradition. The concept of life after death seems to have come to Judaism during the Babylonian captivity, at the same time as they met the concept of powers of good and of evil, of angels and devils. The Pharisees, the mass of the ordinary people, believed in life after death and Jesus belonged to the Pharisee sect. This does not mean that he was a Pharisee, a hypocrite, but that he belonged to the broad group of people who believed in life after death.

The Jews, even today, regard life on earth as being of paramount importance and hold that we should live life in this world as well as we possibly can, with little, if any, thought for another existence after death. I do believe that we survive death in some real ways. Our inborn characteristics are carried by the genes on our chromosomes and our genes survive in our children. Even if we have no children, the genes survive in the children of our siblings and cousins. It is the genes that survive. In this sense, we are part of a flowing river. In the old Celtic tradition it has been said, with some truth, that we can survive death in three ways: by writing a book, by planting a tree and, best of all, by having children.

So, what is my conclusion about my personal life? On the whole, it has been a very happy one. Doctor means 'teacher', and I have tried to be a good one. Serendipity has led to some success with research. I am particularly fortunate in my two wives, in the men and women I have loved, and who have loved me, in being a doctor, and in the very interesting men and women I have met during my lifetime. I hope I shall also survive in the memory of the good I have done in my life and that my mistakes will be forgotten!

I have lent to my friends on a number of occasions a book I have already mentioned by Mika Waltari, *Sinuhe the Egyptian*, based on the life of a physician, Sinuhe, who lived at the time of Amenhotep IV, who changed his name to Akhenaton when he established the new monotheistic religion of Aton. The book ends with the words: 'I have lived in everyone who existed before me and shall live in all who come after me, in human tears and laughter, justice and injustice, in weakness and in strength. Sinuhe, the Egyptian, who lived alone all the days of his life.'

Having written what I thought might well be the last words of my autobiography, I was admitted to the Adelaide Hospital on

12 March 1992. Ian Graham came to see me. I told him that my medical history was good, that I did not smoke, my weight was normal and the only possible warning of heart trouble I had had was when I had been in Turkish Cyprus in May of the previous year. At that time I had been subject to a great deal of frustration because the Turkish-Cypriot administrators refused to collaborate with the Greek Cypriots and blocked my research by not allowing me to see the Turkish MS patients. My blood pressure had gone up and I had noticed some swelling of my ankles.

The following morning I was given cortisone intravenously in case I was allergic to the radiographic contrast medium which would be used to make my coronary arteries visible to X-ray. Under local anaesthetic, a catheter was then inserted into my right femoral artery, in the groin, and pushed up, via the aorta, the main artery of the body, into the right and later into the left coronary artery – the arteries which provide blood to the heart muscle. A radio opaque contrast medium was injected through the catheter into the coronary artery and I was able to watch not only my own electrocardiogram on the screen, showing the heart's pulsations, but also on another screen the catheter in my coronary artery and the outline of the artery. Ian Graham showed me that there was an obstruction to the main branch of the left anterior descending coronary artery. During this time, a film was being taken of the screening of the coronary arteries. The following day Ian came to see me and told me that, except for 90 per cent obstruction of the left anterior descending coronary artery, my coronary arteries were good, and that he thought I was a very good subject for an angioplasty, that is dilation of the blocked artery by means of a balloon being passed into it.

The same afternoon Risteard Mulcahy visited me and lent me an interesting book on the changing pattern of ageing. The book fell open on page 80 and the first thing I read was, 'the left anterior descending artery of the heart is known as the artery of sudden death'. How careful one must be when lending books to patients!

On 16 March, I was transferred by taxi to the coronary care unit at St James's Hospital. This time both Ian Graham and Peter Crean, who was to do the angioplasty, and an anaesthetist, were present. The surgical registrar inserted a canula into a vein in my arm and another canula into the right femoral artery. The room was very cold and I developed a bad shivering attack. This attack probably resulted from a combination of cold and anxiety, because I knew that the blood supply to a large part of my heart muscle would be cut off when the balloon was dilated within the left anterior descending coronary artery.

The anaesthetist then injected into the canula in my arm a sedating and pain-killing injection, cyclomorph. On the X-ray screen, I followed the catheter as it was pushed up from my femoral artery into my aorta and with a little manoeuvring into the left coronary artery and down to the obstruction. A guiding wire was passed through the obstruction and a deflated balloon was pushed along the guiding wire. I was warned that I was going to experience chest pain. The balloon was inflated and after a few seconds I had severe chest pain; watching my cardiograph, I could see that my heartbeat had become very irregular. When the balloon in the coronary artery was deflated, the pain disappeared and the procedure was repeated. In the interval I tried to keep up a quiet conversation and asked why was it that, belonging to a group at low risk of having a heart attack, I had developed such a narrowing of a main coronary artery? Ian Graham replied: 'Ah! I can see a Greek-Cypriot flag on one side of the obstruction and a Turkish-Cypriot flag on the other side. That is the reason!'

When the doctors were satisfied that the blocked artery was sufficiently dilated, the catheter was removed. The canula in my femoral artery was left in place in case the artery closed quickly and the procedure had to be repeated. As I left the room, I was very pleased to be alive.

I was taken by stretcher to the Intensive Coronary Care Unit, where my cardiogram and blood pressure were constantly monitored. I also had an intravenous drip of heparin to discourage clotting in the previously blocked artery. Although I was well looked after and carefully monitored, I noticed as night approached that my blood pressure dropped to a very low level. Next to my bed was a defibrillator, a machine to give a shock to the heart to restart it if the heart stops or fibrillates (an ineffective twitching of the muscle fibres of the heart). During the evening my bed was moved along one place so that a patient whose heart had stopped and who had not regained consciousness could be placed next to the defibrillator. He was unlucky. I did not enquire what procedure he had had. I noticed that my cardiograph was much worse than it had been before the angioplasty; no doubt because of the lack of blood to the heart muscle during the time when the coronary artery was blocked.

The following day I was confined to bed, but the day after that, I was able to get up and return home by car. Faced with my own mortality, I was keenly aware of the beauty of the trees that were coming into leaf. On my first night at home I had an attack of angina for which I needed to use the glyceryl trinitrate spray. I have not had an attack since then and when my cardiogram was repeated a week later, it showed a marked improvement.

I had been warned that an angioplasty is only successful in about 70 per cent of patients and that I would know the result within six months. During the next few months I kept to a diet low in calories and animal fat and lost weight to 140 lbs. Every day I would go for a 40-minute walk. My report 'What Is It Like To Have An Angioplasty?' was published in the Journal of the Royal College of Physicians of London in 1993.

Angioplasty was of special interest to me because when I had practised as a consultant physician in South Africa, from 1947 to 1968, little of the generally successful hi-tech treatment for coronary artery disease was available. The care I had from my cardiologist and the nursing staff in the Adelaide and St James's hospitals was first-class, both in their psychological care and in the medical treatment I received. Perhaps it is a good thing that a doctor should sometimes be the patient.

CHAPTER 27

The End of the Story

A man's character is his fate.
Heraclitus, *On the Universe*

Every year I go to South Africa to see my children and grandchildren. Perhaps this is the time to relate my own attitude towards
relations between white and non-white South Africans. Over the
years my perspective has changed considerably.

I grew up accepting, as did my parents, that the British settled
throughout the world with the highest of motives, which were to
'civilise' the indigenous people of the lands where they settled.
Canada, Australia, South Africa and New Zealand and, in my
father's time, Ireland, had a Viceroy but were largely independent
in their home administration and many other countries throughout
the world were British colonies. It was regarded as regrettable that
the United States had seen fit to break away from England; George
III was considered much to blame for this! The large colonies, such
as India with mixed Hindu and Muslim peoples, were known to
be difficult to rule but, fortunately, Britain kept the internal peace
and defended the country against outside invaders; for example,
they defended India against incursions from Russia on the Afghan
frontier. Stories by Rider Haggard and Rudyard Kipling were
much admired. *Kim* was read by every English schoolboy. It was
believed then, and I still think it was correct, that colonial rule by
Britain was by and large benevolent and honest, not perhaps today
a popular view. Cecil Rhodes was regarded as a hero in my younger
days because not only had he developed the diamond mines at
Kimberley, he had brought Matabeleland and Mashonaland under

British rule as Rhodesia and he had the great dream of white civilisation under Britain 'from the Cape to Cairo'. Today this sounds old-fashioned and we certainly know much more of the other side of the picture.

It was by chance that I was offered a passage as a ship's doctor from Liverpool to South Africa; it might just as easily have been to Australia, New Zealand or Canada. In 1947 there was no question of choosing because paid passages were not available. I knew little about South Africa except that the Boers of the independent Transvaal, with its rich gold reef, and the Orange Free State, had put up a good fight against the British in the Boer War but inevitably they lost. I knew nothing of the British concentration camps during the Boer War in which over 20,000 Boer women and children died from typhoid and other infections. I arrived at the Cape, therefore, in a blissful state of ignorance about the relationship between the different South African races.

While the white population was wealthier than the Coloured, there were a large number of 'poor whites', mostly of Boer origin, who had come into the cities from the country. They had a preference for certain jobs, such as postman. This preference was known as the 'civilised labour policy'. While a sense of colour differences existed at the Cape – for instance a white man would hesitate to marry a Coloured woman – there was no law which prevented intermarriage, and such unions, licit and illicit, in the past had resulted in the formation of the Coloured people. The term 'Coloured', when I lived in South Africa, referred to the people of mixed race who mostly lived in the Cape Province. Those who were white were wealthier and better educated and they owned and controlled most of the land and the business life of the cities. A hierarchy existed with the English-speaking whites of British, Irish and Jewish extraction at the top, then the Afrikaans-speaking whites, the Afrikaners, then the Coloured. The language of the Coloured people was Afrikaans, as was their culture, so the divide between the Afrikaner and the Coloured was not very great. At the base of the hierarchy were the blacks, known as the Bantu (Bantu means 'the people'). It was after the 1948 general election that apartheid laws were introduced restricting the intermingling of white and non-white and disenfranchising the Coloured people at the Cape. The changes, however, were gradual.

The situation in South Africa was rather like that of Ireland in the eighteenth and nineteenth centuries, when the mostly Protestant 'Irish of the Ascendancy', or the 'Castle Irish', who might be invited to receptions by the Viceroy at Dublin Castle, owned the land, and the native Catholic Irish were looked on as being somewhat inferior and uneducated.

It was only when I migrated eastward to Port Elizabeth in 1948 and met with the Bantu that I appreciated the great gulf there was between the way of life of the whites and the blacks. They had come from the countryside to the city to find work, they lived in shacks made of iron and timber with no electricity or sewerage, and the infant death rate among them was high. Tuberculosis, syphilis and gonorrhoea were rampant. In spite of the difference in the standard of living between the whites and the blacks in the 1950s, relations between the races were remarkably good. The poor living conditions among the black population were, and are, softened by the excellent climate and, while there was malnutrition, there was little starvation, although the differences between the way the white and newly urbanised black people lived was great. However, the general feeling among the whites was that it had always been so.

In the late 1950s and 1960s the iniquitous system of apartheid became more and more entrenched, particularly when Hendrik Verwoerd and John Vorster were prime ministers. Nevertheless, because of slowly improving living standards, the black infantile mortality rates fell, resulting in a greatly increased black population in the cities and high unemployment. Under the political impetus of the African Nationalist Congress Party (ANC), and the training of ANC members overseas, generally in communist countries, attitudes hardened on both sides. The white security police became more and more ruthless and did not hesitate to murder the leaders of the ANC when it suited their purpose. The ANC used bombs to disrupt the economy.

I had become very friendly with the cardiologist Moses Suzman. His wife Helen was a founder member of the Progressive Party, founded in 1959. This party, which I supported, later advocated universal suffrage for white and non-white South Africans. Helen is a lady of great courage; among other things, she was involved

in a women's organisation known as the 'Black Sash' which demon-
strated against the apartheid laws and social injustice.

I hope I have now explained how my ideas about race relations
in South Africa have changed. My viewpoint today is still not as
radical as that of some of my friends. For instance, I do not agree
with my very liberal daughter-in-law Charlotte, who would not
visit South Africa, because she believes that not enough has been
done to right the injustice meted out to the black people, although
her husband, Gordon, was born there and loves to visit.

Fortunately, since 1994, under the guidance of Nelson Mandela,
there has been a major shift towards true democracy, but there is
still a long way to go before the non-white south Africans enjoy
the education and standard of living of the white. The change will
depend on many factors, including an appreciation of the need for
family planning to slow down the present population explosion.
Major expenditure will be required on education and public health
to enable the non-white population to take an active part in the
production of wealth in the modern South Africa, so that all South
Africans can enjoy a good standard of living. There are still great
problems: high unemployment, lack of education and the rapid
spread of HIV infection among the non-white population resulting
in AIDS. Fortunately there is a great deal of intrinsic wealth, so
there should be a prosperous future. South Africa will then be able
to assist the impoverished African countries north of the Zambezi.

In 1997, a dramatic and important event was reported: the successful
cloning of a sheep and the birth of 'Dolly', named, it is said, after
the singer Dolly Parton. No doubt humans can and will also be
cloned. It would be the same as having a much younger identical
twin. Although no doubt it can be done, I sincerely hope that the
cloning of humans never becomes a common practice. The even-
tual result might be, for example, a loss of ability to adapt to
changing circumstances because of a lack of biological diversity.

By scientific conviction I agree that a human life starts at the
moment of conception; this is also Catholic teaching. Therefore,
at least theoretically, a deliberate abortion is taking a life, or a form
of murder. It is also forbidden in the Hippocratic oath. Nevertheless

there can be some difficult problems. To take an extreme example, I ask myself what I would do if my own daughter was raped by a stranger suffering from a genetic disorder that was likely to be inherited? In honesty I think I would arrange an abortion, knowing that it is taking a life and breaking the commandment 'Thou shalt not kill'. Less extreme examples than this can also present a problem, and we break this law in other situations, for instance by judicial execution and in war. But 'hard cases make bad law'.

The problem is made much more difficult now that we know that potentially a human being can be grown from any human cell in the body, all of which carry the usual 46 chromosomes. If we grow a small mass of cells from, say, a cell in the lip, have we created a human being? Would it be murder to destroy this mass, perhaps only a millimetre in size? There is no significant difference whether the 46 chromosomes come from one person or from two people because in both cases a new human can be grown. Can we therefore argue that cells grown from a fertilised egg, without any human shape, as in the early stages of a foetus, are different to a small mass of cells grown as a clone?

I see that there is a danger in moving the line from conception to the stage when a foetus is visibly recognisable as a human being because at what point do you decide that there is a change from a mass of cells to a human life? For the present I believe we should say that human life starts at conception and leave to the future the decision about the point at which a duplicating cell becomes human. Dolly has created problems!

In June 1999 Nonie complained of pain in her chest which was at first thought to be due to her osteoporosis. X-ray examination showed multiple areas of cancer, known as secondaries, in her bones. The pain was due to the secondary cancer in her spine. It was not certain where the primary, or origin of the cancer, might be. I had just returned from holiday with Maria, Elizabeth, her husband Michael and Zack in Paphos, Cyprus, when I heard the news about Nonie. I flew to Port Elizabeth so that I could spend time with her. She was receiving excellent care, including much X-ray therapy, at St George's Hospital. She fully understood the situation and her one wish was to die quickly. She was extremely brave and, on returning home from hospital, put her affairs in order, made a new will, which I witnessed, and her funeral arrangements. She was well attended by my son Michael and his efficient wife Jenny. My daughter Jennifer came from Cape Town to stay with her and devoted herself to her care. In spite of many secondaries in her bones, she did not, to her regret, die quickly. It was possible at least to make her life reasonably comfortable with good treatment for pain and with help from the staff of the cancer hospice. I was with Nonie when she died on 4 October 1999. I loved her.

Today a much higher proportion of people will live well beyond retiring age and there will be a major increase in the disorders associated with age. My hope is that we shall be able to prevent and treat these disorders so that old people will still be able to enjoy life, as indeed I do in my eighties, and then, when death is inevitable, die relatively quickly. For the last few years I have had cancer of the prostate, fortunately a strange cancer since it can remain quiescent for some years, as it has with me. I am also somewhat short of breath due to deterioration in the alveoli, or breathing sacs, of the lung. This is a condition known as cryptogenic fibrosing alveolitis. Another sign of advancing age is that the vision in my left eye deteriorated rapidly in 1998. This has been diagnosed as being attributable to 'age-related macular degeneration', the consequence of deteriorating cells of the retina, particularly those affecting central vision. All three conditions from which I suffer are of unknown cause and all three are becoming more common, quite apart from the increase in the number of older people. Environmental factors must be involved and there is a great need for epidemiological studies to find out what they are. When we know what it is in our way of life that is responsible for these disorders, we should be able to prevent and treat them. I was advised that I should, at least for the present, do nothing as far as my cancer is concerned because treatment might do more harm than good; that I should wait until further symptoms develop. This policy, known as 'watchful expectancy', is very difficult for a doctor to accept! X-ray therapy may be required, and I shall be guided by the doctors at the Memorial Sloan-Kettering International Center, New York.

As the reader will know, porphyria and porphyrin metabolism have been a major interest of mine since I first practised in South Africa more than fifty years ago. I wrote to Dr Andrew Smith of Wills Eye Hospital in Philadelphia about the need for epidemiological research into 'age-related macular degeneration' from which I was suffering. He replied and told me of a new treatment on trial for the condition called photodynamic therapy. This was undertaken by giving an intravenous infusion of porphyrin, which made not only the skin but also the blood vessels sensitive to light. Immediately after the porphyrin was given, the blood vessels in the damaged part of the retina were treated by a low-strength laser beam that could affect the now sensitive blood vessels in the affected area of the retina without killing the retinal nerves – a brilliant idea! I flew to Philadelphia and had the treatment. After the infusion of porphyrin I had to protect my skin from light for a few days, wear dark glasses and a broad-brim hat. Strange that porphyrins should be my life interest and in my eighties I am treated with porphyrin! The treatment has helped my vision a little and should prevent further deterioration.

Perhaps I should finish my story with my present resolutions. I am well aware that I devote too much time to research and need to give more time to my practical, humorous and understanding wife Maria, to my children and grandchildren, to work less and play more. I also hope to see many old friends all over the world that I have sadly neglected. I know I have become too introspective. I shall certainly endeavour to be less self-centred, even if this means not carrying out all the research I have in mind. I do not know if I shall succeed. Does the leopard change his spots?

I have seen during my life an extraordinary change in the pattern of illness. When I was a medical student before the war, infections were very often fatal. Doctors were dealing with diphtheria, with streptococcal infections that caused scarlet fever and rheumatic fever, with tuberculosis and syphilis. Many young people died from pneumonia. Today classical pneumonia rarely occurs and many of the bacteria that caused fatal illnesses in the past have lost much of their virulence. A new plague, AIDS, has arisen, and in some areas of Central and Southern Africa and Eastern Asia up to 30 per cent of the population in the prime of life is infected by the virus. Many of the drugs that have been discovered to fight infections, such as the anti-malarial drugs, have become less and less effective because of over-usage. When I was in the RAF, my staphylococcal septicaemia was halted with what today would be a homeopathic amount of penicillin, 16,000 units four-hourly. Today the equivalent injection would be one million units and the effect would be less dramatic than it was fifty years ago.

In 1949 I first wrote about the four out of seven veterinary research workers studying swayback disease in sheep who had developed a neurological disease not dissimilar to MS. I wondered if they had caught an infection from the sheep's brains on which they had been working. In 1985 we followed up what happened to the four research workers; by then they had all died. Probably they had caught a prion disease, similar to scrapie, from the sheep's brains. Perhaps we are too greedy; why did we ever feed grass-eating cattle with feed made from sheep's brain and offal, when we already had mountains of dried milk and unsold butter, so leading to the possibility of an epidemic of Creutzfeldt Jakob disease?

We have tended to forget that we are only part of nature and cannot continue with unlimited consumption and so waste the natural resources of the world. It is necessary to maintain a balance so that our descendants for thousands of years to come will still have the resources they need to survive. The Chinese are much criticised for their strict population control, but have they any option if they want to feed their 1.3 billion people, more than 20 per cent of the world's population, on a limited amount of usable land? The vegetable kingdom is the ultimate source of life on earth, which uses, through porphyrins in chlorophyll, the energy of the sun. The Chinese have long practised, from necessity, what is only now being appreciated in the West: a wise policy of eating in the main a vegetable diet.

Many illnesses in the Western world result from too high a standard of living. It can be argued, and I personally believe it is true, that the population of the world, which will probably double to twelve billion people in fifty years, is already too big if we are to maintain a reasonable balance in nature and keep the world's wonderful diversity. When I first flew to South Africa more than fifty years ago, I watched from the plane herds of elephant, giraffe, zebra and buck. Not many herds can be seen today, even from a low-flying plane, and many species of animal are fast disappearing.

These days I work in an office in my home in Dublin, surrounded by photographs of my family, my books and many files. On the walls hang a number of paintings: Lauries Bay; the old 'Coloured area' of Port Elizabeth with its Malay mosque; a painting of the Georgian building of the Medico-Social Research Board, most picturesquely situated on the Grand Canal in Dublin; and a beautifully woven tapestry presented to me by the Chinese Academy of Medicine. On the bookshelves are the two old Dean family Bibles, one dated 1793, with the names of my Dean ancestors on various pages.

In pride of place is a print of the painting by Holbein of Thomas More, whom I have always regarded as my patron saint. What appeals to me about Thomas More, which I have tried with varying success to emulate, was his ability to be a practical man of affairs and yet to keep to his principles. He was indeed a 'man for all seasons'. Perhaps my sisters Pauline and Helen are right, and the spirit of a man does live after him.

Index

THE TURNSTONE

Tropical Medicine 48–9
in the Republic of Ireland 98–9,
154–73, 177–83, 188–94, 202–8,
222–6, 237–8, 255
resolutions for the future 253
retirement plans 101
retires from Medico-Social Research
Board 207–8
in Rome, meets Pope Pius XII 88–9
joins Royal Air Force as flying officer
29–42
Bitteswell Wellington bomber
station 30–1
Halton air force station 29–30
Officer Training Corps camps
13–14
Waterbeach bomber station 32–9,
40
schizophrenia research 179–80
on serendipity 174
in Sicily 184–6
on his sister, Helen 236
on his sister, Pauline 236
first son delivered stillborn 41
son Gordon Richard's birth 151
in South Africa 49–50, 76–80, 82–3
stays with Afrikaner farming family
56–7
Cape Town 51–4, 55–6, 58–60
Lauries Bay 64–6, 71, 73–5, 83,
85–6, 114, 116, 138, 148, 152–3,
156–7, 232–3
Port Elizabeth 54–9, 61–8, 70–5,
83, 90–1, 101, 107, 109, 113–14,
116, 138, 140–3, 147–8, 152,
251–2
on relationship between white and
black South Africans 247–50
in Spain 221
at Stanley Hospital 20–2
contracts staphylococcal septicaemia
40–1
stroke research 182, 183
suicide research 180–1
trial of (regarding prison brutality
research) 149
in Turkey researching porphyria
105–6

in the US 80–2
wives of see Devlin, Nonie; Von
Braunbruck, Maria
on world population figures 254–5
writings in the face of his possible
death 241–3
in WWII 18–42
Dean, Geoffrey (Geoffrey's grandchild)
230
Dean, Gordon (Geoffrey's cousin) 18, 39,
237
Dean, Gordon Richard (Geoffrey's son)
250
adult life 235
birth 151
education 229, 235
moves to the Republic of Ireland 158,
159
in the Republic of Ireland 229, 255
trips to Cyprus 212
Dean, Helen (Geoffrey's sister) 4, 103,
236, 255
Dean, Jennifer (Geoffrey's daughter) 84,
152
adult life 231
character 86
education 86, 87, 151
left alone in South Africa 156, 158
mother's death 252
Dean, Joe (Geoffrey's uncle) 1, 10–11, 18
Dean, John (Geoffrey's paternal grandfather) 1
Dean, John (Geoffrey's son) 48, 50, 68,
152
adult life 230–1
birth 44
character 86
childhood 74–5
education 86, 87, 151, 156
left in the care of nuns in Port
Elizabeth 59, 60
poliomyelitis infection as child 138
tragic death of sister Patricia 76
Dean, Malcolm (Geoffrey's cousin) 237
Dean, Mary (wife of Joe Dean) 1, 10
Dean, Michael (Geoffrey's son) 152
adult life 231–2
birth 84